Pipers

Frontispiece. William Ross (1823–1891), from Knockbain near Beauly, was one of the foremost Victorian editors of pipe music. He was piper to Queen Victoria from 1854 until his death.

Pipers

*A Guide to the Players and Music
of the Highland Bagpipe*

William Donaldson

Birlinn

First published in Great Britain in 2005 by
Birlinn Limited
West Newington House
10 Newington Road
Edinburgh
EH9 1QS

www.birlinn.co.uk

ISBN 1 84158 411 8

The publisher acknowledges subsidy
from the Scottish Arts Council
towards the publication of this volume

British Library Cataloguing-in-Publication Data

A catalogue record of this book is available
on request from the British Library

Typeset by Hewer Text Ltd, Edinburgh
Printed and bound by Antony Rowe, Chippenham

Contents

Tunes

Illustrations

'What would you choose', said the fairy,
'knowledge without power,
or power without knowledge?'
'Knowledge', said MacCrimmon.

THE PIPES AND THEIR MUSIC

Introduction

Piping is everywhere and nowhere. Big public events and sporting occasions call forth the pipe bands; moments of grief and solemnity, the lone piper. In the summer months it is seldom possible to escape the sound of busking players in central Edinburgh, and at tourist hotspots like Glencoe. Yet you could travel widely throughout the rest of Scotland and, unless you knew where to look, catch neither sight nor sound of this vital and widespread culture. This is because pipers largely play for other pipers who alone are knowledgeable enough to appreciate what they do. Public understanding exists at so low a level that players clamber into the elaborate gear generally deemed essential with a kind of weary fatalism ready to trot out the half-dozen commonplace airs they think the audience might, possibly, know: 'The Green Hills of Tyrol', 'The Barren Rocks of Aden', 'The Nut-Brown Maiden' and, almost inevitably nowadays, the awful 'Amazing Grace'.

Different forms of bagpipe have been played in the West for as far back as history records. The basic idea that the woodwind player can retain a supply of air in an external reservoir has been so useful that many peoples have availed themselves of it. Previous books about piping have often taken a long historical approach, therefore. Likewise, there has been much attention to the wide range of bag- and bellows-pipes preserved in the record all over Europe. But this book is about the music and musicians of the Highland pipe and the relatively recent past, rather than the days when Cleopatra was a kid and the legionary pipers were playing 'The II Trajana Crossing the Nile'.

Scotland has sustained a brilliant line of players and composers who have given it one of the richest of traditional instrumental musics. Players and singers of all sorts throughout the traditional repertoire use pipe tunes, often without any idea that they are doing so. The pipes are frequently considered in a rather compartmentalised way, as if they stood outside the broad current of traditional music. In fact there are rich and fascinating links between the various forms. Pipers frequently also played the fiddle, and fiddlers borrowed all sorts of ideas from pipers. Singers helped themselves freely to the results and dancers conjured

[1]

new formations into existence under their inspiration. The traditional perform-ing arts draw upon a common expressive pool, and piping is central to the whole Scottish repertoire.

Yet there is little public acknowledgement of this, except for a plaque or two and a scatter of memorial benches. The enterprising might seek out the ugly MacCrimmon cairn in Skye, or the cairns to Malcolm MacPherson at Catlodge in Badenoch and to the Bobs of Balmoral on Deeside. But the spaces in Edinburgh, Glasgow, Aberdeen, Oban and Inverness, where the statues of Willie Ross, Donald MacLeod, G. S. McLennan, John MacColl, and John MacDonald should stand, are empty. The tourist information offices know them not. The folk museums teem with material bric-a-brac, but intellectual culture is often poorly represented, indeed unknown to the custodians of the communal past. Enquiries in one west-coast site about a historic local piper, whose name is a household word amongst the knowledgeable, elicited a helpless shrug. As did the name of a leading Gaelic historian and journalist, a founder of the Mòd, who had been born and brought up not two hundred yards from the 'museum's' door.

There are two kinds of piping, the trash and the real stuff; piping for the eye and piping for the ear. Real piping exists in an enclosed and hidden world, at specialist events, mostly competitive, where the audience is made up of other pipers and a few non-playing devotees. Piping takes a vast amount of mental time, and some occupations are better for this than others: policemen used to say traffic duty was just grand for the purpose. Indeed a famous Hebridean piper/ policeman banished to a busy city junction because he hadn't arrested anybody for years ('Well', he said, 'how would *you* like to be arrested?') used to produce spectacular tailbacks on a Saturday afternoon. Deep in some *pìobaireachd*, he had forgotten the traffic was there. The Glasgow force was, and is, famous for pipers; and it is said that instead of being at large apprehending malefactors, they could frequently be found in the back shops of bagpipe firms drinking tea and demonstrating tunes on their truncheons. The finger technique in piping is very demanding and requires more time to perfect than modern life generally allows, so if you see fingers rapidly pattering on worktops, chair arms, poles and bollards, steering wheels, rulers and pencils- any kind of convenient non-sticky edge or surface- you are probably looking at a piper.

It is often assumed that traditional music 'just happens', that it is created by anonymous communal processes in a past so dim and distant that little reliable information can be gained about it. Traditional music is felt to be artless and unpremeditated, unworthy of serious attention or copyright protection and so simple that it can be mastered in about a fortnight by any person of education.

Nothing could be further from the truth.

Traditional music is *made* to happen by countless gifted individuals, and it might be to our advantage if we knew more about them and the world they inhabit, for this knowledge is attainable. The great players and composers of the Highland pipe created a musical world of surpassing loveliness. This book is about who did it, how they did it, and why.

The instrument

The pipes are often referred to in the plural, and the collective noun is a 'stand' or 'set' of pipes (*not* a 'pair' of pipes). In their present form they go back in Scotland until at least the later Middle Ages, and consist of a bag to hold the piper's breath which is placed beneath the arm (usually the left), a blowpipe with a non-return valve, three drones (a bass and two tenors) which rest on the player's shoulder, and a conically-bored chanter with a nine-note scale, which produces the melody. Bags are traditionally made of sheepskin in Scotland (although hide has often been preferred in other climates) and vary in size according to the build of the player. A fabric bag cover is normally used, once almost invariably of tartan, but often nowadays of plush or cord, and the drones are looped together near the top with cords of woven silk or wool, or lengths of ribbon. On ceremonial occasions sumptuous pipe banners decorated with heraldic devices can be worn, attached to the upper sections of the bass drone; but these tend to be rather heavy and awkward (as well as expensive) and are not used in normal playing. The bag does more than just hold air. Various preparations have traditionally been rubbed into it to ensure that it also absorbs moisture, the regulation of which is crucial to steadiness in pitch and tone. But this on its own is seldom enough. Human breath has an unavoidable moisture content so that various ways have to be found of combating this if the instrument is to remain in tune for more than a few minutes at a time. The stream of hot moist air passing from the piper's lungs into a suddenly cooler environment immediately begins to condense, and nowadays various forms of plumbing are resorted to inside the bag to mop this up before it reaches the reeds. Bags made of modern 'breathing' composites are now common, fitted with airtight zips (courtesy of North Sea oil diving technology) which facilitate drying out by giving access to the inside of the bag and the moisture-absorbing devices nowadays found inside. Pipers would look in a traditional bag for suppleness, durability and air-tightness and in the modern synthetics for dependability in use. Blowpipes too have moved with the times, sometimes incorporating clever water-trapping devices, or ball-joint sockets to relieve pressure on the teeth. A good blowpipe should deliver the air to the bag with minimum drag or fuss, be of comfortable length and not leak.

Five short wooden tubes called 'stocks' are attached to the bag and it is through these that the flow of air passes on its outward journey. To them are attached the chanter or melody pipe, drones, and blowpipe. Three drones are the normal pattern nowadays, although a two-tenor configuration seems once to have been used in the Isles. There is no guarantee that all three of the drones are being sounded, by the way: sometimes only two, the bass and one tenor, are reeded up – making for easier tuning and blowing. The drones are made up of jointed sections, two in the tenors and three in the bass, and they are tuned to sound in unison with the low A of the chanter, an octave below the main tonic of the chanter for the tenor drones and two octaves below for the bass drone. A good-quality instrument which has been well reeded-up and properly winded also produces a pronounced series of harmonics above the fundamental, which greatly enriches the tonal colour.

Tuning involves changing the length of the column of air vibrating inside the drones by manipulating the moveable upper joints. This is a complicated business as several things have to happen simultaneously. Subtle movements of hand and discriminations of ear have to take place while physically winding the instrument. This latter is a considerable skill in itself (see below). Good drones are much prized, and those of late Victorian master craftsmen such as Henderson and the MacDougalls of Aberfeldy are still sought out for their superior tonal qualities. Whatever the make, the piper will be looking for a robust and responsive tone, ease of reeding up, steadiness and balance between the drones and chanter. Factors which influence this include the quality of the wood, the subtlety of the bore, and the size of the cheque, since pipe-makers naturally reserve the best of their output for their most expensive instruments.

Reeds

The sound of the pipes originates in the reeds. These have traditionally been made of *arundo donax*, which has been used for instrument- and reed-making since classical antiquity. Pipers call it 'Spanish cane'. It used to be imported as packing around wine barrels, and indicates Scotland's long-standing links with the Mediterranean basin.

The subject of reeds is potentially enormous and a huge amount of lore is connected with them. The ability to get the best out of reeds forms a considerable part of the piper's art. Four reeds are required in all: three drone reeds and one chanter reed. The drone reeds are tubular, sealed at one end, with a single blade, and they are inserted into reed seats in the lower sections of the drones. The vibrating length of the blade (and therefore the pitch, and to some extent also the tone) is regulated in a traditional cane reed by a bridle of waxed or rosined hemp, artfully placed and tensioned so that the reed gives its optimum response, and by various forms of rubber or metal bridle in the modern synthetics. An ideal cane reed would 'strike in' (i.e. begin to sound) reliably without squeaks or grunts, quickly reach a stable plateau in terms of pitch and timbre and then stay there, for a long time. This is not easy to achieve. The ability to get an imperfect medium to behave in this fashion is one of the things which separates the good from the average player. Synthetic reeds, married to the new systems of water-trapping, tend to be more stable but lack, some think, the harmonic richness of the traditional materials.

The chanter reed is also made of cane but is double-bladed, the blades being triangular in shape and bound to a metal staple, the whole assembly being inserted into the reed-seat at the top of the chanter. Having a different configuration from the drone reeds, it behaves differently in playing and some twenty minutes may pass before a stable plateau is reached. Therefore the first thing the listener will hear is a whole sequence of tuning preludes or flourishes while the performer brings the instrument into tune and settles it down. These are often very spectacular, flashing arpeggios and cascades of tricky decorative movements. Some are part of the common inheritance but there is a lot of room for personal taste and some people's tuning flourishes are highly distinctive. There is a clear element of display as well, a desire, human enough, to impress the audience with the sense that one may be a better player than one actually is. It has been said of some pipers that once you have heard them tuning up you have heard the performance.

Chanter reeds come in three strengths, strong, medium and weak, and this is determined by the amount of cane on the blades and the overall profile of the reed which determines the degree of openness at the tip. Strong reeds produce a big, bright, rough timbre that sounds good at about twenty paces and are used mostly by people who play in pipe bands. Left to their own devices, pipers seek out hard reflecting surfaces giving a good natural acoustic, 'rocks, hills, valleys and coves where echoes rebound', and a balanced instrument can be shown off to advantage. But pipe bands often play over grass and the volume of the chanter needs to be increased so that it does not disappear into the ground. Strong reeds are not for the faint-hearted. Big men (the kind where you'll hear people remark that it took two sheep to make them a bag) often produce a big sound; but quite diminutive people can be trained to produce the huge dynamic typical of the top pipe bands. The drawback is that one needs tremendous embouchure and muscle tone to play such instruments steadily, and extended playing, say 45 minutes to an hour, becomes problematic. Good band players are the sprinters of the piping world, specialists in brilliant lung-bursting effort over short distances.

Not everybody wants to play like this, of course, and while many first-rate players do both solo and band work, the lonelier calling of the solo player has its appeal. It is here that the medium-strength reed comes into its own, producing what some regard as a more balanced and cultivated sound. Such instruments are more comfortable to wind and thus to play for longer periods of time, and it is here that the players of *pìobaireachd*, the classical music of the pipe, are mostly to be found. The problem for everybody is that there is no standard chanter. Each make has its own peculiarities and reeds have to be adapted cunningly to suit them, to produce a true scale (many an otherwise fine reed may be uncomfortably flat on one note or sharp on another) and optimum balance and timbre.

[5]

There is much anxious work here with sharp knives, conscious that a false move may undo weeks of effort.

Pipers do not as a rule make their own reeds but get them from various firms of reedmakers around the world. This is a testing relationship, and they can often be heard exclaiming bitterly about the quality of the materials and workmanship, the moral condition and likely destination of the makers. Reeds are so important to the piper, and he has to get so many of them to cooperate sweetly together, that he lives in a permanent froth of anxiety and discontent, illuminated by occasional gleams when something a little better comes along. Since the reed-maker has to sell a certain number of units a week, he tends to work to a 'middle of the road' profile that will suit the dominant band chanter and, hopefully, have enough tolerance to fit a range of other things as well. This can mean difficulty in getting reeds for 'non-standard' (especially older) chanters. It is a bit like computers, really: commercial pressures mean that you upgrade or die, so that to a large extent pitch and timbre in piping are involved in processes of enforced change. Reedmaking and reed-craft encompass a world of arcane knowledge, sometimes jealously guarded. One leading piper dismissed the whole business with a wave of his hand saying, 'ach, the secret of having good reeds is just having thousands of reeds'.

Within the last decade plastic and carbon fibre have become increasingly popular for making drone reeds as absorbency and moisture tolerance became less important thanks to new water-trapping methods. All kinds of – to the traditional eye – strange-looking objects may nowadays be found lurking inside the drone stocks. They help to solve one problem – namely steadiness of pitch – but they create a whole new dimension of technical difficulty. They are not so easy to manipulate as cane reeds; there are problems with striking in and finishing cleanly; and some think they lack the tonal richness of the traditional product. They can be harder to tune, as well, because they reduce the fractional difference in timbre produced by cane reeds and, of course, they have a homogenising effect on tone in general. Unlike the old days when you could tell who was playing immediately they started, even if you couldn't see them, most good players now produce the same bland, almost exquisite tone. And the new-style reeds can be rather costly. At the time of writing nobody has yet managed to perfect a good synthetic chanter reed. Whoever does will probably make a good deal of money.

Chanters

If refractory reeds can strew the hair with premature grey, then chanters run them a close second. Once again, these are made by a variety of makers worldwide and they are all different. Annual sales of new chanters are probably well in excess of 20,000, fuelled by the ceaseless search for the fashionable sound. Bagpipes are sometimes thought to typify the world of 'tradition', sailing down the centuries quite unaffected by the restless change that makes the modern world so disturbing a place to live in. But the pipes have been changing ever since the records begin. Critics at the end of the nineteenth century looked back on the trumpet-tongued instruments of a century before with their huge bore and fantastic carrying tone, in contrast to the poor pinched things – as they thought them – of their own times. Exactly similar views could be heard at the end of the twentieth century, as conservative players shook their heads over degenerate modern methods and sighed for the great days of Henderson and MacDougall.

The pitch of the pipes has probably risen during the past two centuries in the ceaseless search for refinement of tone and an ever 'brighter' sound. Drones can cope with this and many fine old sets are still being played; but chanters have less tolerance and must be replaced. During the 1950s many of the top people played Henderson chanters. Then everybody switched to Hardie; then Sinclairs were all the rage; then Niall ruled the roost and so it went. Each make had its own peculiarities and all required a subtly different kind of reed. The spectacular increase in worldwide demand if one's chanter 'took' created problems for pipe-makers who had to step up production dramatically to meet the demand. There was much anxiety in the performer community that standards were being compromised; that when tools lost their edge the makers ploughed on; that when their supplies of good well-seasoned wood laid up for several years ran out they dunked the stuff in a chemical bath to give it a quick fix, so that the resulting chanters soon warped and went out of tune (even if they had been properly in tune in the first place which some players felt inclined to doubt). One famous piper persuaded to switch to the new pitch regarded his chanter with a jaundiced eye and exclaimed 'My God, the birds were whistling on this thing 24 hours ago'.

Many chanters nowadays, especially in pipe bands, are not made of wood at all but a dense plastic called polypenco. Purists frown on this kind of thing and most of the top performers still favour wood as giving a richer, more subtle timbre. The preferred substance is African Blackwood which was once merely one of a whole suite of tropical hardwoods used for pipe-making, including ebony and cocus wood, before they were wiped out by the piano industry. These replaced native hardwoods such as laburnum and holly during the eighteenth century, being favoured for their brighter, more resonant tone. At about the same time ivory and silver began to be used for ferrules, tuning slides and projecting mounts instead of the native bone and horn.

Styles of manufacture evolve and one can date a pipe fairly accurately by the cut of its drones. Many eighteenth-century instruments had pear-shaped bells before the characteristic drum shape was introduced which survives to the present day. Likewise, the slender drone profile with a neat button mount typical of the nineteenth century tended to thicken, sometimes quite markedly, during the earlier twentieth century. There were distinctive 'Edinburgh' and 'Glasgow' styles. At the same time it was individual turners who bore ultimate responsibility so that it may not be possible to identify a pipe with certainty unless it bears the name of the firm. Not all do. The various mounts and slides are partly for appearance and partly for utility. They secure the ends of the stocks and joints and prevent them from splitting; the ring-caps, of ivory, plastic or metal, which top the drones are necessary to complete the bore; the projecting mounts help get purchase on the joint and protect the drone from unexpected bangs and knocks. Pipes are fairly fragile and a broken joint can be a serious matter, being difficult to replace, especially on an older pipe, in a way which matches the harmonic characteristics of the original.

Good pipes usually look good. They will be beautifully made and mounted with materials of the highest quality. Cheap pipes, by the same token, can usually be spotted at several paces, with their bright over-glossy varnish, wood of doubtful hue, and ferrules and mounts of visibly tawdry materials. Promising years of instability, dull timbre, reeding problems and general heartbreak, instruments like these are fit only as wall decorations in darkened rooms.

Starting to play

The pipes are set going by settling the drones on the left shoulder (or right, for some left-handed players). The appropriate fingers of the left hand are placed on the upper note holes of the chanter. The bag is silently filled with air. Then it is given a brisk push with the free right hand to set the drone reeds going. This hand then settles the bag fully under the left arm ready for playing while the player increases blowing pressure to make the chanter sound. Simultaneously the fingers of the right hand are placed on the lower note holes of the chanter. The instrument is now ready to be tuned. All these things have to happen in rapid succession within about ten seconds, and beginners can find the sequence tricky at first. Indeed the learner has to go through some months of preparation before this stage is even approached.

First of all comes a period of intensive instruction and practice in order to master basic finger technique. For this a quite separate little instrument called a practice chanter is used. This is a miniature version of the pipe chanter. It is blown directly by the mouth through a blowpipe which expands into a cap, containing a reed often nowadays made of plastic. It is a compact, portable, small-voiced instrument which can be played in places the full pipes can not, and is designed to develop a sound and accurate technique. It is a kind of gymnasium for the hands and arms because it is in the bits that cannot be seen inside the piper, between fingertip and shoulder, that the physical basis of technical mastery lies; and it is on the practice chanter that these invisible wonders are conjured into being. Good finger technique is founded upon suppleness, accuracy and strength, and has to be built up and maintained over extended periods of time. The practice chanter is not just for beginners. All pipers have one and continue to use them throughout their careers.

Although the pipes look straightforward and do not have the tangle of rods and levers found on some other woodwind instruments, they are not a simple instrument, or easy to play. The musicologist Percy Scholes pointed out that 'the technique of this instrument is certainly more difficult to acquire in perfection than that of any other instrument of so small a range of notes'. The piper has to keep going, single-handedly, an entire wind section, the equivalent of three bassoons and an oboe. Pipers' fingers have also to move faster than those of other woodwind players to achieve good articulation. It is not just beginners who have to cope with this. Relentless practice is the inescapable burden of all who aspire to excellence. Talent and good fine-motor skills are not enough. One of the great teachers, Lt. John McLennan, wrote to his brilliant son and pupil 'G. S.' McLennan, 'Dear George . . . always recollect that excellence of any sort is beyond the reach of indolence. If you allow yourself to believe that it is impossible for you to do what you see others perform, your despair will not allow you to succeed . . . facility will always come with diligence and labour'. Top players tend to be evasive about the amount of time they devote to the art; but one would expect that to maintain their virtuosic skills would normally take at least three or four hours a day. And instruction never stops; even masters usually have an older master to whom they go for advice and support. Good pipers have to do a dauntingly large number of things well: possess a high-level musical gift, a finely honed finger technique, a huge amount of traditional lore married to more than basic craft skills; and, of course, possess a good deal more time than modern society usually allows. It sounds almost impossible – and for most people it is: which is one reason why master pipers are held in such esteem. The opposite side of the coin, of course – and one which clouds the understanding of many of the potential audience – is that the pipes are an easy instrument to play badly, as a stroll through the tourist hotspots of Scotland on a summer afternoon will quickly confirm. As a result, the pipes have a poor reputation in many quarters, even in Scotland, because atrociously bad playing is all that many people ever get to hear.

Learning the basics

The beginner starts by learning to place the fingers on the chanter. A series of simple scales and runs is used so that he or she can find the holes reliably and sound the notes correctly. Then begins a long (and frustratingly lengthy) pilgrimage through the 'movements' – the many grace notes and ornamental figures which are at once the glory and challenge of piping – leading perhaps to the Promised Land of mouth-watering mastery and international fame, or, more usually, into the weary wilderness that lies somewhere in between.

The journey starts with a series of simple gracenotes called 'cuttings', made by raising and lowering a finger smartly while another note is being sounded. Cuttings are the commonest piping gracenotes and they do two jobs: (a) they add varying force of emphasis to a note – important because the piper does not have other ways of doing this, such as playing more loudly or softly:

and (b) they separate two or more notes at the same pitch – a characteristic blend of elegance and usefulness, so often found in piping:

Then come a whole sequence of more elaborate figures, beginning with the 'doublings' – which are two cuttings at different pitches executed rapidly one after the other, like so:

then 'grips', where a cutting is 'framed' between two notes at a lower pitch, giving a crisp, percussive effect:

and 'throws' which extend the 'grip' principle, and are used when moving emphatically from one melody note to another at a different pitch:

next the 'taorluath', which gives its name to an important form of *pìobaireachd* variation, and is also commonly found in the light music:

and 'crunluath', a word whose meaning is disputed, but may perhaps mean 'the crowning dexterity'. It forms the substance of the later and most technically demanding variations in *pìobaireachd*:

There is an interesting manoeuvre called the 'birl', the bane of many a piping existence, made by striking down-across-and-back on the bottom hole on the chanter with the little finger of the right hand, to produce an effect somewhat thus:

When basic finger technique is well established, a few simple tunes are introduced and the work of integrating ornament and melody begins. Once this is securely grasped, it is time for the pipes themselves. Instructors sometimes move beginners towards this stage via an instrument called a 'goose' which comprises a bag, blow pipe and chanter only. When beginning the full pipe, a common approach is to have only one drone sounding (usually a tenor), to help the learner cope with the increase in physical demand. The novice learns to sound it steadily, to tune it accurately to the chanter and to keep the instrument going for ever-increasing periods of time. When this is achieved, more drones are allowed to sound until the instrument as a whole can be winded steadily and without obvious effort. This takes a good deal of time and practice.

Learning is believed to be most effective in childhood and early teens. It is here, as a general rule, that the foundations of virtuosity are laid and if missed can probably never be made good however ample the musical endowment. This is a common enough phenomenon in music. The composer György Ligeti did not get proper access to a piano until he was fifteen, and quickly learned that his dreams of a career on the concert platform were already hopeless. Turning to composition instead, he produced piano works of the kind of technical demand and complexity that he would have loved to have been able to – but could not – play himself. The ideal pupil would be so deeply drilled that execution would be automatic, and the whole conscious purpose could be focused, undividedly, upon expression. With most of us, however, what should be a tranquil passage through a smiling landscape of technical expansiveness and ease is often littered with minefields, mental hang-ups, fear of momentary loss of control, and unforeseeable acts of God. One famous player became so neurotic about his birl, that his practice chanter was worn into a scoop around his low A, as he battled to ensure that when he reached for the movement it was *always* there.

What can go wrong

So much can go wrong. The writer remembers a notable young player once sailing round the boards at a march-playing competition. He had a solid technique, his instrument was in good order, the weather was fine, and the tune a favourite. All seemed well. Suddenly his chanter ceased to sound, a serious fault at once eliminating him from the prize-list. His brows knitted and he quickly increased the pressure to make the reed start again. The whole sequence should have occupied no more than a fraction of a second. But blow as he might the reed refused to go, and he continued his progress round the platform, his fingers describing elegant parabola, while not a sound came out. And so he had to stop, mortified. A quick inspection revealed what had gone wrong. In seasoning the bag the previous day, he had partially dislodged a solidified wedge of older seasoning which at the moment of crisis had launched itself down the chanter stock and stopped the reed, whereupon the entertainment came to a halt.

Weather can cause all kinds of problems. The pipes are often obliged to play out of doors but respond as well to wet as a grand piano would, while temperature is also important: below about 55 degrees Fahrenheit fingers begin to stiffen up, and close humid weather is desperately uncomfortable to play in.

In the technical sphere, all manner of calamities lie in wait: sealing clamps coming adrift during performance, leading all the air to rush at once from the bag; reeds falling out of their seats, with similar effect; blowpipe valves coming apart; hitherto dependable reeds going suddenly 'out' on essential notes; while several septs of inner demons peculiar to piping gnaw at the performer's consciousness, including creeping mistrust of ear; hysterical loss of embouchure; and the clammy, palsied feeling that afflicts hitherto responsive fingers in conditions of acute stress.

One famous piper was hit by viral illness in middle life, and never thereafter regained complete control of his right hand. There seemed no physical basis for the problem, and his friends induced him to undergo hypnotherapy, but to no avail: the hand had gone and there seemed no obvious way of getting it back. Piping folklore is full of anxiety about loss of mastery, involving things like the dreadful *cruime* or contraction of the tendons said to be hereditary in certain piping families. 'The Cave of Gold' stories also enshrine the notion that pre-eminence is precarious and may come at terrible personal cost. These tell of the famous MacCrimmon pipers and their dealings with the fairies, a pact with the supernatural conferring exceptional skill – for a time – at the cost of the piper's life, to be forfeited on the day when he must return to the enchanted Cave of Gold and confront the, by now deadly, source of his supremacy. The tales of magical chanters being stolen by rivals, or slipping forever beneath the waves after being cursed by their owners, contain a similar suggestion. But of these things the starry-eyed beginner has little inkling when the smiling old man hands him a mountain and says 'could you just hold that for me, laddie?'

Pipers come in all sorts of ages, sizes and temperaments, but tend to be at their peak technically from about their early twenties until about their mid-fifties, although there are many exceptions. The famous G. S. McLennan, who showed precocious talent as a child, was picking up important prizes when barely into his teens. At the other end of the scale, the scarcely less famous Robert Meldrum came within a bar of carrying off the clasp (the top prize in *pìobaireachd* playing) at the age of eighty at the Northern Meeting at Inverness.

Teachers

Instructors come in various sorts and show a variety of styles ranging from the ferocious, through the coolly clinical, to the kindly and gentle. I encountered the ferocious sort first. Pipers were rather rare in my part of the country – where they ran to fiddlers – and, to be sure, the instructor was an incomer, ex-City Police pipe band, recent world champions, and so a crack technician. There were a lot like him in the piping world, as I was to learn: dark, wiry, tigerishly direct and intense, fairly crackling with energy and purpose. And he taught his youthful class with a kind of loving fury. Application and discipline were the watchwords. No tunes till he said. (This was puzzling. How could a tune be a transgression?) And he taught us to write and read bagpipe music with a strict regard to accuracy, and the tunes 'The Green Hills of Tyrol' (every movement to be heard distinctly) and the strathspey 'Lochrell' (with just the right 'lift', to give lightness but not exaggeration), and drove us down the beaten track of cuttings and doublings on our shiny new Robertson chanters (12s/6d a go; now held together forty years later by Blu-Tack and very nearly as battered as its owner) snapping at our heels, everything to be executed smartly, just so, and not one movement to be attempted until the previous one had been thoroughly mastered. 'I never heard such fumbling!', he would cry. 'Do it like this! Again! Again! By God, I'll make pipers of ye yet!' As if he would have his will of us by main force in despite of God and man and the laws of gravity.

The clinician was a solo champion with a glittering competition record, broadcasts and recordings, teaching and recitals all over the world. Suave and self-possessed, he lived in the suburbs of a great city and would greet you with practised courtesy: 'Good morning, Mr. X, and what can I do for you today?' 'Oh dear, Mr. Y', you would begin, as he ushered you to a chair by the fire and installed himself gracefully on the other side, attending with a slight inclination of the head, poised and alert, to whatever it was that ailed you. As you described the condition, he would warm his chanter (his chanter, mark you, not his hands) by the fire, diagnose at once what was wrong, play it back to you as you were doing it (with depressing accuracy), demonstrate what ought to be happening, and then prescribe precise practice routines to bridge the gulf between what was and what ought to have been. The secret of good tone, he said – and his was outstanding – was being exposed to it when young: 'in my father's house I heard nothing else'. Practicality and resourcefulness personified, he was an outstanding example of the application of method to piping. Everything was neat, precise, thoroughly considered, and set well in order. He was the finest technician I ever met, and a man of much dignity. Money never changed hands; the fee would be left discreetly on top of his gleaming pianoforte, and when it was done you descended to the city street as into a lesser world, trying somehow to prevent the magic melting away into the common air.

The kindly tutor was a surprise because he was dauntingly gruff and unapproachable by reputation, and he lived up a strath in seclusion, mysterious, formidable, and not to be tackled lightly – at least according to the folklore. He didn't have a phone and if you wanted a lesson you had to ring the local police to ask if it would be convenient. And in a day or two, you would call back and they would say 'Aye, you're to come at such-and-such a time'. I was moved by a sense that although the vastness of his knowledge was a byword amongst pipers and he was a famous player and pupil of a famous teacher, none of my immediate contemporaries seemed to study with him and I thought if I did not, what might be lost? And so, lugging a bulky pipe case, and wondering what the future had done for me that I should do this for it, I set off on the bus, walking the last mile or so to his cottage on the edge of the wood. There was nobody in. The place was deserted, there was no sign of recent habitation, and I knew that, whatever had happened, I did not think I could do this twice. As I trudged back towards the village, however, a perky little estate car drew up and a bright-eyed, cheerful-looking, elderly man in spruce tweeds jumped out and cried, 'Was I Mr. X?' Alas, I was. 'Mercy man, why didn't you say which bus you were on? I went to pick you up. Thought you hadn't come.' And so back to his snug cottage, a fire raked into vigorous life, biscuits and a dram, and music and much talk. He was of the apostolic succession in piping, one of a line of master teachers going back in unbroken succession for centuries, and although a dazzling light-music player, *pìobaireachd* was his business. He used traditional methods of singing and talk, pausing occasionally to consult a tattered printed volume when I asked for something obscure. Young pipers tended to concentrate on the tunes set for competition in any given year, which meant that large portions of the repertoire were unvisited. It was the latter I was after, and he agreed to help immediately. During the next several years I studied all kinds of things with him. His repertoire was enormous: I only once asked for a tune he did not have. The playing and teaching were mingled with hours of talk, and it became clear that there was more to piping than just music. There was a whole verbal culture as well, involving not merely technical matters about execution and interpretation and stories about the tunes, but all kinds of information, of varying degrees of propriety, about famous pipers living and dead. It was a kind of initiation, an admission to membership – however junior – of an élite and fascinating company. Most obvious of all was his

[14]

own utter commitment to and inexhaustible fascination with the art. He didn't *teach* piping, he *was* piping. His style was unobtrusive, but only one other teacher in any field – and I have been much taught – could induce such vivid contact with the subject matter, or create so enduring a sense of significance and delight. Perhaps because he had himself been ferociously taught – some of the remarks of his teacher, reported with a sigh and shake of the head, could make the listener quail even at the distance of half a century – he was gentleness itself. He smiled frequently and praised much, and he refused to charge for instruction.

Not every tutor, of course, is an effective or enthusiastic communicator; some are laconic, even positively unhelpful. One of piping's most famous families, the Camerons, were notorious for not imparting everything they knew. One player described studying with Sandy Cameron the younger. He would play and Sandy would sit in his armchair, his hand describing gentle curves in the air, shaping the phrase contours and rhythmical pulse, a common method in teaching *pìobaireachd*. If you strayed from the straight and narrow the hand would falter and fall still, and you would think, 'Oh lord, I've lost him'. And when you were done, you would enquire, with some trepidation, 'Well, what did you think?' And after a silence Sandy would say, 'Well, *I* wouldn't play it like that . . .'

Piping 'schools'

Teachers do not come singly; they themselves have had a teacher, and *that* teacher a teacher in turn. So undergoing instruction automatically makes you part of a lineage, and this is intimately bound up with notions of 'power' and 'authority' in piping. Pipers are consequently keen on what folklorists call 'genealogies of learning', i.e. the descent of their own particular line of instruction through a long succession of teachers and pupils. The tradition reached the present through a myriad of such lines, great and small, but there are certain famous families which produced master players and teachers for generation after generation and names like the MacCrimmons, the MacArthurs, the MacKays, Camerons and Mac-Phersons have enormous significance. All serious players like to think that they have one or two of these stowed away in their personal lineage. The most famous family, the MacCrimmons of Skye, were diverting their energies into other fields by the time dependable information about them began to be written down, and most later accounts of them contain a good deal of fanciful speculation. The MacKays, the Camerons and the MacPhersons are historically more recent, covering the period from the later eighteenth to about the middle of the twentieth century. One does not have to be acquainted with piping for very long to hear talk of the Cameron and MacPherson 'schools', for example, and the (largely trivial) differences in style between them. Although often overlooked, the most important of the later families may well have been the McLennans, whose influence was direct and measurable in ways that could not perhaps be said of the others.

Working clothes

Although an inseparable part of the image of piping, the association of the kilt with the pipes is rather arbitrary. At the early competitions of the Highland Society of London in the 1780s, the players wore their everyday clothing. Highland dress was made compulsory when the organisers, more concerned with pageantry than music, sought to attract a wider audience. Eventually the connection became so universally expected that pipers needed to have kilts and associated gear if they intended to play in public. This is why so many of them were in the Volunteer Force and, later, the Territorial Battalions of the Highland Regiments, which provided the requisite paraphernalia (along with other useful considerations such as drink-money and free reeds) in return for agreeably little military duty or commitment.

The kilt, and the 'Highland Dress' of which it forms part, has changed like everything else down the centuries. It reached the modern period in two forms, the *féileadh-mór* and the *féileadh-beag* (anglicised as 'philabeg'). The *féileadh-mór*, or great kilt, was a length of tartan about sixteen feet long by five feet wide. The wearer spread it out on the ground on top of his belt, roughly pleating enough below the belt to cover the lower limbs between knee and waist, then lay down on it, fastened the belt and stood up. The long upper portion could then be arranged in various tasteful ways according to circumstance. It was a flexible contraption, part clothing, part windbreak, umbrella, rucksack and tent. The *féileadh-beag*, ancestor of the modern kilt, was the abbreviated version, with the upper portion removed and the pleating stitched into place around the waist and hips. The kilt was essentially a plebeian garment designed for people whose chief means of getting about was on foot; the upper classes, who rode on horseback, wore outfits resembling tartan jump-suits.

In the nineteenth century Highland dress became spectacularly elaborate and this too became *de rigueur* for pipers, although it was singularly ill-designed for the purpose. It sent out an interesting collection of signals: military threat, implicit in the ostentatious array of swords, dirks, powder horns and pistols; a heroic larger-than-life implication lent by the towering sugar loaf of the feather bonnet and the fluttering ribbons and banners with their echoes of old romance and heraldic chivalry; the full sail of tartan in the kilt and plaid, designed to enhance the physical scale of the performer, and to move with the wind in a complex blending of ideas of the natural and heroic (the Victorian scarf plaid, which still survives in pipe band settings, was purely symbolic, serving no useful purpose whatsoever); the complicated web of belts picked out with regimental or pseudo-regimental insignia, along with various other subtle signs of power tamed and controlled, including spotless white gaiters, acres of brass and silverwork and stiffly belled flashes; and of exaggerated virility, too, which seems the clear implication of the enormous hair sporran. The outfit took a deal of work to keep in order, and many a contortion to clamber into. But here, as in everything, practice counted for much and old hands could get from tangled déshabillé to parade-ground perfect in about seven minutes flat.

The ethos of competition, presided over by landed gentlemen enthusiasts, ensured continuing formality of dress, full 'No. 1s' for military pipers and the equivalent for civilians, leading to the incongruous sight of players promenading the boards on chill September mornings at the Northern Meeting in full evening dress, stiff fronts and wing collars, shoulder plaids and all. Things became more relaxed during the second half of the twentieth century. Indeed many modern pipers seem uncomfortable with the element of display. Left to their own devices, they tend to favour tweeds and tartans so restrained, even drab, that when you see them together at a competition, they look like a convention of Highland bank-managers. The element of display is at its most obvious in the pipe-band world.

The Pipe Band

Today's top pipe bands are the ensemble equivalent of the virtuoso solo performance and attract many fine players. The pipe band, in the modern sense of a dozen or so pipers with their own dedicated corps of drums – say three or four side drums, a couple of tenors and a bass – developed in the closing decades of the nineteenth century as part of the Victorian enthusiasm for public music. It is frequently claimed that the pipe band was invented by the regular army in the mid 1850s, but the evidence points elsewhere. Pipers usually regarded the army as a last resort, preferring careers with landed estates or establishing their own businesses, both of which contexts could provide opportunities for ensemble play.

For most of the 19th century the term 'pipe band' described a group of pipers playing ensemble, *without* drummers. From at least 1820, a big estate like Taymouth, home of the fabulously wealthy Marquesses of Breadalbane, could deploy up to two dozen players to provide lavish entertainments under the direction of famous first pipers like John Bàn MacKenzie and Duncan Mac-Dougall. Later leading players like Duncan Campbell of Foss, Sandy Cameron, Malcolm MacPherson, Peter Henderson, John MacDougall Gillies, William Laurie, John MacColl, and John MacDonald of Inverness, were all connected with the Volunteer Movement where bands were likewise in high demand.

From 1859, as a spontaneous response to fears of French invasion, a 'Volunteer Force' was formed throughout the United Kingdom, drawing on business and professional people and the 'respectable' working class. It was a civilian movement, whose members – quite unlike the twentieth-century Territorial Army with which it is sometimes confused – were not under military discipline and could leave at a fortnight's notice. In Scotland it was particularly popular and was often the focus of whole communities. The Volunteers held balls and dinners, bazaars, picnics and sports meets, blending shooting and drill with a great deal of marching out in their often rather splendid uniforms. For this sort of activity bands were essential. But military and brass bands were expensive, temperamental, and a frequent source of rows and resignations. Pipers were as loud, more affordable, and usually more proficient technically.

One of the earliest illustrations of pipers and drummers playing ensemble as a regular musical formation is a sketch from the *1st Lanark Rifles' Gazette* of 3rd December 1891 showing the corps built up by Pipe-Major Peter Henderson from about 1884. It was also around this time that the first civic bands began. The Govan Police Pipe Band was formed by public subscription in the early 1880s and reached national fame under the greatest of its early pipe-majors, Inspector Alex Hutcheon of Ellon, whose piping and dancing was acclaimed as an inspirational influence on the young. Printed programmes of popular entertainments in the parks show pipers often playing selections alternatively with dancers, or singers, or with military or brass bands. A corps of pipers 'sandwiched' in this way had an obvious opportunity to experiment with rhythmical support from drummers. Impetus may also have come from another hugely popular entertainment, the Volunteer 'march out', described here by leading Glasgow journalist Archibald MacMillan who had a long association with 1st Lanark Volunteers: 'The pipers were at the heid, next the common brass band – the man wi' the biggest drum had the skin o' an elephant or a teegur or something hung in front o' him, tae keep the drum frae breaking his ribs, when he hit it ower hard at the chorus . . . The pipers struck up the "Blue Bonnets", and awa' we marched amid a great ootburst o' applause and waving pocket-napkins . . .', (*Jeems Kaye*, first series, Glasg., 1883, pp.29–33). In accompanying marching columns the drums give the pace and sound continuously, so that whatever is also playing cannot help playing along with them.

The final step, of course, is to detach the pipes and drums as a distinct, separate musical ensemble. In an earlier piece MacMillan reported on the parade for the arrival of the Lords of the High Court of Justiciary on circuit in Glasgow. This provides what seems so far to be the earliest unequivocal reference to what would nowadays be understood as a 'pipe band': 'Then cam' an extraor'nar fine man in kilts, wi' a big feather hat [presumably the drum major], followed by twelve fine braw fallows [sic] playin' the bagpipes an' drums' (*The Bailie*, 04/09/1878, p.11).

In 1878, the Parks Committee of Glasgow Corporation was formed and soon established an extensive programme of summer entertainments. If one had strolled along to Glasgow Green or Kelvingrove of a summer evening, one would probably have found a Volunteer brass or pipe band, or if one was lucky the famous Govan Police pipe band with its team of dancers regaling the public – strapping great fellows bounding like roes to the music of the pipe. In 1887, Govan Police opened the season on 14th May in Elder Park; they also performed every Tuesday evening in George Square alternately with the Blind Asylum Band. At Glasgow Green and Kelvingrove the Royal Scots Band performed with 'Pipers alternately between each piece'. The following year one of the greatest public events in Victorian Scotland, the Glasgow International Exhibition, had guest performances from 'Pipers of the Queens Own Cameron Highlanders', 'Pipers of the 3rd Argyll and Sutherland Highlanders', 'Pipers of the 4th Argyll and Sutherland Highlanders' and Seaforth 'Pipers and Drummers'. So that while the 'pipe band' still generally meant merely a corps of pipers, the modern 'pipe and drum band' was beginning to emerge. By this time Clyde Volunteer Division (Submarine Miners) Royal Engineers had 9 pipers and 5 drummers and the Edinburgh Industrial School had 14 young pipers, and 4 drummers for 'marching purposes only'.

In June 1895, a local correspondent of the *Oban Times* urged that Oban needed to encourage tourists by forming one of the new-style pipe bands, with drummers: 'In Glasgow there are Clan gatherings, pipe music regularly in the parks . . . I know that strangers to Glasgow always go to the park that has for that evening the pipe and drum band . . . in making arrangements "drums" should be bargained for. Pipes without drums have not the military "roll" nor the "roundness" that make the music martial' (01/06/1895, p.3)

Within a few years the 'pipe and drum band' had become the standard form, and the movement was dominated by the police and Volunteer bands. When the Haldane reforms of 1908 disbanded the Volunteer Force and replaced it with the more militaristic Territorial Army, many pipers left, as witnessed by the formation of the City of Glasgow Pipe Band from personnel drawn largely from the 5th and 7th (VB) H.L.I. The loss of the Volunteer network of support is why so many even of the top bands had to struggle in the early years of the 20th century to provide themselves with suitable uniforms, and find somewhere – since they no longer had access to the drill-hall – where they could practice.

The earliest band competitions began in the 1890s at Ibrox and at Bella-houston, both won by the Govan Police. Their only competitor on one occasion was the Wallacestone Colliery Band from Polmont, pioneers in what would become an important tradition of workplace pipe bands. Seventy years later the great Invergordon Distillery Pipe Band took this phase of development to its climax with Donald Shaw Ramsay and Alec Duthart carrying to virtuosic heights the potential of a corps of drums to enhance the rhythm, timbre, texture and dynamic of the modern pipe band.

In the meantime, the movement had expanded to global dimensions. In 1972 over 600 U. K. pipers and drummers flew to Toronto for the Intercontinental Pipe Band championship. By the 2004 World Championships at Glasgow Green, of the fourteen top bands qualifying for the final of the Grade One event, half were from outside Scotland. First was Field Marshal Montgomery from Ulster with Simon Fraser University from Canada in second place. In third place were the 2003 champions, Scotland's famous Shotts and Dykehead Caledonia, one of the most consistently successful competing ensembles. The band started in 1906 in a cart shed at the back of a local hotel and had to save for eight years before it could even afford uniforms. The contrast with the gleaming, commercially sponsored outfit of today is an apt symbol of the achievement of the pipe band movement during the last hundred years.

Early competitions

Competition is the central fact of serious piping life, and most of the contemporary scene springs directly or indirectly from it – so much so that most people wishing to gain access to quality piping for most of the past two centuries would have had to go to a competition to hear it. The big solo events include the Northern Meeting at Inverness and the Argyllshire Gathering at Oban which are held each year in the early autumn, followed by the Glenfiddich Championship at Blair Atholl, a prestigious invitational contest which brings the season to its climax.

Organised modern competitions had their beginning at the Falkirk Tryst in 1781, sponsored by the Highland Society of London which put up the money for running costs, travelling expenses and prizes which included, for the winner, a handsomely-made prize pipe. Falkirk was chosen because the great cattle fairs which were held there brought people together from all over Scotland. Thirteen players turned up in October 1781 for the first event, held at the town's Mason Lodge. They drew lots for the order of play, which took place in the yard behind the building while the judges occupied the lodge-room above where they could not see the players, thus avoiding obvious favouritism. The event was confined to *pìobaireachd*, each contestant played four tunes of his own choice, and it took three days to complete. The Falkirk events were about piping pure and simple. But as the years went on, showbiz came increasingly into the picture, especially after the competitions were transferred to Edinburgh in 1784. Songs and dancing were introduced, and, as they became one of *the* places to see and be seen in Edinburgh's fashionable social calendar, the events became more and more focused on Highland *Kitsch*. All that was required to be a judge was to be a gentleman, an 'enthusiast', and physically present. In some years judges outnumbered competitors.

During the nineteenth century the competition circuit grew as the Highland games movement expanded and the cultural shortcomings of the judging class were increasingly exposed. The habit of having children educated at English public schools such as Eton, Winchester and Harrow (followed up by spells at the universities of Oxford and Cambridge) eliminated Gaelic (or even Scottishness) amongst the native upper class. Benches at piping competitions came to be occupied by an assortment of titled, landed and military types with vaguely Highland connections who were presumed to be 'authorities' *ex officio*, but in most cases were deeply ignorant of the instrument and its music.

At the larger events judges recruited from the landed élite could treat pipers with a high-handedness that was almost feudal. At the Northern Meeting, competitors were required for many years to form up and play in a body down to the field. Unlike the Argyllshire Gathering at Oban where the landed element accompanied the pipers and took their chances with the uncertain autumn weather, at Inverness the pipers had to do it on their own. It was a hated chore and ducked, if possible; but at the end of the 'parade' performers were issued with a ticket and without it they could not compete. Anyway, one year it was lashing with rain and the legendary Willie Ross, then instructor of the Army Class at Edinburgh Castle, was ensconced in a tent tuning up and looking absolutely resplendent. His instrument was going just perfectly. So he dodged the parade and when he presented himself at the boards, he had no card:

'Pipe-Major', said the chief judge, J. P. Grant of Rothiemurchus (a Highland laird built on such emaciatedly Anglo-Norman lines that pipers referred to him as 'Bones'), 'you were absent from parade.'
    'Och yes, sir,' says Willie Ross, 'I just got up late in the train this morning.'
    'I know for a fact, Pipe-Major,' said Grant from a great height, 'that you were in town last night; be off with you, you will not play here today.'

Benches (usually of two or three judges in modern times) have various ways of harassing the player, including 'closing the book', i.e. ostentatiously shutting their notebooks early in the proceedings, as a sign that the performer is no longer considered to be in the running. If things get really bad, a player can be 'waved off the boards' in mid-performance, the chief judge flourishing his handkerchief in a dismissive fashion, indicating to the performer that his continued presence is no longer required. Openly chatting with fellow-judges while somebody is playing is another manoeuvre. Andrew MacDonald, brother of the famous John of Inverness, was an outstanding player (some thought better than his brother) but he disliked competing and did it seldom. When he turned up at a rain-affected Northern Meeting in September 1929, therefore, his lack of current 'form' meant less-than-minute attention from the judges. One of them wrote:

Andrew Macdonald played extraordinarily well . . . I thought he made a mistake in the ground, but we were none of us attending very carefully as we thought he could have no chance.

Such behaviour caused one long-time sufferer to compose a sardonic competition march called 'The Yapping of the Judges' (Bert Barron, *A Piper's Legacy*, p.20). It begins in orthodox fashion but rapidly degenerates into a mocking sequence of basic scale exercises without a gracenote in sight, the notion being that since nobody is listening to you anyway, it does not matter what you play. Since pipers incur a good deal of inconvenience and expense in terms of entrance money, accommodation and transport costs, to say nothing of the pains taken to prepare for the event for weeks in advance, such conduct is not very gratefully received, and there are a number of stories which illustrate the attitude of senior players towards judges whose pretensions outweighed their knowledge. One, appearing before a judge he despised, played slowly up the scale and then back down again, saluted and left. Another, encountering a judge known to insist rigidly on the note-values of the published score, enquired if he should play the page number as well.

Mixed benches of professional players and gentleman amateurs created recurring problems for the amateurs. In 1953, Archibald Campbell, secretary of the music committee of the Piobaireachd Society, wrote to the Society's hon. secretary, George Campbell of Succoth:

> Neither I nor any of my sons, nor Iain [J. P.] Grant, nor Jock Shirvan (nor presumably Archie [Kenneth] or Dougie [Ramsay]) nor (I am told), [Frank] Richardson, nor (I am told) Balfour Paul would judge along with professionals, & I don't know any of the others on our judges list who would do so willingly. I have very wide experience of such judging. In later years I have judged with my very old friend John MacDonald, but always disliked doing it. Alastair Anderson has found judging with [Willie] Ross a most unpleasant experience. It simply does not work.

Likewise, although professional players judging their pupils became an issue later in the twentieth century, gentleman pupils seldom seem to have had qualms about judging their teachers. On one occasion at Oban Sheriff J. P. Grant, himself little more than a beginner as a player, relegated his teacher John MacDonald of Inverness to fourth place in a competition he had otherwise clearly won, because MacDonald played his own setting of 'MacKay's White Banner' and not the prescribed score.

There is a story told of Willie Ross which shows these underlying tensions rather well, by quietly stripping the judge in question of his social standing (which normally, of course, was his only claim to consideration). Willie and some other top pipers were travelling between a couple of big events when their train stopped at a small station and

> Willie happened to notice a billboard up advertising the local games which were being held that afternoon.
> And he also noticed that there were a number of piping events and he turned to his three compatriots and said, 'I think we should get off the train here, boys, and go and take part in these games which should be fairly easy for us'.

Well, when they arrived on the field . . . the only other people there were, as Willie said, 'just locals' who couldn't hold a candle to these chaps. So they entered anyway and they tuned the pipes and, turning round to the piping platform, Willie said to the others, 'Goodness me, just look at the judge. He's a wee man with a bowler hat'.

Willie went up first and identified himself and the judge said, 'Ah, yes'.

'How many tunes have we to put in, sir?'

'Oh, just the one tune. What are you going to play?'

'Oh, I'll play "The Lament for Mary MacLeod"', said Willie.

'Very good', said the judge, 'just once through please.'

So, Willie immediately realised that the chap knew nothing at all about *pìobaireachd*. So, he thought, 'there's no good wasting time here'. So he played the ground and a variation or two, you see, and then came off.

Next, number two went up, you see, and passed Willie on the way and he said, 'Did you break down Willie?'

'No, of course I didn't break down'.

'Well, you didn't seem to be long on the platform then'.

'Well, well', said Willie.

So, this chap went up and went right through his tune. Then the results were given out. Willie got the first prize and two of the other professionals got second and third and the chap who had gone up number two wasn't placed. And he was extremely displeased because he was a very fine player indeed but he got nothing. So he was absolutely furious about this and he said to Willie, 'I don't believe that man knows a thing about *pìobaireachd*'.

'Oh, I don't know', said Willie, 'I don't know.'

So when Willie went back up to play the strathspey and reel he said, 'By the way, sir, competitor number two was extremely displeased that he wasn't placed in the first three'.

'Oh, oh.' So he looked up his wee black book and all he had written in it was the competitor's name and the name of his tune.

'Well, sir', he said, 'he's going to go for you, I think, you know, so if you like I could give you a few notes on his tune if you write them down.'

So he got out his pencil. Willie said, 'Well, of course, his ground was played far too slowly and in his first variation he missed out two bars in the third line. The middle of it wasn't too bad but he must have been nervous by that time knowing that he'd probably gone off and he didn't make much of a job of his crunluath movement. Then, when he came to his crunluath-a-mach, his ending movement, he played far too fast and it was a bit of a mess'.

And the chap is scribbling furiously in his book, you see.

So, when Willie had played his strathspey and reel, he met number two going up and he said to him, 'Go for him. Go for him'.

'By God, I'll go for him.'

So number two went up and the first thing he said before he even talked about the strathspey and reel, he said, 'What was wrong with my *pìobaireachd*?'

And the chap looked up his book and said, 'Well in the first place, your ground was too slow; in the second place, you missed out two bars in your first variation. The middle of your tune wasn't too bad. You obviously got nervous in your crunluath and made a few fumbles there and, of course, your crunluath-a-mach was just terrible, just a mess'.

So, when he came off the platform, having played his strathspey and reel, he met Willie.

'Well, Willie', he said, 'he's maybe a wee man with a bowler hat but he knows his *pìobaireachd.*'

Poor prize money was a long-standing source of discontent. Robert Meldrum whose 'Reminiscences', published in the *Oban Times* in 1940–41, record a long and interesting life as an army pipe-major and competing player, recalled a row at the Northern Meeting in 1885. He had arrived in Inverness to discover that some of the leading players were staging a boycott. Meldrum did not get much time off to compete, so he decided to go ahead and play, a move not at all appreciated by some of his colleagues:

On my arrival, William McLennan met me and asked me what the devil I was doing there.

I replied that I was not afraid of any of them, and asked why I should not be there.

He explained that they had protested against the smallness of the prizes, and that they were not going to play.

I replied that I had paid for my return ticket to Inverness, and was going to play. Eventually Angus Macrae and [John MacDougall] Gillies played, although they had protested, but [John] MacColl and McLennan did not. They got into some trouble for booing those who played. Gillies got the *pìobaireachd* and I was second. The judges praised my playing but for my reed. Someone had removed my own reed and substituted another (27/07/1940, p.3).

Highland Games

But ignorant judges and niggardly financial returns were only some of the tribulations of the competing piper. The Highland games circuit expanded mightily during the Victorian period as industrialisation created a commercial leisure industry to which it was the distinctive Scottish contribution. The Braemar Highland Gathering and the Northern Meeting Games started in the 1830s; but in the 1860s and '70s as the expanding railway and steamship network extended the recreational reach of urban centres, there was a crop of new events, amongst them Ballater, Aboyne, Crieff, Dunoon, and the Argyll-shire Gathering at Oban. The games catered for many tastes and the resulting mixter-maxter of fairground and circus, music hall and menagerie, athletics meet and military tattoo, made a less-than-ideal setting for playing or listening to high-quality bagpipe music. The many other activities going on at the same time – the hubbub of the crowd, the blare of military music, the frequent report of starting pistols, canned music from the neighbouring fairground and, for much of the twentieth century, amplified public address systems – created a cacophonous din that not even the pipes could penetrate. Sometimes the piping was physically separated from the main arena but even so it might still suffer interruption: competitors could find the boards requisitioned to saw the ends off cabers, even while they played. Whoever managed to struggle through the acoustic ruck to win was often then expected to provide music *gratis* for the dancing events.

Large events like these are difficult to run smoothly. Since there will probably be no formal tuning-up facilities, pipers are squirreled away in various nooks and crannies and have to be flushed out and got to the boards in good order by teams of stewards appointed for the purpose. As a result of people 'breaking down' (because they have gone off the tune or committed some fatal disqualifying error) it is difficult for others further down the draw to calculate how much tuning-up time they have got – a matter of considerable importance. Pipers can be strangely hard to find in such circumstances (and when found to browbeat into playing) if stewarding is slack. At Aboyne one year there was great reluctance to begin among the top players who had been drawn early, and in desperation the stewards turned to a local lad called R. B. Nicol (later a famous champion but then at the beginning of his career) and he readily agreed to go first. He had been watching the weather and knew what was going to happen next. The heavens duly opened and he was the only performer to complete his tune in the dry. At Oban the stewarding was done by enthusiastic local lairds whose social clout and habit of command meant they were rather good at it. Willie Ross once reduced a train compartment of pipers coming back from the Argyllshire Gathering to helpless mirth by remarking, out of the blue, 'You can say what you like about Campbells; but by God they're efficient'.

The competition circuit

Success at competition is one of the few indisputable markers of professional eminence for pipers and so they tolerate the frustrations of the circuit for the chance of the top awards. These include the clasp for former winners at the Northern Meeting and the Inverness and Oban gold medals. Competitions take place virtually throughout the year; there are both indoor and outdoor events and the main part of the 'season' runs from about May to September. Pipers compete in different categories for prizes in *pìobaireachd*, for march strathspey and reel playing, for jigs and occasionally hornpipes. These attract distinctive audiences. Some players confine themselves more or less exclusively to the light music and have little taste for *pìobaireachd*. Indeed one famous player who had won all the top awards in *ceòl mór* declared to the writer that in his view people who affected a genuine interest in the stuff were 'nutters'. Head-to-head elimination contests between the top light music players can produce spectacular displays of technical brilliance and fill halls. Visitors to *pìobaireachd* competitions, on the other hand, may find themselves in a cloistered atmosphere in the presence of a mere handful of devotees bent intently over their books of scores in the '*pìobaireachd* appreciation crouch'.

In competition, temperament is important and the unflappably steady, not to say prosaic, player is at a great advantage. The mercurial Bob Brown, who was thought the most expressive *pìobaireachd* player of his generation by those who heard him play well, competed rather seldom and was sometimes so badly affected by nerves that people could receive the impression that he was greatly overrated. Brown said of his own teacher, John MacDonald of Inverness, that you heard him best in his carpet slippers, and the same was probably also true of the pupil.

Competition is sometimes stated to have done much to promote piping, but it tends to focus attention narrowly on those aspects of the art which lend themselves most easily to comparison. Thus, while brilliance of tone may reasonably be rewarded, so frequently are machine-like accuracy of technique and a ploddingly literal approach to expression. This is especially so in *pìobaireachd* where, thanks to the prevailing ethos in judging, some approaches are quite arbitrarily deemed to possess 'authority' while others are not. This fosters an atmosphere in which avoidance of error becomes the major virtue, producing drab safety-first performances which would hardly be tolerable in another setting. In *pìobaireachd* particularly, the fantastically deliberate modern style appears to proceed on the principle that 'anything you can play I can play slower; I can play anything slower than you', the general effect being of laboriousness seven times laboured. Pipers call it 'the dead hand on the chanter', but it is a phenomenon by no means confined to piping. Mendelssohn summed it up well when commenting on the concert keyboard style of his day with its penchant for empty technical display where 'the only thrill in the performance was in the anticipation of an accident'.

It is now quite common in piping magazines to find evaluative comment on performances at the top events, usually written by senior ex-competitors, and mostly from a narrowly technical point of view, along the lines of 'Well, I thought X played his tune quite nicely but his drones drifted a bit towards the end and he missed a doubling at the start of the third part of the strathspey'. But for a long time this kind of thing was rather taboo. The pipes are such a demanding instrument to play well and the upper echelons of piping so often meet in circumstances of personal rivalry that a deal of tact is involved in evaluating one another's play. There is much use of indirect language, therefore, and expressions like 'Aye, man, I liked your tune' (probably implying 'but not the way you played it'); or 'I liked your chanter' ('but not your drones'); or 'Man, you have fingers like lightning' (i.e. 'they never strike in the same place twice'). What seems like praise may indeed be so, but it can be hedged about with all kinds of unspoken qualifications. On the other hand, a typical piece of understatement like 'Aye, that's nae bad' may actually mean something pretty close to 'Yes, good, excellent!' A tutor, glowing with satisfaction (inwardly), may tell his pupil, 'Aye, that'll dee' ('that will do'), a flexible usage indicating anything from its literal surface meaning up to, and including, 'My *word*, that's good!' It has been said that in a laconic culture like Scotland's the mere absence of criticism may constitute the highest praise.

The Music

The Big Music (Ceòl Mór)

Pipe music is divided into two sorts: *pìobaireachd* (pron: '*pee*per-uchk') or *ceòl mór* (pron: 'kyol-more', literally the 'big music'), often described as the classical music of the pipe, and *ceòl beag* (pron: 'kyol-bek', or the 'little music') comprising marches, strathspeys, reels, slow airs, jigs and hornpipes. This latter category, especially nowadays, is a complete misnomer – at least as regards technical difficulty. The 'light music' heard in competition can often make more demands on the player than *pìobaireachd*. The word '*pìobaireachd*' itself, although it has come to be used to denote a special type of pipe music, basically just means 'pipering' or 'what pipers do'. All decent players can do both kinds, although specialism in *pìobaireachd* is sometimes regarded as the preserve of a highly-trained élite. Once upon a time a repertoire of two hundred *pìobaireachd* may not have been uncommon; the lower threshold of mastery nowadays would be around fifty or sixty tunes.

Pìobaireachd has a long and troubled history. It has a reputation for being abstruse and demanding, but this owes more to poor twentieth-century editing and the circumstances of competition than to the intrinsic difficulty of the form. Although some compositions are built upon abstract tonal relationships, many have a richly lyrical strain and are counted amongst the high peaks of Scottish melody.

[27]

Pìobaireachd takes the basic form of a rondo: a theme and variations with periodic return of the theme. It comprises:

– a 'ground' (or *ùrlar*, pron: *oor*lur, which provides the basic theme)

followed by variations of different sorts including perhaps:

– a 'thumb variation' (or *siubhal ordaig*, pron: '*she*well *or*dik') in which high A or high G is substituted for certain notes in the ground
– various other kinds of *siubhal* which involve pairing themal notes from the ground with lower notes on the chanter such as A or G
– a *leumluath* (pron: *lem*la) which combines the themal notes from the ground with a conventional gracenote figure revolving round a tonal centre on E
– a *taorluath* (pron: *toor*la), which combines the themal notes from the ground with a different conventional gracenote combination centring on A
– a *crunluath* (pron: *croon*la), which combines the themal notes from the ground with still different gracenote combinations.

There are other types of variation, but the above are the most common.

In terms of musical organisation *pìobaireachd* follows a number of prescribed patterns of which the simplest is nowadays called 'primary metre'. This involves an asymmetrical phrase pattern within a three-line melody, arranged as follows:

Line 1:   **A**   **A**   **B**
Line 2:   **A**   **B**   **B**
Line 3:   **A**   **B**

'Secondary metre' is made up of four phrases – A, B, C and D – repeated in certain fixed sequences, phrases C and D being twice the length of A and B, so that the pattern of a typical 'secondary *pìobaireachd*' would be:

Line 1:   **A**   **B**   **C**   **D**
Line 2:   **C**   **B**   **A**   **D**
Line 3:   **C**   **D**

This may look 'difficult', but the only point necessary to grasp is that *pìobaireachd* is an extremely regular and rule-bound form, quite the opposite of the wild and artless strains fancifully depicted by Romantic writers.

The various genres of *pìobaireachd* include laments, marches, gathering tunes, salutes, and battle pieces. These imply certain differences in style and the way the tunes are developed. For example, concluding *crunluath a mach* variations, nowadays played throughout the repertoire thanks to the influence of the competition circuit, were traditionally found mainly in gathering and battle tunes of which they were a distinctive marker. There are important differences, too, in the scales or modes considered appropriate for each genre. Although there are nine melody notes available on the chanter, rather few tunes use them all, the majority deploying partial scales gapped at different points, each giving a distinctive emotional flavour. Five- or six-note scales, called 'pentatonic' or 'hexatonic' scales, are common and altogether twenty-four different ones have been described, which gives some idea of the expressive nuance available to the player. This underlies the immediately perceptible differences between a tragic piece like 'The Lament for Patrick òg MacCrimmon' based on a pentatonic modal scale G, A, B, D, E (heightened by the dissonant harmonies of drones tuned to A) and a joyously expansive tune like 'Hail to my Country', which uses a scale, A, B, C, E, F, with very different expressive implications:

'Patrick òg MacCrimmon's Lament', Ground, line 1

'Patrick òg MacCrimmon's Lament', first variation, line 1

'Patrick òg MacCrimmon's Lament', scale

'Hail to my Country', Ground, line 1

'Hail to my Country', first variation, line 1

'Hail to my Country', scale

Naming conventions in *pìobaireachd* are highly formulaic. Even in English, the names are often evocative. Titles like 'Too Long in this Condition', 'The

Desperate Battle of the Birds', 'The Blind Piper's Obstinacy', 'The Finger Lock', 'The Unjust Incarceration', 'Drizzle on the Stone', 'The Carles with the Breeks' and 'My King has Landed in Moidart' have an appealing music of their own.

Those keen to claim great antiquity for the music have fixed upon tune titles ostensibly marking events in the remote past as proof of this and have proceeded to draw from such 'evidence' various largely fanciful conclusions about the evolution of the form. The assumption is that tunes are given to the world by their composers in fixed and final form and are not subject to subsequent re-working. But everything we know about the transmission of music in traditional societies suggests that *pìobaireachd* is likely to have received attention from every creative intelligence through which it passed. Given that there is little written evidence earlier than the eighteenth century and that tune titles frequently vary, such speculation must be treated as doubtful at best.

There are many stories associated with the tunes and sometimes different stories attached to the same tune. In Angus MacKay's *Collection of Ancient Piobaireachd or Highland Pipe Music* (Edinburgh, 1838), Aberdonian journalist and antiquary James Logan gave the story of the famous 'Lament for the Children' which has passed current for most of the past two centuries. It tells how the famous player and composer Patrick Mór MacCrimmon 'was accompanied to church one Sunday by eight sons, who all, with one exception, died within twelve months, on which bereavement he composed a tune called *Cumha na Cloinne*, or Lament for the Children'. But Donald MacDonald, drawing upon the traditions of Skye around 1800, gives quite a different account:

> The subjects of this very plaintive *Piobaireachd*, were three young ladies, two of whom were Campbells, the other, Cameron of Lochiel's daughter. These ladies went to bathe, in a linn of water, near Sir Ewen Cameron's house; Sir Ewen and his lady, wondering why the ladies were so long in returning, sent their servant to ascertain the cause of their delay, who, when she could not find them, returned, and told Cameron and his lady. They became very much alarmed, and proceeded immediately to the linn, in which the ladies had intended to bathe; and, on their looking into it, they beheld, to their great grief, the three ladies, lying lifeless, at the bottom of it. The above air was played, after their corpse, at their funeral, the common custom in those days.

Then there is the famous tune 'Too long in this condition'. According to Donald MacDonald it was 'Composed by Great Peter McCruimen Piper to McLeod of Dunvegan Isle of Skye, After being Stripped of all his Clothes by the English at the Battle of Sheriff-Muir in 1715'. However, the journalist and Celtic scholar Henry Whyte (1852–1913), who wrote under the pen-name 'Fionn', recorded quite a different set of circumstances for the tune:

An old man from Loch Carron told me it was composed by Donald Mór MacCrimmon. He had to flee from Skye on account of some depredation . . . and having fled to Sutherlandshire, he entered the house of a relative named MacKay who was getting married that day. He sat in a corner unnoticed, and nobody heeded him. When the piper began to play Donald was fingering his stick, and the piper observing this knew that he could play. He asked him to do so, but Donald said he could not. The whole company asked him, but he again refused. At last the piper said – 'I am getting 7s 6d for the marriage; I will give you one third of it if you play.' Donald took the pipe and struck up –

> 'S fhada mar so, 's fhada mar so,
>   'S fhada mar so 'tha mi;
> 'S fhada mar so gun bhiadh gun deoch,
>   Air banais Mhic Aoidh tha mi.
> 'S fhada mar so, 's fhada mar so,
>   'S fhada mar so 'tha mi;
> 'S fhada mar so gun bhiadh gun deoch,
>   An tigh mo charaid Mhic Aoidh tha mi.

['Too long am I thus, too long am I thus, too long in this condition; too long am I thus without food or drink at MacKay's wedding. Too long am I thus, too long am I thus, too long in this condition; too long am I thus, wanting food and drink at the house of my friend MacKay']. 'Fionn' continues:

The whole company at once knew that this was the great MacCrimmon; understood the meaning of the tune . . . and he was loyally entertained. (*Oban Times*, 07/06/1890, p.3).

The Light Music (*Ceòl Beag*)

The light music is rich and varied. There are several different kinds of march, for example, including retreat airs, six-eight marches, four-four marches, and two-four marches great and small, each with its own particular idiom, as well as strathspeys, reels, jigs, hornpipes, and various other forms.

One of the simpler forms, the retreat air, springs from an army setting when retreat would be beat of an evening to mark the end of the military day. Most of the good ones were written by people who were professionally or temporarily soldiers. Famous pieces include 'The Green Hills of Tyrol', which is said to have been picked up by sharp-eared pipers listening to other people's military bands in the Crimea. But during the mid-Victorian period much of the light music of the pipe came from the popular song repertoire of Lowland Scotland – 'A man's a man for a' that', 'Because he was a bonnie lad', 'The bonnie house of Airlie', 'Up and waur them a', Willie' and similar tunes filling the published collections. Not surprisingly, those brought up in this ambience sought to develop it further. We see this in the work of John MacLellan of Dunoon (1875–1949), whose lovely retreat airs, including 'Lochanside', 'The Dream Valley of Glendaruel', 'The Highland Brigade at Magersfontein', and 'The Bloody Fields of Flanders' (which was used by Hamish Henderson as the air for his famous song 'Freedom come all ye'), show this quite clearly.

It is sometimes maintained by writers on folk song that words come first and are subsequently fitted with a tune. In Scottish tradition this relationship is usually reversed, instrumental music coming first and only later being matched with words. For example, late eighteenth- and early nineteenth-century Scotland was bursting with brilliant new fiddle tunes, as well as fresh awareness and enthusiasm for the older tradition. Songwriters like Robert Burns, James Hogg and Carolina Oliphant (Lady Nairne) all produced outstanding new sets of words to existing airs. Hogg wrote:

One evening in the winter of 1800, I was sawing away on the fiddle with great energy and elevation, and having executed the strathspey called Athol Cummers, much to my own satisfaction, my mother said to me 'Dear Jimmie, are there ony words to that tune?' – 'No that ever I heard, mother.' – 'O man, it's a shame to hear sic a good tune an' nae words till't. – Gae away ben the house, like a good lad, and mak' me a verse till't.' The request was instantly complied with.

It is interesting, therefore, to watch John MacLellan working in exactly the opposite direction. MacLellan was also a poet and song-writer and with him the words came first. When he had got them, he then evolved a tune to fit. We can see this in 'My Dream Valley on the Road to Glendaruel' which was published in the *Oban Times* in 1942. The words go like this:

> In the gloaming by the river,
> There are scenes that haunt me ever;
> There is peace and love, as in Heaven above,
> In the sweet valley of my dreams.
>
> And there's glory in the morning,
> Dewey flowers the fields adorning,
> And there's love to share, with a maiden fair,
> In the sweet valley of my dreams.
>
> (*Oban Times*, 30/05/1942, p.5)

and the tune, like this:

It will be obvious that MacLellan was very much better as a melodist than as a poet. The tune, with its flowing lyrical quality and that sweet melancholy that marks so much of his work, contrasts quite markedly with the conventional pastel-coloured lyrics and it is interesting to think that MacLellan had to pass through this kind of verbal screen to arrive at the distinctive melody beyond. It may be that for somebody like MacLellan the tune was relatively little trouble; he could conjure it up quite easily once he had done the, for him, hard bit, which was arriving at the words. Typically of a retreat air, 'My Dream Valley on the Road to Glendaruel' is in two parts, the first taking its flavour from the lower register of the chanter, the second developing related or contrasting ideas chiefly in the upper register.

The 6/8 march supplies many of the musical high points of the bagpipe repertoire, and the tune 'Dovecot Park' is one of the classics. It sprang from an episode featuring the famous Pipe-Major Willie Ross. When Willie was – rather suddenly – appointed instructor of the Army Class at Edinburgh Castle in 1919, he had to wait until his flat at the Castle was fixed up and stayed with his friend Pipe-Major James Braidwood at his house 'Dovecot Park'. To commemorate this, Braidwood composed a lovely march tune which he intended to call 'Pipe-Major William Ross's welcome to "Dovecot Park" '; but Willie said 'No, no, never mind the Pipe-Major Ross stuff, just call it "Dovecot Park" '; and so it was:

Various typical features are on display here – such as the development of the tune in four parts rather than two, the relative emphasis given to notes on the bottom hand in parts one and three and to the upper hand in parts two and four and the fixed two-bar motif which recurs at the end of every part. All of this is more or less obvious. Less so, perhaps, is the ingenious network of balancing and contrasting figures which lies at the heart of the tune. The gesture

is repeated no fewer than twenty times in sixty-four bars. The answering figures

are stated with similar frequency. And yet these are approached so cleverly that there is no suggestion of tedium or lack of invention. Maximum effect is achieved with an audacious economy of means. It may look simple, but this is not an easy thing to do.

The 6/8 march is a favourite genre and some of the best-known pipe tunes take this form, including 'The Glendaruel Highlanders' by Alex Fettes of Aberdeen:

This was the theme tune of the famous '1,000 Pipers' March' through Edinburgh in August 1951. It ground to a halt in Princes Street because instead of the anticipated 10,000 crowd, it attracted an audience of a quarter of a million people, swamping the performers, stewards and police; and very nearly the writer himself, then a child, and hanging on to his aunts for dear life at the top of the Mound.

'Farewell to the Creeks' by James Robertson of Banff (also used by Hamish Henderson for his song, 'The 51st Highland Division's Farewell to Sicily') is another classic of the genre:

Many pipe tunes became part of the common stock in this way. They were whistled, played and sung all over Scotland, often acquiring words in the process. Sometimes this was done commercially, as with 'Scotland the Brave'. Its lyrics were hastily improvised by journalist Cliff Hanley (1922–1999) when the leading Scots tenor Robert Wilson wanted to record it as a song:

Its later popularity caused acute embarrassment to the streetwise writer who, assuming it was a one-off and nothing more would be heard of it, cheerfully stuffed it with every cliché he could think of:

> Proudly in gallant fame,
> Scotland, my mountain hame,
> Lang may your proud banners
> Gloriously wave . . .

As he scribbled it down in a pub in Glasgow, he had little inkling that he was penning one of Scotland's national anthems.

But some lyrics were more fragmentary, mere floating strands of popular tradition like those to Black Will MacDonald's tune 'The Highland Division at Wadi Akarit', one of the catchiest things to come out of World War II, which began:

Oh, my dar-ling Flo I love you so...

In Aberdeenshire they sang

> Harry Laader shaved his faader
> Wi' a roosty roosty raazor . . .
>
> (Harry Lauder shaved his father
> With a rusty rusty razor . . .)

to the tune of 'The Barren Rocks of Aden' ('*faa*der' and '*raa*zor' being near-rhymes in that cold county where as a general rule vowels work at about 75% of their advertised rate):

Har-ry Laa-der shaved his faa-der wi' a roos-ty roos-ty raa-zor

There was an alternative verse, in some ways most touching of all – to a player – about the bungling piper who made his best efforts,

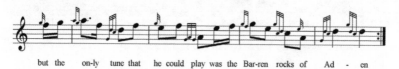

but the on-ly tune that he could play was the Bar-ren rocks of Ad - en

Sometimes the words were rather coarse. Scott Skinner's pipe-march 'The Lovat Scouts' was sung to the following:

Oh my auld wife and your auld wife gaed oot tae sho-vel sn -- aw, says my auld wife tae

your auld wife gie my auld airse a cl -- aw .

'The Barren Rocks' would certainly rank amongst the over-popular airs held in weary disdain by pipers, certain that they will be called for again and again by naïve audiences and harassed pipe-majors. The hate-parade would also include 'The Brown-Haired Maid'. It had words as well, sub-Hebridean maunderings on the lines of:

Ho ro, my nut brown maiden,
Ho ree my nut brown maiden,
Ho ro, ro, maiden,
For she's the maid for me.

The virtue of this stuff lay in its being, perhaps, fractionally less witless than the Metrical Psalms, and it was visited as such upon generations of Scottish schoolchildren. The children, grown up and conscripted into the army, revenged themselves upon it in parodies, like

'Highland Laddie' is another old un-favourite. There are words here again:

Some of these 'top of the flops' are just bad tunes, played more for the sake of their local or historical associations than for any musical merit they might possess. How many people, for example, who had ever been connected with the Gordons and had the slightest musical taste, could hear the regimental march, 'The Cock of the North':

without wincing? It had words, too, beginning 'Auntie Mary had a canary/Up the leg o' her drawers . . .'

Changing repertoire

In the earlier nineteeth century, the light music of the pipe was a cheerful hotch-potch of material drawn from the whole range of Scottish popular tradition, much of it consisting of Lowland song-airs arranged in simple two-part settings, very lightly ornamented. The great age of original composition of light music for the pipes began in the middle of the nineteenth century and continues to the present. A number of factors contributed to this. The expanding games circuit stimulated the growth of a light music repertoire of sufficient technical difficulty to be a test in competition and led to the development of the so-called 'competition' march, strathspey and reel.

One of the results of this was that tunes got bigger. This might happen as a result of original composition; or the compounding of two or three pre-existing airs into a kind of medley; or, most commonly, by the addition of variations to an existing tune. Thus a characteristically two-parted formula evolved into one containing typically four or perhaps as many as six or eight parts. We see this in 'The Breadalbane Fencibles Quickstep', preserved in two-parted form in Angus MacKay's manuscripts and probably written down during the later 1840s. This was superseded within a decade by a six-parted version by Donald Cameron, in which form the tune was transmitted during the following century-and-a-half, as shown in the Tunes section on pages 145–6 below.

In the process of change, the source material could be effectively re-composed, as we see in the famous march 'The 71st Highlanders' by Hugh MacKay dating from 1851 and still in the repertoire of all good players. It seems to have sprung from an earlier tune, 'Lord Lennox's March', a version of which is preserved in the papers of Robert Millar, dated 1838, currently in the National Library of Scotland:

MacKay's '71st Highlanders' begins like this:

Few would doubt that the tune had gained significantly from MacKay's intervention, in particular in the more shapely melodic contour and the heightened tension between the first, second and sixth intervals of the scale. He may have achieved this in a single step; but since tunes receive attention from every creative personality through whom they pass, there may have been intervening stages, now lost. One result of such continual re-making was that standard pieces tended to improve with the passage of time as good ideas were kept and inferior ones discarded. This would go on until nobody thought they could improve on what they had got, or until a change in fashion prompted a rethink about the inherited repertoire.

The construction of variations in competition march tunes, with their characteristic strings of rising and falling semi-quaver runs and rapid stepped figures permitting flashing exchange between the top and bottom hands of the chanter, seems to derive from two main sources, the first being an impressionistic attempt to imitate *pìobaireachd* variations in this new convention. For example, the characteristic

competition march motif swings between the tonic and dominant rather like a spaced-out *crunluath*. Another obvious source is the traditional fiddle repertoire where the habit of expanding melodies by the addition of strings of conventional variations had long been in use. Since pipers frequently also played the fiddle, and the fiddlers may have got the basic idea from pipers in the first place, this is a further illustration of the various traditional performing arts drawing upon a common expressive pool, overlapping and enriching one another in interesting ways. The most obvious development of all, perhaps, was in tonality, the competition march in particular frequently using the whole range of notes available on the chanter rather than the gapped pentatonic and hexatonic (five-and-six note) scales which had tended to predominate hitherto.

As the 'competition march' developed as a form, its characteristic idiom continued to evolve. One can see this by comparing the tunes of John Bàn MacKenzie (1796–1864), one of the early pioneers, with those of John MacColl (1860–1943), who as a composer was perhaps the best of a gifted late-Victorian generation. As we see in the appendix of tunes, MacKenzie's pieces were typically built from recurring blocks of angular figures organised in rigid double tonic sequences, while MacColl's have a much more sophisticated and through-composed feel. As time went on there was increasing use of tricky ornament and figures difficult of execution. This feature was probably carried to its highest point by G. S. McLennan, the most brilliant technician of his generation. When he played, conservatives used to grumble that they could hardly hear the tune for the doublings. Indeed, it is said that early in his career McLennan lost a number of prizes in competition because the judges considered his style over-elaborate. The spread of the new style also helped separate the masters from the merely good players in competition: McLennan had been a child prodigy and could do this kind of thing with ease, but not everybody was similarly endowed.

Thus the 'competition march' came into being. It happened quickly, going from obscure beginnings to maturity as a form within two generations at most. Yet it was to have a lengthy creative lifespan and become one of the most distinctive of the many contributions pipers have made to Scottish culture.

After a while, however, the new conventions began themselves to sound 'conventional' and there was much exploration of fresh tonal and rhythmical effects, typical of the ceaseless quest for the new that marks pipe music throughout its history. This is well illustrated by the twentieth-century compositions of Peter MacLeod. Their innovative approach to rhythm and interval can be seen in a tune like 'Hugh Kennedy, M.A. B.Sc.' which is built on two contrasting scales:

↑C borrowed from contrasting scale

MacLeod cheekily fills in the gap in the second scale with material from the first in a way that would probably have made John MacKenzie gasp. In a further development of the typical approach in John Bàn's days, bars 5–6 are not a simple repeat, but a clever development of the material first stated in bars 1–2. Compositions like 'Hugh Kennedy' are notably innovative, but others conforming to a more traditional aesthetic still found novel and attractive things to say. William Laurie's 'Captain Carswell' was one of the great hits of World War I (which, alas, claimed the life of its gifted composer) and is still widely played. Its first measure is formed on a perfect gapped pentatonic scale:

'Captain Carswell', scale

It is possible in the space available to give only a glimpse of this major form, which is well represented in *Pipe-Major W. Ross's Collection of Highland Bagpipe Music* (5 vols., London, 1923–1950) and whose high points include tunes like 'The Abercairney Highlanders', 'Bonnie Anne', 'Brigadier General Ronald Cheape of Tiroran', 'Charles Edward Hope Vere', 'The Edinburgh Volunteers', 'The Glengarry Gathering', 'Highland Wedding', 'The Stirlingshire Militia', 'The Argyllshire Gathering', 'Pipe-Major John Stewart', 'The Lochaber Gathering', 'The Braes of Castle Grant', 'The Crags of Stirling', 'Lord Alexander Kennedy', 'The 71st Highlanders', 'Donald Cameron', 'The Ross Shire Volunteers', 'Mrs. John MacColl', 'John MacFadyen of Melfort', 'Arthur Bignold of Lochrosque', 'The Braes of Brecklet', 'The Conundrum', 'Millbank Cottage', 'MacLean of Pennycross', 'The Atholl Highlanders March to Loch Katrine', 'The Hon. Miss Elspeth Campbell', 'Leaving Glenurquhart', 'John MacColl's March to Kilbowie Cottage', 'John MacDonald of Glencoe', 'The Balmoral Highlanders', and 'The Inverness Gathering'.

Tune titles in the light music are highly conventional and involve formulae such as 'X's welcome to Y', or 'A leaving B' or similar movement between places such as 'Cairo to Tunis', or 'Kantara to El Arish'. Tunes may be dedicated to institutions, events and (very commonly) to people. But the music is largely abstract and non-referential: it does not seek, generally speaking, to evoke or describe, or find musical equivalents for events in the outside world. There are a number of exceptions to this rule, like G. S. McLennan's mighty reel 'The Little Cascade', which he composed, according to the folklore, while listening to a dripping tap as he lay on his deathbed (though parts of the tune had been in existence for at least ten years); or the invocation of birdsong in Donald MacPherson's jig 'The Curlew', which came to him when listening to one on a fishing trip. But there is no essential quality of the remarkable Elspeth Campbell expressed, or even aimed at, in the tune which bears her name, and the same is true for most such pieces. There may be an element of irony or insider humour, such as the reel 'The Old Ruins' which apparently refers to somebody's teeth; the classic modern hornpipe 'Duncan Johnstone' was so called because its composer, Donald MacLeod, played it to Johnstone when it was spanking new and asked what he thought of it:

'It's the worst tune I ever heard in my life', said Johnstone, provokingly.
'Well, there you go', said MacLeod, 'we'll call it "Duncan Johnstone"'.

The question, 'What's in a name?' is not always an easy one to answer. The great majority of tune titles are arbitrary and offer little guide to interpretation. At the same time, titles sometimes give an ironic inflection to the melodies to which they are attached. At weddings you can sometimes hear 'I'll ne'er gang back to yon toun', a lovely old piece which her brother recalled Caroline Oliphant – Lady Nairne – playing as a girl on the harpsichord. But you need to know the words to realise that the song cynically questions the institution of marriage and the possibility of finding happiness within it. The regular army did this kind of thing quite frequently, with regimental duty tunes like 'Sleep Dearie, Sleep' for lights out; 'O but ye've been lang in comin'' for playing in a draft, or 'Happy we've been a' thegither' for playing out a draft. During the First World War the famous William Laurie when pipe major of the 8th Argyll and Sutherland Highlanders led the pipes and drums at a formal parade when a man from his native Ballachulish was being reduced to the ranks in front of the whole battalion for some misdemeanour, most thought unfairly. On leading off the parade, Laurie turned to the band and said 'Don't play', and the whole battalion marched off the square in total silence; when they reached the road 'A man's a man for a' that' struck up.

Composition in light music

Many pipers, perhaps most, compose. There is no formal instruction in this aspect of the art, but with increasing experience the player becomes conscious of the musical conventions involved, with what has been done with them and with what might remain to be said. The poet Robert Burns taught himself in this way, studying songs at the plough, trying to figure out how they worked, what sorts of things they talked about and in what manner, what pleased him and what didn't and why this might be. Not everybody can be a Burns, of course; the best that most of us can hope for is, in Robert Tannahill's phrase, 'to be reckoned respectable amongst the minor bards of the country'. Indeed the beginner in composition quickly becomes aware of major musical intelligences amongst his predecessors, giants in terms of talent, the latchets of whose shoes he or she is not fit to unloose.

The composer working within the traditional idiom has got two difficult goals to achieve. While manipulating a highly conventional set of phrase materials and structural procedures, he or she must say something sufficiently new to attract the interest of a highly knowledgeable audience, while at the same time framing the material in such a way that it sufficiently resembles the inherited repertoire to gain acceptance. The very best composers, like G. S. McLennan and Donald MacLeod, do this so effectively that they can induce the audience to widen their view of what might be considered 'traditional' at a stroke. But usually the process of change is slower and more cumulative.

The musical picture of the world changes from generation to generation and there is much creative re-interpretation, ranging from tiny decisions about accent or ornament to major stylistic change within the genres. Dvořák once said that any fool could write a tune: melody just 'came', mysterious, unbidden, an act of God. It was what you then did with it – the bit where *art*, in the sense of conscious intelligence and skill, came into play – that sorted out the real composers from the duds. But things are not quite like this on the Highland pipe. Working with a solo instrument with invariable timbre and dynamic, the piper is compelled first and foremost to be a melodist: building a tonal collage from fragmentary phrase materials, as an orchestral composer may do, is not an option. Getting a complete part, never mind a whole tune, in a single intuitive flash seems highly uncommon. More frequently, perhaps, an interesting phrase may enter the mind, and then become the focus of conscious shaping to evolve a complete whole from the tiny inspirational part, trying all the while to steer a delicate course between cliché on the one hand and breach of idiom on the other. At any given time the best has already been achieved and all the easy effects have been used up. So that while the past is a constant guide and inspiration, it can also be a burden and may, indeed, entirely frustrate the expressive urge.

Methods of composition vary. Donald Shaw Ramsay used to do it while driving. G. S. McLennan sat down with large sheets of music manuscript paper and relentlessly worked out the various possibilities. Some people extemporise on practice chanters; others pace to and fro crooning to themselves. Nor are they always conscious of the quality of what they achieve. Tunes may undergo tinkering for lengthy periods before the composer thinks 'yes; that will do'. Again, there are exceptions. Judging by his written commentaries, G. S. seems to have known at once when he was on to something good and Donald MacLeod seems to have been quick to discard what he thought inferior. There is probably a lot of waste in this way: you may quickly find yourself in a blind alley from which there seems no acceptable way out, at least not one apparent to an ordinary talent – which is maybe why that wonderful tune you are struggling to write has not been written by somebody else first. Of course, the beautiful, elusive phrase that may be the start of something exceptional must be written down before it escapes. Any kind of surface will do at a pinch, even an arm or a hand. One of the 'Larks of Dean', a fascinating community of plebeian musicians in nineteenth-century England, preserved a new tune on the back of a spade. Timothy Swan of Massachusetts, a notable composer in the New England shape-note or 'Sacred Harp' tradition, wrote down one of his new hymns in the sand, as he lay on the beach recovering from a hangover.

Of course, not every one is a hit. Composers can turn out tune after solidly competent tune for years before coming up with perhaps a single outstandingly lovely piece – if they are lucky. Alexander MacLeod, Pipe-Major of the 26th Cameronians, composer of 'The Drunken Piper' – the tune to which 'The Reel of the 51st Division' is danced – had about three excellent tunes in him including the fine 6/8 marches 'The Wee Sergeant' and the still-unpublished 'Convention at Bonar Bridge', but had to thrash about through hundreds of nearly-good pieces to get at them. As paper got cheaper during the Victorian period, pipers could afford to doodle in this way, as the contents of his manuscript collection entitled 'A. MacLeod's Light Music', now in the National Library of Scotland, bear witness. A number of tunes were the work of more than one composer. The first two parts of 'The Barren Rocks' were by A. McKellar, Pipe-Major of the 78th, when they were lying at Aden, the last two parts being added by a later hand.

G. S. McLennan's private papers show him working his way through jig after theoretical jig, systematically mapping out every possible grouping of intervals and rhythms and arranging the results in numerical sequence. Eventually there were more than fifty of these. Number 47 was the classic 'Jig of Slurs':

This seems little different from the ruthless exploitation of resources one might see in a professional composer at any time, especially during the baroque period, when it was said, rather cruelly, of Vivaldi, that he composed the same tune four hundred times.

Yet not even the greatest is immune from the misconceived or banal, and the decision of his regiment to publish G. S. McLennan's rejects could be viewed in a number of lights. In composition what you do not say is almost as important as what you do. One thinks of the large number of pieces left unpublished by Donald MacLeod. Restraint is an enormous virtue. The classic beginner's fault is over-elaboration, squandering as many ideas on one tune (where they simply get in one another's way) as would fill half a collection.

Success also has its perils. The struggle to find a distinctive 'voice' runs the risk that after a while everything you say sounds very much like what you said before, and although your work may continue to achieve a high level technically, it may lose its capacity to surprise and delight. The great 'cellist Rostropovich, spotting a bass player of his acquaintance who had just performed in a new orchestral piece by Shostakovich, eagerly enquired what it was like and was told: 'Well . . . there *are* one or two good bits, but the rest just sounds like Shostakovich'. In the end creative exhaustion can overtake even the most exciting of talents. One thinks of Brian Wilson in his solitary studio conjuring the choirboys-in-bluejeans effects of The Beach Boys into such magical existence, duelling probably not so much with Lennon and McCartney, as the music press suggested, as with himself. Eventually he reached the outer limits of even his creativity. After 'Good Vibrations' and 'Heroes and Villains', what was there left for anybody of that generation to say – unless they re-invented the whole genre?

There are two tendencies at work here. One is the urge to conserve, to view the achievement of the past as definitive and to approach it in a custodial, curatorial spirit; the other is to rush headlong into innovation, and violently break asunder the stylistic shackles of the past. The tension between these opposing impulses is the source of much creativity in music but partisans of either camp can take a dim view of the other. The American composer Roy Harris famously dismissed a modish jazz-influenced piece by his colleague Aaron Copland as 'whorehouse music'. Similar reflections may occur to the conservatively minded listening to some of the spectacularly innovative light music for the pipe of the later twentieth and early twenty-first centuries.

Composition in *pìobaireachd*

The golden age of composition in *pìobaireachd* was probably the seventeenth and eighteenth centuries. Non-playing 'patrons' later tried to discourage composition on the grounds that 'tradition' belonged to the past and all the present was entitled to do was preserve it and pass it on unaltered. But composition did continue and continues to the present day. The nineteenth century produced some lovely pieces, amongst them C. S. Thomason's 'Hail to my Country' quoted above. In the twentieth century highlights include William MacLean's great 'Lament for the Earl of Seafield' (published in the *Cabar Feidh Collection*, London, 1984) and G. S. McLennan's previously unknown nameless 'Piobaireachd' which is preserved in the Alfred E. Milne Manuscript and appears here for the first time (see Tune appendix). MacLean looked back, challenging the great works of the past on their own ground. McLennan showed the idiom continuing to evolve as he accommodated it to his characteristically lyrical and melodic style.

The *pìobaireachd* composer works out a tone row in the chosen form ('primary', 'secondary', or whatever) and in an appropriate scale for the mood of the piece. The tricky bit is to make sure that there is enough musical tension to sustain what may be quite a long tune and to support the variations chosen to set off the melody. 'The Lament for Miss Emma Haldane', another unknown and previously unpublished late-Victorian *pìobaireachd*, a version of which is preserved in the David Glen Papers, illustrates this quite well:

Emma Haldane, ground, line 1

Emma Haldane, tone row, line 1

Since this is a primary *pìobaireachd*, a piper familiar with the structure needs to remember only the A and B phrases and also to have the elementary resourcefulness to be able to cobble the B phrases together when they are repeated in line two.

The next problem is how to develop the tune. A thumb variation might sound rather nice in this kind of context, perhaps as follows:

Emma Haldane, thumb variation, line 1

If one cared to, this could be doubled, perhaps along the lines of:

Emma Haldane, thumb variation, doubling, line 1

A *siubhal* would be the next logical step with a singling (changing the line ending a bit, just to vary the beaten track):

Emma Haldane, siubhal, line 1

then a doubling to balance the two thumb variations and keep everything nice and symmetrical:

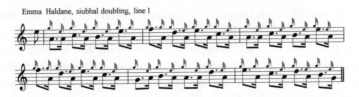

Emma Haldane, siubhal doubling, line 1

The player could then proceed to a set of standard taorluath and crunluath variations, repeating the ground between them if desired:

Emma Haldane, taorluath singling, line 1

Emma Haldane, crunluath singling, line 1

If it was felt that the tune was outstaying its welcome, the player might choose to drop a variation – perhaps the *siubhal* – or thin out the variations, playing only a singling in each case and/or the repeat of the ground between the *taorluath* and *crunluath* variations.

As in all composition, one of two things happen to the composer's efforts. They enter a Darwinian struggle with the existing tune population and the fittest survive. Well-adapted tunes are taken up by other players and continue to evolve; they receive further artistic attention which can go on, if a tune becomes a standard, over quite long periods of time. Or they fall dead from the chanter and are never heard of again.

What to look and listen for

In developing the skills of knowledgeable listening, huge gains in appreciation are possible. However, you may find yourself gradually exchanging a condition of childlike wonder for an understanding so refined and severe that practically nothing pleases you. There are two different fields here, and two slightly different sets of skills.

In solo playing, the performer should seem well in command of his or her instrument: somebody who appears to have trouble with blowing is unlikely to be playing well. Watch for noticeable upper body movement, probably indicating a diaphragm being made to work too hard. Stiff, awkward-looking fingers raised exaggeratedly clear of the chanter are, likewise, unlikely to belong to a good player. Posture can *sometimes* be an indicator of relative skill. Although the size of the bag can be adjusted to the performer, the pipes themselves come in standard sizes and the match with the human frame can be rather approximate. The carriage should be upright, natural and relaxed. But what should be and what is, do not always coincide. One can sometimes see queer contortions, therefore: the left shoulder thrown forward, thrusting the bass drone up against the piper's ear and carrying the tenors out from the body, straining the spine and left shoulder. Tall players have a tendency to cant forward from the hips, leading one to fear a sudden gust of wind from behind tumbling instrument and performer together into the audience. Sometimes the chin is thrust down into the chest so that the performer seems to have no neck. Or the head is twisted round with eyes raised heavenwards as if contemplating the ineffable. Chanters ought to be held more or less vertically but they often assume improbable angles, sometimes in the 'round-the-corner' style turned away from the player and almost parallel with the ground. But such signals can be hard to interpret. By no means every piper who does this kind of thing is a bad player, indeed sometimes quite the contrary.

There should not be (but there often is) obtrusively vigorous stamping or beating of the foot, or bobbing about like a cork in a bucket. One must allow for the context, however: in competitive band work, the time is taken from the pipe-major's foot and no other feet should move. In solo playing, competition marches are played more slowly than one can comfortably march to, and competition strathspeys and reels are played at tempi slower than would be normal in the dance. Playing strathspeys and reels, the piper stands still, but in competition he or she is expected to march to marches. Few performers carry it off with fluency, still less elegance, at the tempi involved. R. B. Nicol of Balmoral, who had been pipe-major of the 2nd Gordons during the Second World War and had given the subject considerable study, detected a deeper cause at work here. He traced it to the decline of the tackety boot. Pipers had taken to wearing light city shoes which disrupted the natural rhythm of walking; as a result, he said, the art of marching was quite lost. The marks of a good solo pipe would include a robust, sweet-sounding chanter, well balanced between top and bottom hands, i.e. with no enormous change in timbre and dynamic between the lower and upper registers. The drones should have a solid 'wall of sound' feel, firm and rich in tone and, even more importantly, should balance and blend well harmonically with the chanter. Squeaks and chokes are tell-tale signs of inaccurate fingering or unsteady winding.

The pipe-band world exists in a different dimension from solo piping and is a huge subject in itself. But a number of things will help you spot a good pipe band. Bands with a huge age differential – venerable pipe-majors followed by an assortment of longs and shorts, including small figures trotting along in the back row hardly able to wind their instruments – are unlikely to be up to much musically. (Starting too early with a band is said to ruin many a promising player.) Money follows success: a good band will *look* good. Beware, therefore, of the shambling and the shabby – the music is probably on a par with the appearance. One must be careful with the military, though: their marching, dressing and deportment are generally rather good, but they tend to be limited musically. In the army pipers are increasingly expected to act as soldiers first and musicians third or fourth. The cutting edge of the pipe band as a musical form lies in the civilian sector and always has.

One should listen for a robust steady sound, good integration between pipe and drum corps with the pitch of the drums reflecting that of the pipes and not proceeding as a separate department. Relations between the two sections can be difficult. Pipers long complained about drums 'drowning out pipe music', although this would refer more to the old, low-pitched rope-tensioned drums, rather than the modern kit which has been likened to a centipede jitterbugging on glass. Some object to playing with drummers at all. It is a curiously lopsided arrangement, even today. Most pipers have little knowledge of drumming but drummers need to know quite a lot about piping, if they are to create musically appropriate scores. Chief amongst the great names of the last half-century was Alex Duthart who was central to the evolution of the modern style. He was much influenced by jazz and apparently also by Continental drumming techniques with their subtle rhythmical patterns and varied dynamic – giving, as the maestro remarked, 'a much more swingin' sound, sir'. Silky power should ooze from a good side-drum section like liquid honey. The bass corps should provide rhythmic punctuation, but not obtrusively. The pipe chanters should sound as one, drones likewise, the latter to be in tune with the chanters at the beginning and staying there. There should be a good clean start and finish, without groans or squeaks, and good attack in between. Bands are ranked for competitive purposes in grades from One down to Four. To play in a crack Grade One band is the ambition of many, especially younger, players. All good pipe-majors are also good players, although they may not have the time to pursue solo careers. What they do is exceptionally skilled: they have lots of pipes to look after as well as their own, and in modern conditions they may also have general oversight of a feeder band at a lower grade and a juvenile band beneath that, feeding the feeder. They tend to be busy people, therefore, and are held in at least as much regard as the top solo masters.

As in solo piping, competition is the lifeblood of serious band work and the major championships such as the British, European and World's are keenly contested by ensembles from all over the globe. In the last two decades of the twentieth century bands from outside Scotland became major competitive forces. The top ensembles included Simon Fraser University and 78th Fraser Highlanders of Canada, the Field-Marshal Montgomery from Northern Ireland, the Strathclyde Police, Scottish Power, and Shotts and Dykehead Caledonia from Scotland.

The competition repertoire had been stabilising since before World War I and by the 1960s had settled into a rather sterile mould. Band after band slogged its way through the same few heavy competition marches, strathspeys and reels like 'Donald Cameron', 'Blair Drummond' and 'Pretty Marion'. Some thought the form could not continue unless it succeeded in re-inventing itself. But few can have foreseen the dramatic effect upon the whole concept of pipe band music which arose from the adoption of a medley format in the 1970s. This produced an amazing ferment of fresh composition and arrangement which showed little sign of faltering into the following century.

Suddenly it became possible to do all kinds of hitherto forbidden things. Circumstances led to the writer being pipe-major of a university band in the early '70s, and all kinds of harmonic possibilities and new drum settings were tried out. But even so there were bridges too far. He remembers trying to interest his amiable but obtuse drum corps in a different kind of timbre to accompany a set of jigs. The existing sound as it came out of the box was wonderfully crisp and compelling, the kind of thing that would make any right-thinking person want to seize his musket and advance at once towards the French at a brisk pace. But he had something darker, more primitive in view, with a whiff of the 'Rite of Spring' about it and a hint too of the tempestuous torrent conjured by North-East fishers from deep, old-fashioned rope-tensioned drums in their winter temperance walks; but all raised – if it could be managed – to a still higher intensity. If one could have the lead tip fall out, maybe, march out, up, back, in the best stiff, Highland Div. fashion, and then address a slackened-off tenor with reversed sticks . . . producing something throbbing, insistent, tumultuous, full of, um, orgiastic abandon . . . yet within a tight framework, bulled, precise, controlled, so that the contrast would be almost unbearably intense and . . . Anyway, he introduced this modest proposal to them, concluding 'Can do?'

'Na', they said, at once, 'ye'll brak the drumheid'.

'Weel, weel,' he said, 'we'll get a new een. It'll be *sensational*, min; jist awa' wi't'.

'Na, we're nae deein' it'.

'But this', he cried, 'is mutiny'.

'Aye', they said, 'and be damned t'ye.'

And so, concluding it was futile to beat his head against a brick wall of irremovable biological limitation, he retired from the field, reflecting that there had been worse losses at Hochkirch.

A final point may be appropriate here, which often puzzles the outsider – the pipes do not sound nearly so loud if you are actually playing them. There is an eye in the hurricane and the piper is tranquilly in the middle of it. By the same token, *playing* in a pipe band, even in a confined space, is unproblematic; *listening* to a pipe band in an enclosed space is like being nailed to the wall.

Pipers and print

Popular instrumental collections had included tunes playable on the pipes since the seventeemth century, but it was fairly late before books of music specifically for the pipes became available. The first published bagpipe music appears in the books of Joseph (1739–1763) and Patrick MacDonald (1729–1824), Scotland's musical brothers Grimm, whose *Compleat Theory of the Scots Highland Bagpipe* (written about 1760 but not published until 1803) and *Highland Vocal Airs* (1783) were the earliest publications specifically devoted to Highland music. *Highland Vocal Airs* was crammed with song tunes and instrumental pieces and was very influential. It was used as a source by Robert Burns and went through five editions in its compiler's lifetime. The *Compleat Theory* was written while Joseph MacDonald was serving with the East India Company, the manuscript returning to his brother Patrick after Joseph's tragically early death in Calcutta in 1763. But Joseph's book gave short examples mainly, and Patrick's settings gave only the outlines of the melodies so that they could be played on violin or keyboards.

The founding father of published bagpipe music proper was Donald Mac-Donald (1767–1840), a Skyeman long resident in Edinburgh as a bagpipe maker and teacher. It was MacDonald who pioneered the convention that melody note stems should point down and gracenote stems up. This has governed all written pipe music subsequently and greatly improves ease of reading in what would otherwise be a dense and cluttered medium. MacDonald's *Collection of the Ancient Martial Music of Caledonia* (1818/19 and later editions) contained 23 *piobaireachd* and a selection of strathspeys, reels, jigs, and song airs from Uist and Skye. Since pipe music was frequently played on keyboards at this period, MacDonald printed a left-hand accompaniment with instructions for non-pipers on how to handle the melody lines (i.e. to play the melody notes only, leaving out the grace notes). The settings show him thinking harmonically for an instrument with which he was not intimately familiar, although the settings do have a certain rugged charm – indeed the faster, later movements with their rocking left-hand accompaniment can sound intriguingly like boogie-woogie, if played up to time:

Would it be entirely fanciful to suppose that on hot summer nights this stuff came wafting out of the windows of Scots settlers all over the American South and quick ears were pricking up and wondering, 'Hey, what dem crazy cats do?'

Ancient Martial Music was published by subscription at a guinea. Printing and paper were dear, so that in the early days publications were expensive and were issued in small numbers. Until the print revolution in mid-Victorian Scotland, pipers mainly worked with manuscript. There was nothing unusual about this. The average print-run of a Beethoven sonata was one hundred copies, and they were so costly that people of modest means, like Franz Schubert, could not afford to buy them. Even in Vienna, the centre of the cultivated music world, it was still cheaper to use manuscript, and this was long the case in piping.

MacDonald's successor, Angus MacKay, also published his influential *Collection of Ancient Piobaireachd or Highland Pipe Music* (Edinburgh, 1838 and later editions) by subscription, for a market made up largely of well-heeled connoisseurs. Although there were a number of subsequent reprints, second-hand copies became so scarce that they were changing hands for up to £10.00 by the 1890s. The breakthrough came in the 1870s when machine-made paper and power-driven presses brought prices dramatically down. As soon as it became affordable by pipers, the open market was able to sustain large quantities of pipe music in print. The pioneers were Glasgow pipemaker Donald MacPhee (1842–1880), who brought out his *Collection of Piobaireachd* in 1879 covering the central core of the repertoire, and David Glen (1853–1916) of Edinburgh, whose firm David Glen and Sons quickly became the leading publishers of bagpipe music in Scotland. Glen's scores were carefully edited and physically well produced. He was quick to adopt the latest marketing techniques, publishing serially to spread costs. His *Collection of Ancient Piobaireachd* was issued in seven volumes between 1880 and 1907 and eventually contained one hundred tunes. Glen also produced an enormously popular collection of light music on the same principles – *David Glen's Collection of Highland Bagpipe Music* (Edinburgh, 1876–1900) which ran to seventeen volumes in all, eventually containing more than a thousand tunes.

There were major contributions also by Queen Victoria's piper, William Ross (1823–1891), a grand-nephew of John Bàn MacKenzie and editor of *Ross's Collection . . . Pipe Music* (London, 1869 and later editions), which contained numerous examples of *pìobaireachd* very attractively arranged, along with a large quantity of light music. Another important figure was Charles Simeon Thomason (1833–1911), who developed a new abbreviated system of notation which enabled him to publish virtually the whole repertoire in a single volume. His *Ceol Mor* (London, 1900 and later editions) quickly became one of the classic sources.

In the light music of the pipe, the twentieth century was even richer than the nineteenth, so much so that by the century's end new collections were appearing at the rate of about one a month. The outstanding examples are *Pipe Major William Ross's Collection of Highland Bagpipe Music* (5 vols., London, 1923–

1950) which defined the core competition repertoire during the following two generations, and *Pipe Major Donald MacLeod's Collection of Music for the Highland Bagpipe* (5 vols., Glasgow, 1954 and following) which was another great landmark. This contained both stylishly set traditional tunes and also many original compositions by MacLeod himself who was by far the best composer of his generation.

In *pìobaireachd*, the situation was more problematic. The great age of the *pìobaireachd* editors came in the nineteenth century when outstanding figures like Donald MacDonald, Angus MacKay, William Ross, Donald MacPhee, David Glen, and C. S. Thomason established the conventions which enabled the music to be written in staff notation, and committed most of the repertoire (some 400 tunes in all) to print. The old pipers are nowadays regarded as mighty figures but in their own day their standing was sometimes not very high. Being plebeians (except for Thomason who was a Major-General), their activities created a swarm of middlemen, 'patrons', promoters, and enablers who took it upon themselves to interpret the music to wider audiences. Antiquaries like James Logan (who wrote the notes and introductions for Angus MacKay's *Ancient Piobaireachd*) usually had a different agenda from the master pipers. They were frequently enthusiasts for fashionable aspects of 'Celtic' culture and personally knew little about the pipes and their music. Since they tended to write anonymously, however, their opinions were often attributed to the master players themselves and this led to serious misunderstanding later on. The mediators liked to picture *pìobaireachd* as the creation of a dim romantic past which had been handed down unchanged for centuries. This typifies the written parts of Donald MacDonald's *Ancient Martial Music*, and Logan took a similar approach in MacKay's book. But tune titles provide little guide to age. Attempts to trace the historical development of the music by using them to establish a chronological sequence have ended in failure, as they were bound to do, seeing that titles vary, and that anything in the nature of folklore is as 'old' as the day it is first written down. At least the antiquaries stuck to words and did not try to interfere with the music – that came later.

At the beginning of the twentieth century, pipers had access to more than 270 different published *pìobaireachd* settings distributed amongst the collections of MacKay, MacPhee, Ross, Thomason and Glen, settings which were musical and varied and offered a substantial degree of artistic choice, an enormous achievement in little more than a generation.

But in 1903 the Piobaireachd Society was founded and all this changed.

Patrons and print

Anybody who cares to take in one or two piping competitions at the games in summer or at the indoor events at other times of year must be struck by the generally musical and appealing way the light music is played, in contrast with the plodding, unmusical way that *pìobaireachd* is played by the very same pipers. Why is this?

The strange disjunction between light music and *pìobaireachd* is a classic example of externally imposed change on a traditional art form. While the light music remained in the control of the pipers, *pìobaireachd* was much altered by the intervention of self-appointed regulatory bodies whose aim was 'rescue' and 'preservation' but who came close to stifling the art as an expressive form.

This began with the aristocratic Highland Societies of London and Scotland which were founded respectively in 1778 and 1784. Moved by the fashionable theory that traditional arts were intrinsically at risk, they assumed (wrongly) that the music of the pipe must be dying and duly set about 'preserving' it. To this end they introduced competitions and attempted to standardise the music and introduce 'scientific' staff notation. Their main concern was not artistic but military. The Highland Societies were quasi-governmental agencies founded to promote the economic and military exploitation of the Highlands in the post-Culloden generations; their goal was a steady flow of pipers into the army to maintain the fighting efficiency of the Highland corps.

The Highland Societies began the piping competitions at Falkirk in 1781, and presided over their later transformation into Highland vaudeville to meet the tastes of fashionable Edinburgh audiences. The Highland Society of London paid for writing down 30 *pìobaireachd* from the repertoire of their piper, Angus MacArthur, but their attempts to publish the resulting manuscript came to nothing. They did little other collecting and failed to preserve such material as they did get. They did not respond to requests for assistance in publishing seminal works such as Joseph MacDonald's *Compleat Theory of the Scots Highland Bagpipe* (1803) and Donald MacDonald's *Ancient Martial Music of Caledonia* (1818–19?). They refused to buy the extensive *pìobaireachd* manuscripts of Angus McKay when they were offered to them, although these contained virtually the whole of the tradition as it was then known. Their attempts to revive the MacCrimmon college as a school of military piping ended in failure. When a leading piper offered to 'translate' the Nether Lorn Canntaireachd for them, they refused even to listen. The history of the Highland Societies' involvement with the pipe is a catalogue of pennypinching and missed opportunities. The frequently repeated claim that the music would have died without their intervention is not supported by the evidence.

The cry of 'rescue' and 'preservation' was to guide their successor organisation, the Piobaireachd Society of Scotland, founded in 1903. The original members of the Piobaireachd Society were also landed, titled and military people. They did not insist on ability to play the pipes and few had much knowledge of the music. Membership was by invitation. It was for gentlemen only and professional players were barred. Like their predecessors in the Highland Societies, the Piobaireachd Society's founders assumed that the music was in danger – an odd conclusion in view of the healthy condition of the published repertoire and the substantial body of written and orally transmitted material known to have been in the hands of contemporary master teachers. Even more curiously, the founders of the Piobaireachd Society thought that the music could be 'rescued' by people like themselves. A genuine expert like Angus Cameron (winner of the Edinburgh prize pipe in 1794) could – accurately – assure Scottish judge and diarist Henry Cockburn whom he entertained at his inn at Ballachulish in 1841 that the music of the pipe took 'a deal of edication' (i.e. a lifetime's learning); but to some members of the Piobaireachd Society a few weeks on the practice chanter with 'Pipey X or Y' was considered quite sufficient to make one an 'authority'. They proceeded, thus equipped, to publish their own arrangements of the classic tunes, enforce the playing of these in competition, and sit in judgement on the resulting performances.

The pipers' eventual submission to this bizarre state of affairs tells us much about the distribution of social power in twentieth-century Scotland. It may be difficult for people whose contact with the country has not been direct to realise exactly what is implied by a word like 'gentry'. After all, Scotland has long prided itself on its populist and 'democratic' credentials. Robert Burns's famous song, 'A Man's a Man for a' that', was sung, with great feeling, at the first session of the recently restored Scottish Parliament, and many Scots can quote bits of the Burns-inspired collective ideal which views Scotland as the definitively egalitarian community: 'Princes and lords are but the breath of kings; An honest man's the noblest work of God'; 'The rank is but the guinea stamp, the man's the gowd [gold] for a' that'. They like to picture themselves as the praetorian guard of the democratic intellect, as wild unbridled Celts, untamed hairy Picts and so on. But the truth is that by the beginning of the twentieth century Scotland supported an exceptionally meek and biddable society with a strongly top-down command structure. At the head of this came the landed élite whose feudal powers had been deliberately left intact by the Act of Union with England in 1707 (to ensure the acquiescence of the Scottish ruling class in this profoundly unpopular measure) and had suffered little diminution in the meantime. Educated mainly in England and also largely resident there, they were alien in language, outlook and social mores. The founders of the Piobaireachd Society, the brothers John, Angus and Archibald Campbell of Kilberry, were typical of this pattern.

Their estate lay in Knapdale, in south-west Argyllshire, between Kintyre and Lorn. It was a fairly modest affair with a rather gloomy neo-Baronial castle served by a single-track road and nowadays to all appearances going rapidly back to the birch. Its surroundings, however, were spectacular. It commanded, in anything like decent weather, quite stunning views across the Sound to the Paps of Jura and a varied and lovely panoply of water, wood, and hill. The eldest of the Kilberrys, John, was a soldier, a Sandhurst man and intelligence specialist who later commanded the 8th Argyll and Sutherland Highlanders; Angus, the brains of the family, was a London barrister; and Archibald, the youngest, who was to become the Society's editor and control its affairs for much of the twentieth century, went on from Harrow and Cambridge to become a judge in the Imperial service in India. All three had taken up piping as an adult enthusiasm under the inspiration of the 'Celtic Twilight' movement and with reforming zeal set themselves to 'rescue' an art they casually presumed was dying. The problem as the Campbells saw it was that only about a dozen or so tunes were ever heard in competition at the games. They thought that this was the fault of pipers who were prepared to jog along from year to year offering the same old stuff whenever they mounted the boards, and the reason they did this was because the actual repertoire had shrunk to dangerously narrow proportions.

It now seems clear that they were mistaken and that the tradition was sustained in its entirety by contemporary master players. The reason why so few tunes were heard in public lay with the bench rather than the performers, the latter being reluctant to put themselves at a disadvantage by offering tunes with which they knew the judges were unfamiliar. The ignorance of their own class (typified by one contemporary 'judge' who declared 'I always ask for "McIntosh's Lament": it is a tune I think I understand thoroughly') was a thing the brothers could do little about but their social standing gave them considerable scope to influence what pipers did. So, starting at precisely the wrong end of the problem, they set busily to work.

Their interest had been aroused by the publication in 1900 of C. S. Thomason's *Ceol Mor*, which suggested to them the true extent of the repertoire, and they were keen that more of it should be heard in public. They decided to form a small society to promote Thomason's work, issuing half-a-dozen of the more unusual tunes from it each year and using their contacts at premier events like the Argyllshire Gathering and the Northern Meeting to ensure that these were set for competition. Thomason was offered, and accepted, the Society's presidency.

Although intended as little more than a study group at first, the Piobaireachd Society proved an idea whose time had come, and the original tightly-knit circle of friends and neighbours from southern Argyll was quickly swamped by heavyweight Scottish aristocracy, people like the Dukes of Argyll and Hamilton, the Marquesses of Graham, Tullibardine and Bute, the Earl of Dunmore, and a crowd of the greater gentry. The Society's meetings were transferred to London, and it began to fill up with the friends and hangers on of the great, genteel and well-heeled enough, but having little personal knowledge of the pipe and its culture. The Kilberrys were outmanoeuvred and outvoted by a powerful faction opposed to Thomason's new notational system (although its compression was such that it enabled the set tunes to be reproduced and distributed free to intending competitors). The dissidents, led by Captain William Stewart of Ensay, staged a palace revolution at the Annual General Meeting at Oban in September 1904. Thomason was deposed as president in favour of the Earl of Dunmore (a neighbour of Ensay's who owned most of Harris and of whom it was said by Col. Jock MacDonald that he had difficulty distinguishing one end of a chanter from the other), the traditional MacDonald/MacKay style of notation was re-adopted, and the Kilberry brothers and their supporters resigned. Stewart became secretary of the Society and editor of its 'official' settings. A world of trouble descended on his shoulders, for in many quarters Thomason had been a much-liked and respected man. Five volumes of set tunes were issued by the new regime between 1905 and 1912 and were castigated in the press for their musical incompetence and bungled Gaelic. One of the *Oban Times*'s frequent correspondents, Donald MacFarlane, who used the pen name 'Loch Sloy', wrote with prophetic insight that 'Under all the criticism the Society is prospering. Yes, and it will prosper so long as it has money to launch out, no matter how many write against it; but such prosperity is not very creditable to us as a musical community' (10/08/1907, p.3).

When Ensay died in 1908, there were few left in the Society who could even begin to edit the scores, and following protracted negotiations a deal was struck in 1911 under which the Kilberrys re-joined. John Campbell became vice-president. Archibald Campbell and his friend John Peter Grant of Rothiemurchus became joint secretaries of the powerful music committee which prepared and published the annual set tunes. Angus Campbell, in many ways the moving force behind the Society as originally conceived, had died in 1908 at the age of 35. As a source of influence, the Society was now very much worth re-joining. In 1909, Simon Fraser, 14th Lord Lovat (1871–1933), who had followed Dunmore as president upon the latter's death in 1907, had got the War Office to agree that military pipers could reach the rank of pipe-major only following training and certification by the Society, strengthening its already strong ties with the army. This was to be the cornerstone of its teaching strategy for the next fifty years.

After the delays and confusions of the First World War the Society began to issue its *Second Series* (15 vols., 1925–) with Archibald Campbell acting as sole editor from Volume 2 (1928) to Volume 9 (1957), which contained most of the important tunes. High competence in law or military affairs counted for little when it came to music, however, and the Society's editors were to prove severely limited in this respect throughout the twentieth century. Archibald Campbell often boasted about his superiority to other editors but he made little attempt to meet even basic scholarly standards, such as reproducing the music accurately, giving a full account of sources consulted and identifying and explaining editorial changes. He felt able, following a few weeks of instruction from Alexander Cameron (the younger), John MacDougall Gillies and John MacDonald of Inverness, to substitute his own ideas of what the music should sound like for what it actually said in the sources. Copies of the originals lay before him as he worked, as is clear from his editorial files now in the National Library of Scotland. While there was a carefully maintained appearance of scholarship, Campbell – acting independently of the committee which was supposed to oversee his work – intervened freely in the text, making numerous silent changes to note values in a way that coarsened expression and disrupted the rhythmical flow of the melodies. Had Campbell merely been musically inadequate, the situation might not have been so grave, but he frequently stated in the editorial notes that his personal arrangements were the work of famous dead master players, and the Society (assuming that he was accurate and trustworthy) published them as such.

Pipers had always intervened creatively in the music, but there were three crucial differences here: the settings were presented as

- the result of scrupulous scholarship, following careful deliberation by the music committee in consultation with leading pipers. [This was untrue.]
- the sole accurate channel of transmission, because, Campbell said, Angus MacKay was full of mistakes and all later piper-editors had copied MacKay. [This was also untrue.]
- essential to the rescue of the art since *pìobaireachd* was couched in a demanding and abstruse musical language which, by implication, could not be trusted to mere pipers. [This was untrue as well.]

These three basic tenets – supposed corruption in transmission, supposed incompetence of pipers and the supposedly superior scholarship of the ruling class – form the basis of the 'authority' claimed for the publications of the Society.

This did not happen without protest, of course, but since only Campbell had access to all the sources, it was difficult to mount a challenge on the basis of the written evidence. Those who complained were branded as 'cranks' and 'heretics' and step by step were marginalised and silenced. People objecting from inside the Society received similarly short shrift, like Somerled MacDonald who was removed from the judges' panel at the Northern Meeting, while Seton Gordon discovered that his place on the music committee had been given to one of Campbell's sons. Only once did Archibald Campbell cite a living teacher, John MacDonald of Inverness, as a source for his settings (in the *Kilberry Book of Ceol Mor* published in 1948) and his claim was angrily rejected by MacDonald: 'Yes I have a copy of "Kilberry's Book",' he wrote, 'and my opinion of it is that it is the beginning of the end, of our traditional Piobaireachd playing as handed down to us'.

Campbell's crude and unmusical style was followed by his successors. After his death in 1963, leadership of the Society was assumed by his son James (1916–2003), who became joint editor along with Archibald Kenneth of Stronachullin (1915–1989), nephew of the Society's President, J. Graham-Campbell of Shirvan. Unlike Archibald Campbell who was described as a very poor and laborious player, Archie Kenneth seems to have been a competent traditional musician. He had played the accordion since childhood, and some of his light music pieces, like 'The Back of the Moon' and 'The Lady in the Bottle', became favourites with pipers. As an editor of *pìobaireachd*, however, his musical instincts deserted him. He looks like a classic embodiment of the light-music/*pìobaireachd* split which had been growing ever since the Society started. It seems obvious from the time values of his grounds that he did not expect *pìobaireachd* to resemble 'music' in any ordinary sense. He closely followed the conventions established by his predecessor and the volumes for which he assumed responsibility were, if anything, of an even poorer quality musically than Campbell's had been. At the same time Kenneth realised that Campbell's scores were a good deal less accurate than had been supposed, but sensing that the implications might be explosive, he did not pursue the issue. He commented that 'to revise over freely would be rather a confession of inadequacy in the first instance', and began to promote the idea of Gaelic song as a means of rescuing the idiom of *ceòl mór*.

At the beginning of the twentieth century, before the formation of the Society, more than 270 *pìobaireachd* had been available to the performer in a variety of musically pleasing published settings. But by 1930, this had sunk to the three dozen poorly edited scores contained in the first three volumes of the *Pìobaireachd Society Collection* (second series). By 1960, after more than half-a-century of publishing activity, the number was 149 tunes, contained in volumes one to nine of the second series and the *Kilberry Book of Ceol Mor*, also edited by Archibald Campbell and published by the Society. The key moment had come on 1st April 1905 when a series of advertisements placed in the *Oban Times* warned pipers that only the Society's settings, played as written, would be accepted at competitions under its control. Since these quickly came to include, directly or indirectly, the whole of the senior competition circuit, this became in effect a ban on the existing published scores. Publication of *pìobaireachd* in the open market duly came to a halt and for most of the twentieth century the Piobaireachd Society's books were the only ones available. Archibald Campbell wrote in 1956 that 'we are absolutely the only suppliers of such music today', and his arrangements continued to be prescribed for use in competition throughout the twentieth century although they were – by far – the least accurate or musical of any of the published sources.

Without the institutional power of the Piobaireachd Society, none of this would have come to pass. Left to their own devices, it seems highly doubtful that pipers would have chosen to play Campbell if they could have played Thomason, Glen, MacPhee or Ross instead. Indeed it is unlikely that Campbell's scores would ever have seen the light of day, still less achieved the monopoly they enjoyed, without the sponsorship of the Society and the context of 'authority' and control it was able to create which enabled his work to circulate with very little criticism or scrutiny. One of the many damaging results was that Campbell's scores were accepted as the reliable starting point for future enquiry, as we see in a number of important later twentieth-century publications. To be sure, their musical incoherence was difficult to overlook, but this was assumed to be confirmation of the view that the art had indeed required 'rescue' because incompetent pipers had failed to sustain it adequately over the centuries; not because – as was the case – it had been effectively subverted by a small group of people in the space of little more than three decades.

It is interesting to reflect on the numbers involved. The Society's opening meeting in Edinburgh on 19th January 1903 was attended by five people. The founding members numbered just eighteen. The Society is a closed one: its finances and archival holdings are not made public. For many years it relied for its influence on close links with the army, receiving an annual grant from the War Office and having numerous Scottish regiments and individual officers as members. As the influence of the military declined with the ending of National Service and cutbacks in the Territorial Army, the Society began to forge closer links with enthusiasts in the academic world and drew the upper echelons of the performer community within its sphere of influence. Shortly after the deaths of Archibald Campbell and J. P. Grant in 1963, a number of leading professional pipers were invited to join, including in 1964 John MacFadyen and Seumas MacNeill (who later became its Honorary Secretary), Pipe-Major Donald MacLeod in 1966, James McIntosh in 1972, R. B. Nicol of Balmoral in 1974, and Donald MacPherson, Iain Morrison and John Wilson of Toronto soon afterwards. Although these were people of exceptional gifts and experience, it is not evident that they were able to exert significant influence on the Society's approach to the music, which remained firmly in the hands of the amateurs.

A number of academics from various subject areas were recruited in the early 1970s including Peter Cooke (ethnomusicology), Roderick Cannon (chemistry) and Professor Alex. Haddow (medicine), the first two going on to exert a considerable influence on the Society's affairs. Yet it was its dominant role in the competition circuit that underpinned its success and enabled it to establish an eventually world-wide power base. As increasing numbers of *pìobaireachd* students turned to Scotland for accreditation, the Society joined with the College of Piping, the Army School of Piping, and later the National Piping Centre, to set up 'The Institute of Piping' to establish a single graded programme of certification for players and teachers. The Society gave subsidies to the Northern Meeting, the Argyllshire Gathering, The Royal Scottish Pipers' Society and the College of Piping. Its members were also active in numerous key areas of Scottish life. Directly or indirectly by the end of the twentieth century the Society was able to influence powerfully

- the accreditation of top players;
- who could judge in senior competitions, what tunes would be played and what settings permitted;
- qualification as pipe-major and hence access to higher non-commissioned rank in the regular army;

- the publishing of *pìobaireachd* and the collection of manuscripts;
- the flow of information in the public domain through its links with the College of Piping and the BBC, and teaching and research in academic institutions.

Towards the end of the twentieth century the Society began to publish some of the important *pìobaireachd* manuscripts, although this object had been amongst its stated goals since 1903. These were, in 1994, Joseph MacDonald's *Compleat Theory of the Scots Highland Bagpipe*, edited by the Society's music secretary, Roderick D. Cannon, and in 2001 the MacArthur/MacGregor manuscript in association with the John MacFadyen Memorial Trust and the Universities of Glasgow and Aberdeen with the title *The Music of Scotland Ceòl na h-Albainn* [sic] *The MacArthur-MacGregor Manuscript of Piobaireachd (1820)*. A facsimile and transcripts of thirty settings from Angus MacArthur were accompanied by several chapters of commentary by Dutch linguistic scholar and *pìobaireachd* enthusiast Frans Buisman (1942–2002) which, although they made some interesting points, blended minute textual analysis with passages of airy speculation and were written in a style so opaque that it is unlikely that the message reached many of the intended audience. Thus the Society began to move into the vacuum created by the historically limited interest in traditional instrumental music of the Scottish higher education sector. This enabled it to present itself as a 'scholarly' body to academics who did not know their Campbells from their Camerons (but did not know that they did not know).

As a publishing and regulatory institution the Piobaireachd Society's standing continued to rest on the assumed integrity of Archibald Campbell's scores. Yet none of the editors of the *Pìobaireachd Society Collection* (second series) reached an acceptable standard at any point, and it did not seem clear as the twentieth century drew to a close that the lessons of the past had been learned. For the senior competitions in 2000 the Society issued a number of scores, ostensibly from original manuscript and scarce published sources. Competitors were encouraged to believe that they were playing historic settings by famous figures like Angus MacArthur or Niel MacLeod of Gesto, when they were in fact playing modern Campbell-style arrangements by the Society's editors. This was defended on the dubious grounds that the meaning of the old scores was uncertain and that modern pipers, accustomed only to seeing Kilberry, would be unable to interpret them. Surveying such practices within the context of the previous century, a former president of the Society was moved to comment: 'Serious pipers have been deprived of too much of the priceless heritage which should have been handed down to them, and which was simply distorted and deformed to conform to the ideas of men unqualified to act in their name. What is at stake is the credibility of the current system'.

At the dawn of the twenty-first century this monolithic structure was unexpectedly challenged by a group of enthusiasts in the United States associated with the Bagpipe Museum of Ellicott City, Maryland, and the label 'Ceol Sean' of Springfield, Illinois, who began to issue 'reprints' of the classic old published collections in CD ROM form, selling for a few dollars apiece into a worldwide market hungry for material which had long been virtually unobtainable. This potentially revolutionary advance solved at a stroke the traditional problems of issuing bagpipe music in hard copy, namely its bulk and its expense, and took to the brink of realisation the old dream of bringing the historic published corpus in its entirety 'within reach of poor pipers'. The modest levels of capitalisation involved also meant that the classic repertoire could be maintained 'in print' indefinitely, without institutional sponsorship or state subsidy, banishing the problems of access to the old sources which had hampered intelligent enquiry into the music for most of the twentieth-century.

Oral tradition

Much of the information we receive in everyday life comes to us orally/aurally, i.e. through talk and listening. But 'Oral Tradition' is a grander concept and a thing to conjure with in piping. It has a long and complicated history and some curious outcomes have flowed – and continue to flow – from its misapplication.

Pipers are sometimes thought to have a particularly close relation with the oral mode because they do not visibly play from written or printed scores. All this usually means is that the piper is playing from exactly such a source previously memorised because the instrument and the circumstances in which it is often played inhibit the carrying of written music.

Much of the light music repertoire is probably *learned* orally/aurally, the player referring to written sources only for the fine detail, ornament and such; but things are different in *pìobaireachd*. Despite the lip service paid to it by the Scots intelligentsia, *pìobaireachd* obtrudes rather little into the consciousness of the nation, so that opportunities to learn by oral/aural means were relatively limited until the spread of piping tapes and CDs from the 1970s onwards.

The romantic view which pictures 'oral tradition' as a creative process, by means of which an idealised common people leave their collective footprint upon cultural history, descends from the works of James MacPherson, Sir Walter Scott, and the brothers Grimm. It sounds complicated, but in practice it boils down to a series of – highly doubtful – generalisations. The central notion is that writing and print are corrupting agencies, since writing things down preserves what had been multiple, fluid texts in a single 'authoritative' form, and prevents their further development. Folklorists have therefore tended to act on the principle 'oral good; written bad'. A number of consequences follow, one of the most important being an assumption that since cities have been hotbeds of modernity, superficial literacy, and commercial popular culture, they must be inimical to 'tradition'. Therefore the deep countryside – the more 'remote' the better – should form the proper sphere of operations for fieldworkers and their tape recorders. A moment's reflection on jazz and blues and the part played in their creation by cities like St. Louis, Chicago, New York and New Orleans suggests what a questionable proposition this is.

When the University of Edinburgh's School of Scottish Studies started in 1951 with folklorists Hamish Henderson and Calum MacLean, it was north and west that the tape recorders tended to head. The apparent assumption was that anything recorded in 'remote' areas or from marginalised social groups would yield 'authentic' results. MacLean entertained a romantic enthusiasm for *pìobaireachd*, describing it as 'Scotland's finest contribution to the culture of Europe', and recounted in his book *The Highlands* (1959) his meeting with an informant called Donald Kennedy, a prolific tradition-bearer and piper:

> He was full of the traditions of the island [Shona] and the surrounding district and was an excellent story-teller. Mrs. Maclellan herself sang and her son, a very fine piper, is, incidentally, a direct descendant of Ronald Macdonald (Raghnall MacAilein Oig), a noted hero and piper of Arisaig who lived away back in the seventeenth century. In that Shona family a piping tradition has lasted two centuries and probably more. [Kennedy began to recount the story of the Flame of Wrath for Squinting Peter, but MacLean's machine broke down before completing the story] . . . I still have not got the end of the tale, but I have never heard the story from anyone else and, as far as I am aware, it has never been in print. The story has evidently been in Kennedy's family right down from the time of Ronald Macdonald of Arisaig, who flourished somewhat later than Domhnall Mór MacCrimmon. Thus does one piping family preserve the traditions of another (pp.48–9).

In actuality, Kennedy's story (with the exception that he substitutes MacRaes for MacKays) was, incident for incident, that published by the Aberdonian journalist James Logan in Angus MacKay's *Ancient Piobaireachd* (1838 and later editions).

Perspectives derived from folklore and folklife studies perpetuated the assumption that 'tradition' was a rural phenomenon, rather quaint and remote from the way most people have lived in the West during the past two centuries. This has had a particularly distorting effect in piping, which long ago migrated to the towns and cities. Glasgow had become the centre of the piping world by 1900 at the latest. The School of Scottish Studies is also responsible for the modern form of the notion that the written sources for *piobaireachd* were so corrupt that they could not be relied upon as a guide to proper idiom – although nobody seems to have seriously examined the evidence – and that recourse must therefore be had to the 'pure' unsullied idiom of Gaelic song. There seems to have been little awareness of how doubtful a proposition this might prove, in view not only of the steady promotion of 'bookish' styles by the *Mòd* (the great annual festival of Gaelic song) since its inception in 1892, but also of the fact that the leading Highland paper, the *Oban Times*, had been pumping out printed versions of Gaelic songs in large quantities ever since the 1870s. Like many other popular papers, the *Oban Times* acted as a song-exchange: people wrote in with queries, citing variant versions or stray verses, and usually received numerous replies from other readers. Tunes were also given in tonic sol-fa notation (because it could be done cheaply using a standard case of font), and this went on, week in week out, for upwards of half-a-century. The thesis that while in some mysterious way the sources for instrumental music were 'corrupted' by writing and print while those for song were not, seems entirely unsustainable.

The twentieth-century assumption, that people who did not read books therefore read nothing at all, also enters the equation. Although books were expensive, most Victorians still read hugely, contemporary newspapers supplying not only news and current affairs, but also vast amounts of recreational reading matter of every kind. In addition to songs, the *Oban Times*, drawing upon a network of reader-informants from all over the Highlands and the worldwide Gaelic diaspora, published an enormous range of material, year after year, concerning the language, literature, folklore and music of the Highlands. There were tales and songs, folkloristic belief and practice, every aspect of material culture, countless contributions on place names and history, Gaelic idiom, vocabulary and orthography. At some stage the possibility may have to be faced that much of what has been gathered up into the tape-recorded archives of the School of Scottish Studies during the past half-century, far from being unsullied oral testimony, may be little more than oralised transcripts from the columns of the *Oban Times*.

The assumption is that writing and print is damaging to 'tradition' because it offers a 'fixed' text in place of the creatively fluid variants which are felt to be the preserve of oral composition and transmission. But the evidence entirely fails to bear this out. There is no sign that print or writing interfered with the continuous process of artistically positive change. Indeed the continuous remaking of inherited material, thought characteristic of oral cultures, is exactly replicated in the written and printed sources for the music of the pipe. It seems clear, likewise, that the common notion that the hallmarks of 'tradition' are fixity and resistance to change is not supported by the evidence. But this merely tends to confirm what we may already have suspected, namely that our concept of 'tradition', which requires it at the same time to be creatively fluid *and* fixed and unchanging, must be fundamentally flawed.

Superficial notions of orality underpin the legitimacy of large sections of the modern piping establishment. For example, the striking differences between the Piobaireachd Society's scores and the rest of the written tradition are sometimes explained on the grounds that what Archibald Campbell wrote down was 'oral tradition', i.e. that what he committed to paper was the way that the leading contemporary pipers actually played. The evidence, including that of Campbell's own teachers, gives no support to this idea. Yet for three generations people have taught and played Campbell's settings in the belief that they were really playing MacDougall Gillies, or Sandy Cameron, or some other great master, overriding their often highly-developed musical sense in the process.

In an attempt to get round the problem, 'oral tradition' is sometimes invoked in a different way. Much faith has been placed in the line of instruction that came down through John MacDonald of Inverness, in the belief that it somehow escaped the influence of Campbell's scores and preserved the pure idiom intact. Thus the teaching tapes of 'traditionally' trained players like R. U. Brown, R. B. Nicol and Donald MacLeod (now being released in commercial CD form) are seen as a talisman against 'the modern corruptions' and a hot-line to the MacCrimmons. But Brown, Nicol and MacLeod were taught to *win* in a context dominated by the Piobaireachd Society's scores. Brown and Nicol were sent to study with John MacDonald of Inverness at the behest of the Society, and however much MacDonald may have tried to draw a line in the sand and preserve as much of the music as possible, and however much he is known to have also used Thomason, Glen, Ross and Angus MacKay, he based his teaching on the Piobaireachd Society scores. We know he did so because he wrote to Seton Gordon in 1949 that – such was his disgust at the newly published *Kilberry Book of Ceol Mor* – he was no longer going to do it. Archibald Campbell's influence seems obvious in the recordings of Brown, Nicol and MacLeod – for example, in their timing of the frequently occurring echo-beat movements. The written record prior to the Piobaireachd Society shows these being timed in a number of different ways to reflect the rhythmical context and melodic contour, but MacDonald's pupils invariably played the standardised and unidiomatic form written by Campbell, most prominently the unattractive introductory gesture on A. The evidence suggests that a whole range of artistically pleasing musical effects available to the *piobaireachd* player at the beginning of the 20th century was not transmitted by John MacDonald of Inverness. The Nicol component of the current 'Masters of Piobaireachd' series is based (at least in part) on recordings made by a pupil during which he systematically sang his way, tune after tune, through the *Piobaireachd Society Collection* (second series) in the winter of 1974–5. The 'oral' dimension so energetically promoted in recent years may therefore not be the broad unproblematic highway to the past that some have supposed.

Women in piping

Women have a long and intimate involvement with the music of the pipe as players, teachers, composers and tradition-bearers, although for many years they did not have a public role.

Duncan Ross, the Duke of Argyll's piper, told how his own teacher, John Bàn MacKenzie, had studied with John MacKay of Raasay, and that 'MacKay used to turn his back to the pupils, and play the tunes. MacKay's sister used to sit by the fire, and dictate the words of Canntaireachd, and sing them as the piper played'. The folklore says that the MacCrimmon daughters notated and taught. One, Elizabeth MacCrimmon, is said to have married Duncan Rankin, piper to the laird of Coll, and 'on one occasion in Grisipool House, Coll, during her husband's temporary illness, played in the passage during dinner, and none of the gentlemen present distinguished any difference, though her husband was one of the greatest pipers in the Highlands in his time, having come through both the great seminaries in Mull and Skye, with the highest proficiency . . .'. Pipe-Major Willie Ross was largely taught by his mother, Mary Collie. Many young players in the North-East were trained by Bessie Brown, sister of the famous R. U. Brown of Balmoral.

Women have figured, too, as composers of pipe music. Helen MacDonald (*c.* 1884 – 1975), sister of John MacDonald of Inverness, was organist at the kirk of Craigellachie, and composed the 3rd and 4th parts of the classic competition strathspey 'The Caledonian Society of London'. She had strong opinions on the light music of the day, dismissing the compositions of John MacColl and William Laurie as having 'nae *bite*'. Agnes MacLauchlan, scion of a famous piping family, married the composer Donald MacPhedran who 'had a style peculiar to himself which to a great extent he acquired through his wife, who was a sister of the famous John MacLachlan, piper to Poltalloch, and the foremost piper of his day'. Her own compositions include the rather attractive 6/8 tune entitled 'Jeanie's March' published in *Donald MacPhedran's Collection* (*c.* 1906):

Jeanie's March   Mrs. McPhedran

The classic 6/8 march, 'The Scottish Horse' (first published in Glen's *Edinburgh Collection*, vol.6, 1904, p.1), was also composed by a woman, Kitty

Ramsay, the Marchioness of Tullibardine (1874–1960), a fascinating multi-talented gentlewoman who had studied composition under Sir Hubert Parry at the Royal College of Music, entered politics (first female Scottish MP; one of the first women in British politics to hold ministerial rank) and, following her principled stand against the fascists in Spain and Germany, became famous as the 'Red Duchess' of Atholl.

Women were barred from the Royal Scottish Pipers' Society, although interestingly not from the Piobaireachd Society, whose general committee was graced for a number of years by Lady Elspeth Campbell, the bagpipe-playing daughter of Lord Archibald Campbell and niece of the Duke of Argyll.

As tradition-bearers women were very important. There must have been many like Nell Ackroyd, sister of the composer John Mackay of Strathhalladale, who went to South Africa with her husband Pipe-Major George Ackroyd in 1938 and in many ways was nearly as knowledgeable as he was regarding bagpipe music, although she did not play the instrument. It is said that 'to hear her "Canntaireachd", a set of Ceol Beag, was to listen to one who was fully aware of the gracing and delicate phrasing of the music'.

Women seem often to have played pipe music on keyboards, including Eliza Ross on Raasay who transcribed several pieces of *ceòl mór* from the playing of the famous John MacKay. Then there was Marianne MacLean of Torloisk in Mull, a harper and keyboard player whom contemporaries considered one of the greatest authorities on Highland music of her day. She married into the Clephane family of Fife, themselves quite notable as musicians, and her damning verdict on Sir Walter Scott's piper on a visit to Abbotsford in 1819 is still recorded:

> Mrs. Clephane thought poorly of John of Skye's piping. 'Is he not an elegant man?' Scott tried to wheedle her. 'He is a pretty man; but he understands little of his pipe,' Mrs. Clephane said firmly. 'His drones are not in tune with his chanter. He wants the Highland style altogether.'
> (Edgar Johnson, *Sir Walter Scott the Great Unknown*, i, 683)

In the early years of the nineteenth century, Janet MacLeod and her sisters in Skye were formally taught to play *pìobaireachd* on the fortepiano by their father, Niel MacLeod of Gesto, bagpipe music editor and friend of the later MacCrimmons. Willie Ross's daughter, Cecily, won at the *Mòd* in 1924 playing marches, strathspeys and reels on the piano.

Teaching on the pipes might be discouraged, however, or even withheld from women. The traditional singer Lizzie Higgins, daughter of the famous Jeannie Robertson, was passionately fond of pipe music, and despite her father's opposition was secretly taught by her uncles. When her father found out, he burnt her chanter, declaring that 'he would have no *she-pipers* in his house'. In return, he systematically taught her the traditional song repertoire, hour after hour, nuance after nuance, as a result of which she became a leading interpreter of traditional balladry in a style strongly influenced by pipe idiom. Others have been less fortunate. In its early years the College of Piping refused to take female pupils. The first woman to win a professional contest in Scotland was Edith MacPherson, a pupil of John MacDonald of Inverness, who won the open piobaireachd at Glenurquhart and Invergordon and was runner up for the Dunvegan Medal at the Skye Gathering in the 1940s. But when one considers that female players were barred from competing at major events such as Oban and Inverness until as late as 1976, their limited success at the highest levels had obvious roots in institutional conservatism. Not until 2003 did a woman take first prize in an important open competition, when the Irish player, Margaret Houlihan, took the 'A' grade Strathspey and Reel at the Argyllshire Gathering at Oban.

Female players have often had to cope with attitudes ranging from edgy defensiveness to positive misogyny. In his student days, the writer was fortunate to know a player who went on, thanks to the university's Officer Training Corps, to become the first female pipe-major in the British Army, and who was also the first female 'lone piper' at the Edinburgh Military Tattoo. While the band was being inspected during rehearsals by a harassed Scots Guards officer, who found their student casualness something of a cross, he reached her and exploded:

'And you, get your hair cut! Good God, man, you look like a bloody woman!'

– receiving the cool retort:

'Sir, I *am* a woman . . .'

If you were a *grande dame* you could, like Lady Elspeth Campbell (another connection of the house of Atholl – she was one of the many mistresses of Duchess Kitty's father-in-law, the wayward 7th Duke), make your voice heard in the councils of the *Mòd* and of the Piobaireachd Society. If you were a writer (once again with the right kind of connections), you could become editor of the *Oban Times*. One wonders how many pipers writing to that leading source of information on the instrument and its music knew that their 'Dear Sir' was actually 'Dear Madam', in the person of Mrs. Flora MacAulay, sister of the paper's owner, Duncan Cameron, and editor from 1903–1952. She lived in the upper flat of the *Oban Times* building on the esplanade and personally directed every aspect of the paper. Its rapid loss of interest in piping following her death indicates how much it had relied on her personal support. The editor of one of the best of the post-war piping magazines, *International Piper,* was also a woman, Mrs. Christine MacLellan, wife of Capt. John MacLellan, Director of the Army School of Piping. There have been female antiquaries and historians like Mairi A. MacDonald who fought so long – and ultimately successfully – for her father Alexander MacDonald's reputation when his edition of Joseph MacDonald's *Compleat Theory* (Glasgow 1927) was scurrilously attacked after his death. If you were wealthy, you could be a patron and benefactor. People interested in Scottish traditional music are greatly indebted to Lady Dorothea ('Dertha') Stewart Murray (another of that interesting generation of the Atholl family, sister-in-law of the Duchess Kitty), whose famous wedding-march was written by Willie Ross's great-uncle, Aeneas Rose. She bought the great John Glen collection of old Scottish music books and manuscripts and presented it to the nation when the National Library of Scotland was created in 1927.

Although women have often enjoyed low visibility in what was, and to some extent still remains, a strongly patriarchal society, their role in piping was a good deal more important than the public record might suggest. Nowadays, of course, women are found as solo players and in a lot of the top pipe bands; but for many years they had to be content with a vital, if largely invisible, role behind the scenes. When the Bucksburn and District Pipe Band got costly new uniforms around 1970, women stayed up sewing all night before a big event so they would have new bag covers to go with them. Similar stories could probably be told of most of the top outfits from the early twentieth century onwards. Bearing in mind that a big ensemble has running costs of upwards of £10,000 a year, without largely female organisation, fundraising and support the modern competing pipe band would probably never have developed.

Official support: institutions, information

This may remind us of the largely informal nature of support for piping during the past two centuries. There is a Royal Scottish National Orchestra, a Scottish Opera, Scottish Ballet, and the beginnings of a National Theatre, but there has been little institutional support for any of the activities described above. Local and individual effort, fundraising and organisation has underpinned almost everything.

Access to good-quality teaching is important at every level, and several tutors may contribute to the making of a master player. Until the final quarter of the twentieth century, however, when some local authorities began to appoint peripatetic teachers of piping, this could be very largely a lottery, a simple accident of birth or geography. It takes a lot of resources: time, knowledge, skill, and money too, since instruments are expensive and tuition has usually to be paid for. Not all families have the means, or the desire, to secure this for their children. While the music of the pipes has flourished during the past two centuries – this has been very much against the grain of 'official' Scotland. The days of Presbyterian severity, which led to instrument-burning in the Isles and similar acts of piety, have receded, but the church was hostile to the pipes for many years, although it later became a significant sponsor of the art through its youth wing, the Boys' Brigade and its many pipe bands.

Hostility towards the pipes has marked a wide range of Scottish institutions. For a long time the schools did not, generally speaking, consider the pipes a 'proper instrument' and steered musically gifted children towards the 'cello or the French horn. Indeed, the notion that the pipes were vulgar and 'low' was the normal response of middle-class Scotland. In one Scottish university a few years ago, the music department offered practice facilities to all members of staff, but excluded pipers on the grounds that the instrument was too disruptive for other users (although it produces fewer decibels than a concert grand). The Crown itself, although presented as a supporter of piping (H. M. the Queen is patron of the Piobaireachd Society and annually attends the Braemar Highland Gathering), has done little to encourage the art. This has been the case from the later eighteenth century, when royal inaction frustrated attempts to re-start the MacCrimmon college, down to recent times when, in 1958, R. B. Nicol's classes in South Uist ended because the Balmoral estate had first call on his services as a gamekeeper during the summer. It is believed that a year later royal opposition prevented R. U. Brown succeeding Willie Ross in a new full-time post which would have given him general oversight of all army piping, a proposal winning otherwise universal approval.

In an attempt to tackle the prevailing culture of official neglect, The College of Piping was founded in Glasgow in 1948 by a small band of enthusiasts led by Thomas Pearston and Seumas MacNeill. The College attempted to gain institutional credibility by introducing a standardised system of graded assessment and certification, but it existed outside the formal education system and failed for many years to secure grant aid either from the local authority or the Scottish Education Department. The College achieved much in the city of Glasgow and its immediate hinterland, but it was several decades before it developed any kind of national reach, and elsewhere teaching and learning went on on a largely informal basis.

During the later decades of the twentieth century official support continued to be patchy or non-existent. A survey in the early 1980s reported that only eight full-time piping teachers were employed by local education authorities throughout Scotland (five of them in the Western Isles). Scottish Arts Council funding was received only by the Royal Scottish Pipers' Society, an Edinburgh-based group of about 300 gentleman amateurs, for their concert programmes.

The Scottish tourist authorities appear to know little about piping. Enquiries directed to one Scottish Tourist Information Office in a major Scottish city in 2002 elicited the response that they had everything else . . . i.e., fiddle, accordion, traditional singers, Scottish Country Dancing and so on, but nothing about piping, and when asked about indoor events commented, 'Don't you think the pipes sound better outside? Would you ever send anybody to an indoor performance of piping?'

Libraries vary considerably in quality and extent of holdings. One of the best places is the Mitchell in Glasgow, although its facilities are slowly being eroded by years of local authority under-funding. Its special remit is Glasgow publications and so it has a lot of pipe music, although some titles in the catalogue can no longer be produced, a situation reflected in a number of other libraries.

The Mitchell's imposing neo-classical façade fronts the roaring trench of the Glasgow freeway which will conduct you from the outskirts of the city to the snug inner recesses of the library in about twenty minutes flat. Its holdings and supportive staff make the Mitchell a superior setting for traditional music enquiries.

Then there is the National Library of Scotland (NLS), whose brutal façade rears up from a tangle of streets in the heart of central Edinburgh, abutting straight on to the pavement – no lawns, no statues, no fountains, no parking. It resembles a huge filing cabinet with a small reading room perched on top, so there are lots of stairs; things have to be fetched from remote locations, and ordered by certain times of day. The National is the library of libraries in Scotland, but it is not a very inviting place. There is a noticeable security presence and you will be asked about the nature of your business and if you could not do it elsewhere. In the 1930s Archibald Campbell deposited copies of the Donald MacDonald and Angus MacKay manuscripts here. Although this placed them, technically, in the public domain, he might as well have put them on the back of the moon as far as most pipers were concerned. The NLS preserved the atmosphere of the lordly Advocates' Library from which it had sprung, and while you might not positively be refused admission, it was not the sort of place where you would feel comfortable wearing cheap boots and a celluloid collar. The National Library has also been chronically underfunded from the outset, and recent further budget cuts have resulted in the curtailment of the science and music departments. The latter, once a never-failing source of lovingly accumulated knowledge and expertise on Scottish music, has been converted into a tearoom where vending machines dispense filled rolls, Caramel Wafers and cans of IRN-BRU.

An hour or so's journey north from Edinburgh brings one to the large and excellent Wighton Collection of Scottish traditional music at Dundee City Library, an airy, capacious, intelligently thought-out affair, framed in a pleasing, late-modernist style and well worth a visit. It has lifts and parking spaces, ample life-support facilities and a commanding prospect of the silvery Tay. The staff are helpful, and the catalogue can be consulted online.

Taken together, the libraries of Scotland have substantial holdings relating to the pipe and its music, but no single site has a complete spread of sources. Indeed, with the exception of the Mitchell Library, what is there seems to have accumulated largely by accident, as a result of gifts and deposits rather than a coherent and systematic acquisitions policy. For example, no complete run of *The Piping Times* is held by any library north of the Forth. The full extent of the National Library's own holdings of pipe music can be discovered only by consulting a typescript checklist in a battered ringbinder in the manuscript department's North Reading Room. The library's online catalogue is of limited use here, shortage of funds having restricted the digitisation programme.

The writer was once informed by the music department of a Scottish university, 'Oh, we don't do *Scottish* music here!', and this seems to have reflected the general situation for much of the twentieth century. There was little academic support for the study of piping at a serious level: the entire tally seems to have been a couple of Ph.D. theses (one on *canntaireachd*, another on the tradition in South Uist) and two M.Litt.s (one on the impact of the Highland Societies and one on links between *piobaireachd* and Gaelic song), all sustained at Edinburgh. There is no national archive. Collection of such material was discouraged by the National Archives of Scotland, and the Royal Scottish Museums long found it impossible – for reasons baffling to an outsider – to display their extensive holdings of piping material.

Right at the century's end, however, there were signs of a possible change in official attitudes: the National Piping Centre was created in Glasgow, located in a tiny restored 'Greek' Thomson church in Cowcaddens. It is thought that the intention was to absorb the College of Piping to forge a single centre for the teaching and learning of piping in Glasgow, and the story of how the city ended up with two separate and rival institutions is said to be an interesting one. The National Piping Centre enjoyed links with the Scottish Executive and also with the Royal Scottish Academy of Music and Drama, to which it contributed the piping element of new degree-level studies in traditional music. There was a good deal of emphasis on multi-instrumentalism and ensemble play, and it remains to be seen whether the system can produce real pipers rather than simply swelling the ranks of the folk-rock bands.

The IT revolution has affected piping along with everything else, and websites now offer a good deal of information on the subject. At the time of writing, the best site is *Piper & Drummer Online* which hosts the first piping e-journal based, like its hard-copy namesake, in Toronto. Imaginative and well-designed and covering virtually the whole range of the subject, it is a convincing demonstration of the power and flexibility of the medium – most obviously in being substantially bigger than its print equivalent, and offering instant access to dozens of interesting back files in a way that would be impossible in print. The technology means that breaking stories can be posted as they occur. *P&D Online* is the fastest thing in piping journalism. Indeed a B.B.C. Scotland correspondent recently got the results of a big competition at Cowal more quickly in Toronto than he could get them from Dunoon. It also provides a comprehensive set of links to related sites.

– *Piper & Drummer Online* can be found at *http://www.piperanddrummer.com*
– The most comprehensive general site is 'The Bagpipe Web Directory', which has excellent links, interesting discussion forums, piping photographs, news and results. It can be found at *http://www.bobdunsire.com/bagpipeweb/*

And what about language?

The terms of art in piping come in three languages, English, Scots and Gaelic. Once nearly all Highland pipers would have been Gaelic speakers, but this has gradually ceased to be the case from the early nineteenth century onwards as piping became an urban phenomenon, and the language – deliberately undermined by the anglicising Scottish education system – began to shrink, probably beyond the point of recovery. The number of native speakers currently stands at about 58,000 and is rapidly declining.

This is a vexed matter in some ways, thanks to long-standing cultural tensions between Highland and Lowland Scotland. Once upon a time everybody in the country spoke Gaelic either in its p- or q- Celtic forms (q-Celtic being the root of modern Scots Gaelic, and p-Celtic, the ancestor of Welsh, which was once spoken all over the Central Belt, the Lothians and Dumfries and Galloway). But by the eighteenth century the long official campaign against the language and its institutions had restricted it to the mountainous north and west of the country and produced the classic Highland/Lowland divide so beloved of novelists and historians like Sir Walter Scott. Subsequent major population movement changed this once again. Romantic writers on the Highland Clearances like to picture hazardous sea passages to exile in far-flung places (as Highland landlords emptied the straths of people, wielding a theory of property very similar to that which underpinned the institution of slavery in the Confederacy), there clinging to their distinctive language and culture, their hearts still true, still Highland, and in dreams dutifully beholding the Hebrides.

But, as in most real human situations, people usually had to go for the cheapest option, and it was overwhelmingly to the nearby Lowlands of Scotland, unromantic locations like Greenock, Dundee and Glasgow, that the displaced Highland population went. There they gradually acquired the protective colouring of Lowland society, its language (Scots) and its traditional cultural prejudices – which were significantly anti-Gaelic and anti-Highland. But music took little account of such barriers. There was a common instrumental culture throughout Scotland. Highlanders had for centuries borrowed Lowland tunes, and vice versa, and such was the vitality of the common idiom that piping was to flourish mightily in the Lowland towns and cities, more so, in some respects, than it had in the Highlands.

There was a good deal of seasonal migration which also helped to facilitate the exchange of tunes. Considerable numbers of East-Coast fishermen went to the West Coast every year. The writer's grandfather could find his way unerringly in the dark and without navigation lights round every sea loch in the West likely to contain herring. Likewise, large numbers of Highland people found seasonal employment in the Lowlands at the harvesting and fishing, year after year. The 'Heilan' deems' used to sing at the gutting. On Sundays you could hear the very free West-Coast style in psalmody (little admired locally and described by one who heard it as 'it wizna lik' the soun' o' human craturs'). Northeasters quickly picked up the more lively *puirt a beul*-type stuff, and you could hear them sing snatches of things like 'Let us take the High Road', spot-on in point of musical style, but couched in the most wonderfully approximate Gaelic:

Gaavishing an rachetmower   Gaavishing an rachetmower   Gaavishingan rachetmower   Olkima lecaachay!

The writer's mother used to speak fondly of 'Tonalt' who came down to help crew her father's drifter for many summers, and what a nice man he was, and used to slip the children cans of condensed milk and things, and when they teased him about his accent used to declare – perhaps accurately enough – 'Ach I can spoke ta England as good as yourself and twice as more!'

Anyway, most people would think it an advantage to be able to use some of the basic terms of art with at least a nod in the direction of the original sound systems, and the following table may be of some assistance. Take care, though: equivalent spellings are approximate, and will inevitably be coloured by those of your own speech community.

There is a copious list of terms of art (many of them little used now) in Edward Dwelly's *Illustrated Gaelic-English Dictionary* (1901–11 and later editions) under the heading *pìob*. The instrument itself is called the *pìob mhór* (pron. peep voar), the great pipe, *mór* meaning 'big'. The essential items are as follows (stressed syllables are italicised):

- cumha (pron *coo*-a), a lament
- failte (*falt*-che), a welcome
- cruinneachadh (pron: '*croon*-uchuh'), a gathering (the 'ch' pronounced in the guttural Scots fashion, 'och/loch')
- ùrlar, (pron. '*oor*-lur'), the ground or main theme of a *pìobaireachd*
- siubhal, (pron. '*shew*-ell'), a common variation type in *pìobaireachd*
- taorluath (*toor*-la), a technical term for a movement common both to *pìobaireachd* and the light music
- crunluath (*croon*-la), the final variation/s in a *pìobaireachd*

The taorluath and crunluath variations each come in several different sorts, depending on the kind of tune, namely

- taorluath/crunluath fosgailte (*toor*-la, *croon*-la *fos*-kiltche)
- taorluath/crunluath breabach (*toor*-la, *croon*-la *bre*-bach – 'ch' pronounced here, once again, in the guttural Scots fashion as in 'och', or 'loch')
- taorluath/crunluath a mach (*toor*-la, *croon*-la *a mach* – 'ch' also pronounced here in the 'och'/'loch' pattern)

Many English speakers find Gaelic a difficult language to learn. Vocabulary presents one problem – familiar-looking terms that give a foothold in French, German, Spanish, or the Scandinavian languages are sadly lacking in Gaelic, rather few words from which have passed into modern English or Scots. The nouns decline with insouciant waywardness, although they do occur in only two genders. But then there is word order . . . The standard subject/verb/object structure which shapes most people's thinking about the world and the way it works, is replaced in Gaelic by a highly unusual verb/subject/object arrangement, creating a multitude of pitfalls for the unwary. Unlike most western European languages, where you can juggle with key grammatical components as you go, in Gaelic you have to have the structure of what you are going to say clearly in mind before you start, because the verb comes at the beginning and many of the verbs are irregular. In languages like English or Spanish a noun is a sturdy thing, clear-cut, as matter-of-fact as a leg of mutton; but in Gaelic it dissolves under the slightest provocation into a mist of aspiration, changing its sound – sometimes quite significantly – in the process . . . and native speakers go so fast, seeming to outside listeners to pronounce, at most, about one syllable in three that . . . oh dear . . . and there is no straightforward way of saying 'yes' or 'no' . . . and as for counting . . . not in four twenty years and a ten would you get the hang of it. One exasperated learner was moved to declare, 'Gaelic a *language*? Tush, man – it's a string of irregularities held together by an exception'.

The subject is important because there is frequent blurring between language and music, which has a direct bearing on the pipes, most noticeably the notion that language and music are related in some deep but obscure way, and that because Gaelic is fading, the skids must also be under the music of the pipe. Since the latter is in a condition of almost indecent health, this would seem to be a very doubtful proposition. Then there is the notion that native Gaelic speakers possess, by virtue of that fact, superior insight into the music; but this, too, will hardly bear examination. The pipes have long been an all-Scottish phenomenon with free passage of tunes between the different language communities for centuries. Indeed song airs from the Lowland tradition constituted a substantial proportion of the light music of the Highland pipe for much of the nineteenth century, as one can see in *Uilleam* Ross's *Collection* (1869 and later editions), and similar published works.

The pipes and other instruments

About the year 1900 the military got the notion that it might be good to have pipe and brass-wind regimental bands playing ensemble. The people concerned had little choice in the matter: 'just cut along and play with those chaps, pipey', they were told, and so some way had to be found of doing it. If they thought their commanders were potty, or comically deficient in musical taste – and probably both – who will say they were wrong? Yet the resulting tonal Corrievrechan survives in military contexts, and does not seem to displease too violently audiences in search of a little 'traditional' pageantry at events like the Edinburgh Military Tattoo.

Somewhat later, the advent of amplifiers, synthesisers and midi-devices gave birth to the folk-rock movement, which, in Scotland, led to electric ceilidh-bands quite often featuring the pipes in an ensemble role. The resulting 'Rock 'n' Reel' where instruments of shudderingly different tonality and timbre were yoked together, with the pipes electronically subdued to their surroundings, was frequently also characterised by frenetically rapid tempi, crassly thickened textures, grossly inappropriate harmonies, and repetitive and insensitive percussion lines flattening out the rhythms they ought to have been illuminating. Maybe there should be a word for it: 'Cel-tack', perhaps, on analogy with 'Muzak' (adjective, 'Cel-tacky'). It seems obvious from the success of groups playing this stuff that not everybody found the results tedious, misconceived, or distressing, and it oozes from radio stations and P.A. systems all over Scotland. Nor perhaps should the gloomy conservative consider it a uniquely bad development. Traditional music has been ground in the mills of contemporary fashion at every period of which we have knowledge. What is Scottish folk-rock, after all, but Marjory Kennedy-Fraser with attitude?

Piping and the media

During the past half-century the Scottish education service has consistently failed to teach young Scots – including those who went on to work in the media – anything much about the place they live in. As a result, the Scottish press-corps, with a few honourable exceptions, does not know enough about the country to report it intelligently. This has created a kind of national amnesia difficult for people brought up in normal communities to appreciate, and it has had consequences for the pipes along with everything else.

Although there is a modest amount of specialist programming devoted to piping by B.B.C. Radio Scotland, coverage in the rest of the media has existed in one of two modes: either not at all, or with such sneering vulgarity and/or crass ignorance that one generally wishes they hadn't bothered. A quick survey of the Scottish press reveals the commoner clichés:

- 'Skirl o' the pipes!' and variants. (If pipes are skirling there is something very wrong with the way they are being played or have been set up, or both.)
- Sniggering puns used to describe piping controversies, such as 'Sharp note sends Angus reeling!'
- Weary visual stereotypes such as showing players surrounded by grimacing people with fingers in their ears.

The constant drip-feed of disparagement encourages an attitude that the pipes exist somehow outside the normal order of things and the ordinary rules of social life. One famous player got so fed up with people accosting him when they saw the distinctive coffin-shaped case in which the instrument is carried with 'Haw, erra piper!' and then proceeding to dance and caper and make silly bagpipe noises, that he bought a large executive briefcase into which, with a little ingenuity, the instrument snugly fitted. (It is not recorded whether he was then followed about by people crying 'Haw, erra executive!', capering and crowing 'Salaried man, haw, haw, haw!' and making jocular collar-and-tie gestures.)

Conventional beliefs in piping

There are a number of ideas and assumptions for which there is little or no evidence, yet which recur frequently, and provide a continuing obstacle to understanding. Amongst them

— *that the Pipes were banned after the '45.* This is a popular fantasy, originating in an anonymous commentator in the early nineteenth century and much repeated later – perhaps because it invests the subject with a kind of 'rebel chic'. But there is no mention of the pipes in any of the three Disarming Acts following the '45, and the activities of the main teaching families seem to have continued largely undisturbed.

— *that the army 'rescued' piping.* Although this may have seemed a plausible notion in the heavily militarised society which Britain was to become during the first half of the twentieth century, there is little evidence to support this contention in the key period from about 1780 to 1914. Although the 'rescuers' wanted to promote piping to keep the Highland regiments in fighting fettle, the most vital parts of piping tradition exist apart from the regular army and have done so at all periods.

— *that pipe music needed 'rescuing' at all.* This conclusion was based on a flawed notion of 'tradition', such that if a thing was deemed 'traditional' it was bound therefore to be in a moribund condition. There is no evidence to support this idea; and much, on the contrary, that it was entirely misconceived.

— *that piping was severely damaged during the nineteenth century by the Free Church's ban on secular music.* This is untrue even of isolated West-Coast and Island communities: you could destroy the instruments, but unless you killed the people, you could not destroy the music. Meantime the other 99.5% of the tradition was alive and well in towns and cities where it was immune from clerical censure.

— *that those who speak Gaelic or have Highland blood have a closer affinity with the music.* This is the racial theory, which has its roots in the Victorian movement known as 'The Celtic Twilight'; it seems as improbable as the notion of requiring to learn Scots in order to play 'Jenny dang the weaver'.

– *that the Scots, by their irresponsible penchant for technical innovation and fresh composition, had thereby corrupted piping 'tradition' with the result that the latter existed in a pure and 'authentic' form only in Nova Scotia, Australia, or wherever the writer happened to be at the time, and that this would be confirmed as soon as he or she could find the evidence.* This requires 'tradition' – in the face of all evidence to the contrary – to be unchanging and static. The notion of a purer 'traditional' style does not seem to involve much beyond playing simple tunes with much spirit but little art – a thing that could probably be heard down the Royal Scottish Pipers any Friday night.

– *that the master pipers played only pìobaireachd.* This is the notion that 'there was never a reel at Boreraig'. There is no evidence to support this; and much circumstantial evidence to the contrary. To accompany dancing over a period of several hours the Highland pipe is not an option; for this, pipers seem to have used bellows-blown pipes, as Calum Pìobaire did. It had other advantages: you could smoke or have a dram while playing, things which are difficult – although not impossible – on the great pipe.

– *that pìobaireachd was invented by the MacCrimmons.* This notion grew by a process of fanciful elaboration during the later nineteenth and twentieth centuries by writers working in an area where there was much enthusiasm and few or no facts. There is no evidence to support this contention.

– *that pìobaireachd is 'different' from normal music, and operates according to an aesthetic of its own, difficult, obscure, and understood only by a handful of 'experts'.* Although this might seem plausible enough to those who had heard pipers play only the Piobaireachd Society's scores, the older written and published sources do not support this notion.

– *that the Piobaireachd Society rescued the key piping manuscripts and preserved them for the future.* This was already being effectively done by pipers. The Society seems actually to have lost papers, and withdrew much of the remainder from circulation for considerable periods. Papers of major figures like John MacDonald of Inverness, General C. S. Thomason, and John MacDougall Gillies were taken by the Society after their deaths, and it is not known what the Society still possesses, where it might be, or what proportion has later been returned to the public domain. R. B. Nicol destroyed his extensive correspondence with his teacher John MacDonald shortly before he died. Robert Reid, the leading pupil of John MacDougall Gillies, gave instructions, likewise, that his papers should be destroyed on his death.

– *that it is impossible to write down pìobaireachd adequately in staff notation.* This is a defence often heard by players forced to interpret very freely the Piobaireachd Society's rhythmically distorted scores in an attempt to make musical sense of them in ignorance of the earlier printed and written scores which, thanks to the Society's monopolistic activities, have been unavailable for most of the past hundred years.

– *that royalty and aristocracy have within historically recent times been effective patrons of pipers.* They employed them as servants or gamekeepers with an additional role as 'pipers'. In R. U. Brown and R. B. Nicol's day there was little *pìobaireachd* at Balmoral; they paraded round the dining table on high days and holidays wearing silly hats and even sillier socks and the startling pale grey 'Balmoral' tartan designed by Victoria's Prince Albert, playing 'lollipops' from the light music repertoire like mess-night in one of the more benighted Highland regiments. Although the music of the pipe had accompanied the British royals through large stretches of their lives from the days of Angus MacKay onwards, it is not clear that this resulted in very much knowledge, taste or judgement of the art, although, to be sure, Willie Ross did manage to get Edward VIII to play a bit, but it seems to have been at a pretty low level.

And finally: If I see a piper should I ask, 'Hey can I have a go?'

Absolutely not. Do not even think about it. Because

– pipes are very personal and rather fragile possessions, not the sort of thing you want ham-fisted strangers monkeying about with;
– they are frequently also rather costly;
– you may be unhygienic: the player has no idea where you've been or what you might be carrying; and
– it is pointless in any case, as you will fail to make the instrument sound for more than a second or two at most, and will look like a complete fool as you juggle with its various bits and pieces.
– You may also (and deservedly) slip a disc.

If you want to learn to play the pipes, buy a practice chanter and find a teacher.

PIPERS

To understand a tradition we need to know who made it, and how. This section, then, looks at the lives of some of the men and women who created and sustained the music of the Highland bagpipe during the last three centuries.

DYNASTIES

The MacCrimmons

Much stress has been laid on the role of piping dynasties in the creation and dissemination of the music but a good deal of our information, especially about the earlier pipers, is at best approximate. The idea of families of brilliantly endowed teachers and composers following one another in strict succession back into the misty reaches of time fitted neatly into the romanticised notion of Highland society which developed during the nineteenth century; but the evidence is fragmentary and, for times much earlier than about 1700, largely traditional. The MacCrimmons of Skye are nowadays regarded as piping's royal family, but it was only from about the middle of the nineteenth century that they began to appear routinely in written sources as pre-eminent players, composers and teachers. The account was expanded by subsequent writers step by step until it reached its current position in which they are considered – on the basis of very little evidence – as the leading composers of *pìobaireachd* and the inventors of the form. Similarly, the MacCrimmon 'succession' was extended to push the foundation of their college ever further back in time, and there was much fanciful speculation about their origins – that they had originally been Irish, Norse, or even Italian (the latter based on a strained interpretation of their patronymic as 'son of the man of Cremona'). If so, the man from Cremona must have been an energetic fellow because there were MacCrimmons all over the place – in Skye and Harris, in Speyside and Aberdeenshire, and above all in Glenelg, where they were so numerous that it is said that at the Rout of Glaisbheinn, 81 John MacCrimmons fell.

In the earliest accounts of the music, only a handful of tunes are attributed to

MacCrimmon composers; but during the nineteenth and twentieth centuries, the MacCrimmon 'repertoire' grew as many tunes connected with Skye or the MacLeods were casually attributed to them. The competition for The Silver Chanter, a leading invitational event held annually at Dunvegan Castle, stipulates that contestants must play a 'MacCrimmon' *pìobaireachd*; but the tunes nowadays recognised as such have seldom any tangible connection with the family.

Similarly, the 'MacCrimmon crest' – 'a hand holding a pipe chanter, with the motto "Cogadh no Sith" – Peace or war . . . The bearings . . . on a field argent, a chevron azure, charged with a lion passant or, between three cross croslets fitchee, gules' – made its first appearance in *The Clans of the Scottish Highlands* in 1847, and probably sprang from the fertile brain of the book's compiler, Aberdonian journalist James Logan. Yet there are references to MacCrimmon pipers in historical documents from various parts of Scotland from the sixteenth century onwards. While the succession in the important Skye family is largely conjectural, we know a good deal about at least one of its later members, namely Donald Roy MacCrimmon (died 1825), who emigrated to Carolina and fought gallantly in the American Wars of Independence, where

> He cut his way through Parties of the Rebels, & eluded their pursuit when 500 Dollars were offered for his Head. In the course of his Service he personally wrested in single Combat their Swords from three Commanding officers of the Enemy, laying their owners prostrate on the Earth, & seized three Stand of Colours. He also at the head of six men compelled the Surrender of a Privateer fully armed (quoted in Donaldson, *Highland Pipe*, p.92).

On his return to Scotland, Donald Roy was involved in ultimately abortive attempts to re-establish the MacCrimmon college on an official basis as an Army School of Piping.

The MacArthurs

The other major Skye dynasty, the MacArthurs, who taught at Hungladder in Trotternish, were said to have been pipers to the MacDonalds of the Isles. They are much less involved in glamorous wish-fulfilment than the MacCrimmons, but are still a name to conjure with in piping. They begin to appear in the records from the earlier years of the seventeenth century onwards. The most important of them, Charles MacArthur (*c.*1700–1780), was said to have rivalled his teacher, Patrick òg MacCrimmon. His eloquent tombstone –

Here ly
the remains of
Charles Mac
Karter whose
fame as an hon
est man and
remarkable pip
er will surv
this generation
for his manners
were easy & re
gular as his
music & the
the [sic] melody of
his fingers will

— stops abruptly at the point the mason had reached when, as is said, Donald MacArthur, the dedicatee's son, was drowned in the Minch ferrying cattle between the Uists and Skye. In the following generation, the important members were Charles's nephews: John, usually called 'Professor MacArthur' (died 1790), who settled in Edinburgh, and helped organise the early Highland Society competitions, and Angus (died *c.*?1820) who became piper to Lord MacDonald and lived in London from 1796 onwards as piper to the Highland Society. Angus was a fine composer whose 'Lament for Lady MacDonald' is still regarded as a classic. He was also the source of the rich MacArthur stylings preserved in the so-called 'Highland Society of London's Manuscript' which has recently been published as *The MacArthur-MacGregor Manuscript of Piobaireachd* (Universities of Glasgow and Aberdeen, 2001).

The MacKays of Gairloch

The MacKays of Gairloch were another famous family, to whose chief member, Iain Dall MacKay (1656–1754), we owe the poem 'Cumha Choire an Easain' and the famous 'Lament for Patrick òg MacCrimmon'.

The MacGregors

The teaching families were by no means concentrated in the West. One of the greatest came from Perthshire, the MacGregor pipers, usually called *clann an sgeulaiche* (children of the storyteller), centred on the beautiful vale of Fortingall at the foot of Glenlyon. The family enter the record in the early eighteenth century as pipers to the Dukes of Atholl and other Perthshire lairds and their teaching network was widely extended. One of them, John MacGregor, played at Culloden. Several of the family attended the early competitions of the Highland Society of London, of whom John MacGregor (c. 1781–1822), son of Patrick MacGregor who won the first of the Falkirk competitions in 1781, was probably the most prominent. An accomplished multi-instrumentalist, he also played the flageolet, flute and bellows pipes and settled in London as piper to the Highland Society in 1806. He was Angus MacArthur's amanuensis when the 'Highland Society of London's MS' was compiled in 1820 containing some 30 *pìobaireachd*. John MacGregor collapsed and died playing at the Society's Ne'er Day dinner in London in 1822. MacGregor pipers of this line continued in Breadalbane until at least the early twentieth century and included Neil MacGregor (1861–1921) who was piper to Menzies of Menzies and pipe-major of the Aberfeldy Pipe Band.

Other famous teaching families include the Rankines in Mull, the Campbells in Argyll, the MacIntyres in Rannoch, the Bruces in Skye and Glenelg, the Cummings in Strathspey, the MacRaes in Kintail, the McLennans and Camerons in Strathconon and elsewhere, and the MacPhersons centred in Badenoch.

WORDS VERSUS NOTES

Pipe music was not written down until a relatively late stage, and for some time it hung in the balance whether it was to be represented by words – following the native *canntaireachd* tradition – or in some form of staff notation. Incomparably the greatest of those who chose the former route was Colin Mór Campbell of Nether Lorn.

Colin Mór Campbell

Of Colin Campbell we know relatively little, except that he must have been one of the most remarkable people in Scotland during the closing years of the eighteenth century. He invented, or perfected, the fascinating system of verbal notation known as the 'Nether Lorn Canntaireachd' (pron: *can*-tchir-uchk), the medium in which the largest of the earlier classic collections of *pìobaireachd* is preserved

Nearly all pipers use a form of *canntaireachd* (or singing) when conveying tunes. The idea is basically onomatopoeic, i.e. teachers sing in such a way as to represent roughly what the piece would sound like if it were actually being played. They do this for the same reasons that master teachers of other instruments sing to their pupils, because it conveys expressive nuance without having to warm up fingers and instruments first, by which time the point might perhaps be lost. The teacher chooses from a range of possible vocables and there is a good deal of variety as a result. The system has therefore to be adapted if it is to form the basis of a consistent written notation. There developed accordingly written forms of *canntaireachd* of varying degrees of systematisation, and these may have been in use from the seventeenth century onwards. The basic principle is simple: melody notes broadly speaking are represented by vowels and diphthongs; gracenotes by consonants. The system is very compact. Colin Mór could get even quite lengthy tunes on to three or four quarto pages in his clear italic hand. The end result looked like this:

'9.   Called Tharrin Mach bhat Mhic Cload
1st   Hintradre hintrahodin Two times himtodre chetrahodroo
2d   Hintradre hintrahodin himtodre chetrahodro himtodre chetrahodroo
3d   Hintradre hintrahodin himtodre chetrahodroo
D 1st Hintradili hintrahodin Two times himtodili chetrahodroo
2d   Hintradili hintrahodin himtodili chetrahodro himtodili chetrahodroo
3d   Hintradili hintrahodin himtodili chetrahodroo' [etc.]

These are the opening sections of the tune now known as 'Lament for MacDonald's Tutor' (Colin Mór's title, '*Tharrin Mach bhat Mhic Cload*', would be 'The Pulling out of MacLeod's Galley'). A piper familiar with the system and how the music *ought* to sound (considerations applying also to staff notation) could realise the first line something like this:

Colin's father, Donald Campbell, was, as a young man, apparently, piper to a leading Jacobite, Alexander MacDonald of Glenaladale in the braes of Glenfinnan, and is said to have piped Prince Charles Edward Stuart ashore when he landed from France in 1745. He later rescued the wounded Glenaladale from Culloden. In the light of this, it is interesting that he should afterwards be found working in Easdale in south-west Argyll for Colin Campbell of Carwhin, who had served for the government in the Argyllshire Militia during the Rising. At any rate, it is with this district that his son Colin Mór is traditionally associated and he is thought to have succeeded his father as piper, firstly to Carwhin and then to the latter's son, John, 4th Earl of Breadalbane.

Easdale lies about 16 miles south-west of Oban on the fringe of the Inner Hebrides, amidst the beautiful tangle of islands, sea lochs and straths that make up the province of Nether Lorn. The islands of Easdale and neighbouring Ellenabeich were opened up for commercial slate quarrying in 1744 by Campbell of Carwhin who was then factor of the western portion of the vast Breadalbane estates, and heir presumptive to the Breadalbane earldom. He lived at Ardmaddie

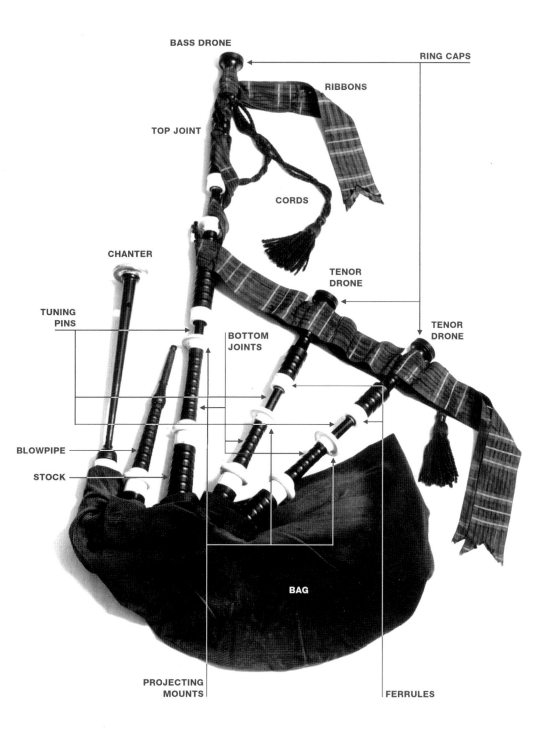

BASS DRONE

RING CAPS

RIBBONS

TOP JOINT

CORDS

CHANTER

TENOR DRONE

TUNING PINS

BOTTOM JOINTS

TENOR DRONE

BLOWPIPE

STOCK

BAG

PROJECTING MOUNTS

FERRULES

The author's pipes, made in the early 1900s by the leading Glasgow firm of Pipe-Major Peter Henderson (1851–1903). The drones are of ebony, then a popular wood because of its density and mellow tone; the mounts are ivory. The chanter is from the firm of Pipe-Major Robert Hardie (1921–1990).

The practice chanter which pipers use to develop and maintain finger technique can have a wider role. The instrument illustrated doubled as a shawm in the 1960s early music revival to record a piece by Perotinus Magnus of the 12th-century school of Notre Dame.

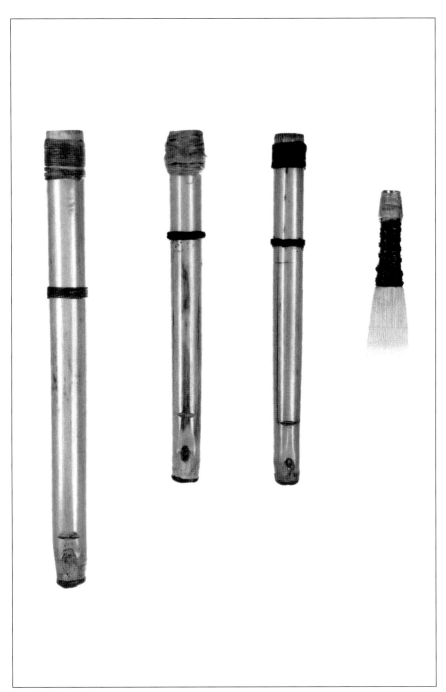

Reeds are traditionally made of Spanish cane. Drone reeds are cylindrical, with a tongue cut in the length and tied by a bridle of waxed thread: these are by Hepburns of Turriff. The chanter reed consists of two triangular blades bound to a copper staple: the above is by Megarrity-Ross of Long Beach, California.

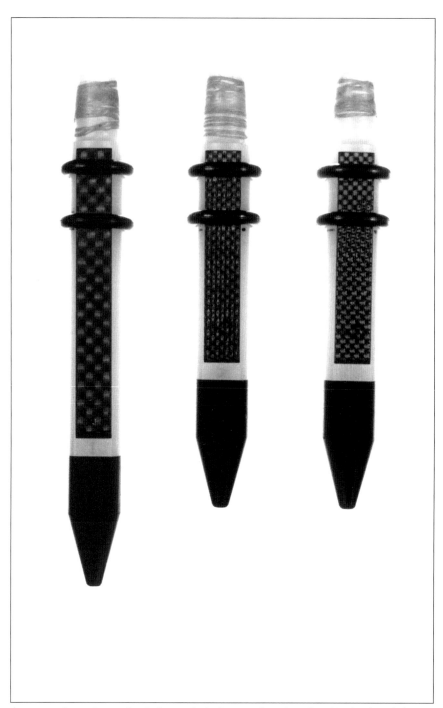

A recent welcome innovation is the synthetic drone reed, such as these 'Rockets' made by Mark Lee of Cleveland, Ohio, which have high specification glass-epoxy bodies and carbon-fibre blades, and rival the tonal qualities of the best traditional reeds.

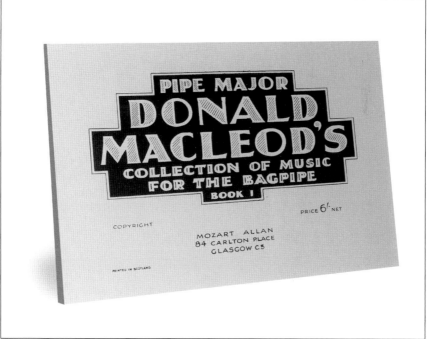

(This and the two following) A few of the many published collections from the rich light music repertoire. Singers and players from all areas of Scottish traditional music use compositions by pipers, often without being aware that they are doing so.

This is one of David Glen's (1853-1916) wide range of well-produced and affordable light music publications for pipers.

In the 1980s Pipe Major Ian Duncan and his brother Gordon pioneered fresh approaches to repertoire with the Vale of Atholl band from Pitlochry.

Seumas MacNeill (1917-1996) was joint principal, with Thomas Pearston, of the College of Piping which they founded in Glasgow in 1944.

Captain John A. MacLellan (1921-1991) was in 1959 appointed as the first full time Director of the Army School of Piping.

David Glen (1853–1916) published large collections of quality pipe music at affordable prices. His outstanding *Collection of Ancient Piobaireachd* (left) became unobtainable after it was banned from use in competition. It has recently been re-published in CD ROM form by Ceol Sean of Springfield, Illinois, in collaboration with the Bagpipe Museum of Ellicott City, Maryland.

The old Masonic Lodge, Falkirk, where from 1781 to 1783 Glasgow Gaelic Club organised the early piping competitions. At first these were relaxed events, spread over two or three days with pipers wearing everyday clothing. In 1784 they were moved to Edinburgh and, under the Highland Societies of London and Scotland, became part of the 'Celtic' entertainments laid on for the gentry during the Edinburgh season.

No. X.

Played by Patrick M'Crimmon, commonly called
LASSAN PHADRIG CHIEGCH.

I hintoradin hiento, hodrovao hieinto,
    hintoradin ha botrie, oddin drao bodrie, ochin to,
    ha bodrie oddin hintoradin, hodrova ochin to,
    hintoradin, ha bodrie oddin, drao bodrie, ochin to,
    hodrova ochin to, hievi, hieo, hiento,
    ho bodrie oddin, hintoradin, hodrova ochin to,
    hintoradin, habodrie oddin, drao bodrie, ochin to,
    biedrieo drao hodra biedrieo hoichin dro ochin to.

1st Var.   I hinininda, hiendo, hodro hoho hieindo,
    hininindo, hinininda, hininindi, hieindo,
    hininindi, hinininda, ho dro ho ho hiendo,
    hininindo, hinininda, hininindi, hiendo,
    ho dro ho ho hiendo, hinininda hiendo,
    hininindi, hinininda, ho dro ho ho hiendo,
    hininindo, hinininda, hininindi, hiendo,
    hininindi, hinininda ho dro ho ho hiendo.

Double.   I hinininda, hininindo, ho dro ho ho, hininindo,
    hininindo, hinininda, hininindi, hininindo,
    hininindi, hinininda, ho dro ho ho, hininindo,
    hininindo, hinininda, hininindi, hininindo,
    ho dro ho ho, hininindo, hinininda, hininindo,
    hininindi, hinininda, ho dro ho ho, hininindo,
    hininindo, hinininda, hininindi, hininindo,

'A Flame of Wrath for Squinting Peter' (nowadays known as 'Duntroon's Salute') from *Pibereach or pipe tunes, as taught verbally by the McCrimmen pipers in Skye to their apprentices* (1828). This pamphlet containing 20 tunes is the only original publication in the medium of 'canntaireachd' (the verbal notation system) and was published by Niel MacLeod of Gesto (c.1754–1836). *Canntaireachd* was displaced by the staff notation system developed by Gesto's friend and fellow Skyeman, Donald MacDonald (1767–1840).

TOP LEFT. An early portrait of a piper, John MacGregor (*c.* 1785/6–1861), of the famous teaching family, *clann an sgeulaiche* (children of the story teller), from Fortingall in Perthshire, winner of the prize pipe at Edinburgh in 1811, and cousin of the John MacGregor who was compiler of the important MacArthur/MacGregor manuscript.

TOP RIGHT. Angus MacKay (1813–1859), son of John MacKay of Raasay (1767-1848), won the prize pipe at the Highland Society of London's Edinburgh competitions in 1835 and his *Ancient Piobaireachd* was published in 1838. This became one of the leading 19th-century editions. MacKay was first piper to Queen Victoria from 1843 to 1854.

LEFT. This is the earliest known photograph of a piper and shows John Bàn MacKenzie (1796–1864), one of the greatest Victorian players and composer of 'His Father's Lament for Donald MacKenzie'. This is one of four calotypes of John Bàn (i.e. 'fair John') made by David Octavius Hill and Robert Adamson *c.* 1847.

Donald Cameron (*c.* 1810-1868) came from the Strathpeffer district and was a pupil of John Bàn MacKenzie. Donald Cameron was the greatest champion piper of his generation and an influential teacher, founder of the so-called 'Cameron school'. He is pictured here with his son Keith (1855–1899), and pupil Donald MacKay (1845–1893), nephew of Angus MacKay, who helped C. S. Thomason to produce *Ceol Mor*.

Alexander ('Sandy') Cameron (1821–1871), brother of Donald Cameron, was himself a champion piper and friend and teacher of Malcolm MacPherson.

Malcolm MacPherson (1838–1898), known to pipers as 'Calum Piobaire' (Malcolm the Piper), was the pivotal figure in the famous MacPherson dynasty of *piobaireachd* players and teachers. In early life he played with Sandy Cameron in the Greenock Rifle Volunteers.

Highland games, old style – The Braemar Highland Gathering, 1st September 1864. The Royal Party is seated front right watching the piper and dancers perform a foursome reel. Many leading pipers were also skilled Highland dancers.

The front cover of *Ross's Collection of Pipe Music* shows William Ross (1823–1891) before Balmoral Castle, with the conventional imagery used to depict pipers at this period. The book itself is of high quality, one of the great collections of *piobaireachd* and light music, and includes many stylings from Alexander MacDonald (1836–1883), father of John of Inverness.

Charles Simeon Thomason (1833–1911) was brought up on Speyside. His pioneering *Ceol Mor* is the largest edition ever published. A pupil of Sandy MacLennan, Sandy Cameron (the elder) and Donald MacKay, he was also a composer and his tune 'Hail to my Country' is one of the loveliest 19th-century *piobaireachds*.

Thomason built Laggan House on the River Spey in Moray, near his boyhood home at Wester Elchies which was a centre of traditional music. His grandfather, J. W. Grant of Elchies and Carron, was a pupil of Donald MacDonald and inherited MacDonald's music manuscripts. Thomason's uncle, William Grant, gifted the family's Guarnerius fiddle to the celebrated James Scott Skinner when the latter was working under his patronage as a dancing master on Speyside.

Colin Cameron (1843–1916), eldest of the three sons of Donald Cameron, was considered the greatest authority on *piobaireachd* of his generation. As well as advising the two leading Victorian editors, C. S. Thomason and David Glen, he made his own important manuscript collection which has yet to be published.

Sandy Cameron, the younger (1848–1923), was piper to the Marquis of Huntly and later to the Provost of Glasgow. His chief pupil was John MacDougall Gillies (1855–1925). Sandy excelled at tunes with complicated left-hand work and was also a talented dancer. G. S. McLennan wrote for him the classic reel 'Alick Cameron. Champion Piper'.

John MacDougall Gillies (1855–1925) learned his early piping in Aberdeen and with Sandy Cameron the younger at Aboyne and went on to a distinguished solo career. After moving to Glasgow he became Pipe Major of the 5th H.L.I. Volunteer Band which dominated the early competition scene.

Ronald MacKenzie (1842–1916), nephew and pupil of John Bàn MacKenzie, was a master player and teacher by whom the 'MacKenzie style' was passed on into the 20th-century. He compiled a large and important manuscript collection, as yet unpublished.

Angus MacPherson (1877–1976), son of Malcolm MacPherson (*Calum Pìobaire*) and Angus's son, Malcolm Ross MacPherson (1906–1966). Angus was piper to the millionaire philanthropist Andrew Carnegie at Skibo Castle, while Malcolm Ross MacPherson was in turn a leading performer of the next generation.

The pipes and drums of the 1st Lanark Rifles, under Pipe-Major Peter Henderson. It is not certain when or where pipers and drummers first began to play together as a separate musical formation. This sketch, dated 1891, is a rare early image of the modern-style pipe band.

Leading pipers at the Highland Games at Birnam *c.* 1898. Standing, *left to right*, are Willie Ross, Jack MacDougall Gillies and David C. Mather. Gavin MacDougall of Aberfeldy, a leading pipe maker, is on the far right. Seated, *from the left*, are Angus Macrae of Callander and John MacColl of Oban; the slight, tanned figure in the middle is James Center of Edinburgh; George. S. McLennan is on the far right.

LEFT. Sandy MacLennan (1811–1902) was a son of master teacher Donald MacLennan of Moy. He was also a pupil of Donald Cameron and great-uncle of George S. McLennan.

RIGHT. Lieutenant John McLennan (centre) (1843–1923), key representative of a major piping family, was brought up in the Black Isle and later became a superintendent of police in Edinburgh. He taught his gifted son George Stewart McLennan (1883–1929) who stands on his left. To his right is an equally famous master player and teacher, John MacDonald of Inverness (1865–1953).

William Collie Ross of Glen Strathfarrar (1878–1966), as Pipe-Major of the 2nd Scots Guards in 1909. He was one of the greatest editors. composers, teachers and players of the 20th century. From 1919 to 1958 he was employed by the Piobaireachd Society to run the Army School of Piping at Edinburgh Castle.

'The World's Pipe Major', Willie Ross, at Edinburgh Castle in 1934, teaching the Pipe Majors' course. This laid considerable stress on the development of musical literacy in players who were often largely orally-trained.

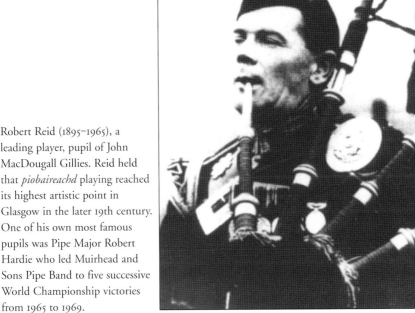

Robert Reid (1895–1965), a leading player, pupil of John MacDougall Gillies. Reid held that *piobaireachd* playing reached its highest artistic point in Glasgow in the later 19th century. One of his own most famous pupils was Pipe Major Robert Hardie who led Muirhead and Sons Pipe Band to five successive World Championship victories from 1965 to 1969.

'He's going to be some player that laddie' predicted the legendary Sandy Cameron. Robert Bell Nicol (1905–1978), aged eleven. By the 1960s Nicol and his colleague R. U. Brown were famous worldwide as the 'Bobs of Balmoral'.

MacLeod of MacLeod (second from left) landing with John MacDonald, the brothers Angus and John MacPherson, and Robert Reid, to inaugurate the MacCrimmon Cairn at Boreraig, Isle of Skye, on Wednesday, 2nd August, 1933.

Solo competitor on 'the boards' at Braemar Highland Games. Pipers often prefer a site like this, away from the din of the main games arena.

Archibald Campbell, Kilberry, (1877–1963), judging at the games. Campbell gained enormous influence through his position as a senior piping judge and secretary of the music committee of the Piobaireachd Society which enabled him to pass off his own musically limited scores as the 'authentic' tradition of master players.

Sheriff John Peter Grant of Rothiemurchus (1885–1963), President of the Piobaireachd Society, shown second from the right, with three leading pupils of John MacDonald at a meeting of Inverness Piping Society. From the left are Donald MacLeod (1916–1982), Robert Bell Nicol (1905–78) and Robert Urquhart Brown (1906–1972).

Student pipers lead the celebration at Aberdeen University in 1967 on the election of new Rector, Frank Thomson, leading businessman and founder of the famous Invergordon Distillery Pipe Band.

The first world bagpipe endurance record is established in 1969 when four student pipers play continuously for 50 hours to raise funds for the University of Aberdeen's annual charities campaign. The record was the brainchild of Donald MacArthur Grant, second left.

Bob Brown (left) and Bob Nicol in November 1971 judging at a competition in St. Andrews organised by Pipe-Major Bert Barron.

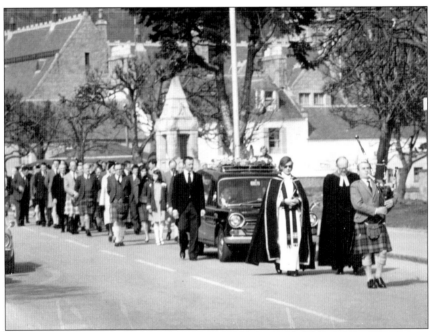

The funeral of Robert Bell Nicol, 8th April, 1978. After requiem mass at St Nathalan's Church the cortège is piped through the village of Ballater by Norman Meldrum on its way to Durris Churchyard.

House across the Sound of Seil, which was where his son John, the 4th Earl, was born and brought up and latterly preferred to live rather than at the family's much grander home at Taymouth in Perthshire.

The quarries went on to prosper mightily under the direction of the brilliant engineer John Whyte, father of Henry Whyte (1852–1913), the Gaelic scholar, journalist and piping historian 'Fionn', who spent his childhood in the house which is at the time of writing the Inshaig Park Hotel. Soon Easdale slate was roofing buildings all over the world, in England, Norway, New Zealand, Australia, the West Indies, Canada and the eastern USA. It was the industrial powerhouse of the Western Highlands, and by the middle of the nineteenth century the Marquesses of Breadalbane were clearing from it half a million pounds a year in profit. In 1861 the population of Oban was 600; that of Easdale and district was 3000.

The Sound of Seil separated two different worlds: on the one hand the beautiful wooded strath of Ardmaddie with its great house and gardens looking out across the inner isles, embodying just about everything people think of when they imagine the 'romantic' western Highlands; on the other, and conveniently out of sight, was the overcrowded, typhus-ridden industrial township on Easdale, which was where the money came from and which looked like a Victorian mill town improbably dropped down in the Inner Hebrides. Nowadays, the island presents a scene of devastation. Its lowering black rocks, great flooded quarries vanishing into unimaginable bluish-black depths and rows of beetling industrial cottages decked out as holiday homes make it an unsettling place even on a fine day.

It is thought that one of the original three volumes of 'Colin Campbell's Instrumental Book' was lost, but, even so, the surviving volumes still contain 169 tunes, some 70 of these not recorded in other sources. When complete, it must have been the largest manuscript collection of *ceòl mór* ever assembled. In addition, the organisation of the collection is extremely lucid and systematic. It is based on opening formulae, tunes beginning on low pitched notes coming first, and then progressing in an orderly fashion up the chanter in a way which makes the typically quite haphazard arrangement of later *pìobaireachd* collections look distinctly casual. Best of all, perhaps, is the marvellous wit and invention of Colin Campbell's arrangements.

The surviving two volumes remained with the family until Miss Ann Campbell of Oban sold them in 1909 to John Bartholomew of Glenorchard, a leading member of the Piobaireachd Society. There was frequent citation of the Nether Lorn Canntaireachd in the *Piobaireachd Society's Collection* (second series), but these scores did not always represent the work of Colin Mór, being sometimes simply translations into Nether Lorn vocables of the facing staff notation text. In addition, the settings arranged in staff notation from the Nether Lorn manuscript by Piobaireachd Society editors are of insufficient quality musically to give an adequate idea of Colin Campbell's ability.

As a result, this oldest of the written collections remains unpublished and little known.

Niel MacLeod of Gesto (c. 1754–1836)

Niel MacLeod of Gesto in Skye was one of the dwindling band of the native upper class who continued to contribute actively to the traditional performing arts. Although head of a leading cadet branch of the MacLeods of MacLeod (Gesto was second only to Talisker in importance), a half-pay captain of Independents and a Justice of the Peace, he was a friend of Donald MacDonald, and of the Bruces and MacCrimmons. Iain Dubh MacCrimmon's pupil Alexander Bruce was his personal piper.

MacLeod was himself a fine musician, passionately fond of *pìobaireachd*, and his house, lying snugly by the shore of the beautiful little bay of Gesto looking out to Loch Bracadale, was a centre of Highland musical culture. His daughter Ann (born 1797) was later to record that she had 'frequently been wakened at four in the morning by John MacCrimmon's pipes'. Gesto had been a player until a lung condition forced him to give it up, but he taught the pipes to four of his sons as well as teaching his daughter, Janet (1799–1882), to play *pìobaireachd* on the piano. His grandson, Keith Norman MacDonald, recorded that she

> was a splendid player of pipe music, far and away the best in Skye. She could play 'A Ghlas Mheur,' and many other pibrochs, taught by her father . . . she mentioned how cross he used to get if she struck a wrong note on the piano, and how patiently he would play it over on the chanter or pipes . . . she never knew such an authority on pipe music as her father (*Oban Times*, 13/07/1912, p.3).

When the musician Alexander Campbell was collecting traditional material for the Highland Society of Scotland in the summer of 1815 (published as *Albyn's Anthology*, 1816–18), Gesto was one of the two piping authorities he was directed to go and see. The other was Donald Roy MacCrimmon. Campbell recorded Gaelic songs from Janet and Ann MacLeod and their mother, Flora MacKinnon of Corry, and pipe music from Gesto himself. He wrote:

> Captain Niel MacLeod of Gesto . . . communicated to me his knowledge of the theory & practice of The Great Highland Bag-pipe, as it is called, in the manner he had acquired his knowledge of it from the famous MacCrummons of Skye.
> . . . Captain M'Leod permitted me to transcribe from his MS two popular pipe-pieces or Gatherings, in those sort of Syllables by which Pipers fix in their memory the *themes & variations* of the various

compositions performed on the Bag-pipe. After transcribing those syllables, I printed down opposite to each its appropriate tone, & duration, agreeably to the rules of *rhythmus* & *melody*; by means of which, the music of this martial instrument may be played by any one the least conversant in the ordinary signs of notation . . . Having accomplished the business which consumed so much of Gesto's time I bid adieu to Mrs. McLeod, & their numerous family. He himself kindly accompanied me to the summit of the hill that rises above the bay, on the margin of which his house is so pleasantly situated.

But these idyllic scenes were soon to be disrupted. The later eighteenth century was a time of gathering crisis in Skye as the profligacy of the largely absentee 22nd and 23rd lairds, popularly known as 'MacLeod the bad' and 'MacLeod the mad', came close to ruining the house of Dunvegan. Southern marriages and education contrived to make Dunvegan appear a delightful haven of English refinement to Dr. Samuel Johnson on his Highland tour in contrast to the dismal Scotchery all around. He wrote:

> Lady *MacLeod*, who had lived many years in *England*, was newly come hither with her son and four daughters, who knew all the arts of southern elegance, and all the modes of English economy (Samuel Johnson, *A Journey to the Western Islands, &c., 'Dunvegan' section*).

It was only a little way geographically – little more than ten miles as the crow flies – between Gesto and Dunvegan; but the cultural distance was enormous.

Gesto's relations with the chiefly family were not cordial. His name was conspicuously absent from the list of gentlemen of the Clan MacLeod acting as guarantors for the Dunvegan family's gambling and political debts, and he fought and won a bitter lawsuit with them when, hungry for revenue, they tried to encroach upon his lands. This took him frequently to Edinburgh, where he was a familiar figure. There he employed the writer Alex. MacGregor, then a student of divinity, to copy law papers for him, and the latter left a lively account of his patron describing him as a

> tall, gaunt, thin-faced man, with long nose, grey hair, white hat, tartan trousers, and plaid . . . He knew, I believe, almost every piobaireachd in existence – the names, the composers, their origin, and the causes for composing them. When strolling to and from the Advocates' Library, he very frequently called on, and sat for hours with old John Macdonald, the father of Donald Macdonald, pipe-major to the Highland Society . . . He would make Donald . . . play 'piobaireachds' to him, all of which he himself could articulate with his pliant lips in the MacCrimmon noting

style. He had a large manuscript collection of the MacCrimmons' 'piobaireachds', as noted by themselves, and part of it was apparently very old and yellow in the paper from age, with some of the writing getting dim. Other parts were evidently more modern, and on different paper . . . Donald Ban MacCrimmon, who was killed at the rout of Moy, the day before the battle of Culloden, was (Gesto said) one of the best of the MacCrimmon performers; but the best of them all was Padruig Mor MacCruimean. For many ages these pipers noted down their piobaireachds, and Padruig Mor had a daughter who was very expert at noting, and could also play herself when asked as a favour to do so. I should think that the manuscript I saw with him would contain upwards of two hundred 'piobaireachds' from the bulk of it, and out of that manuscript he selected twenty or so, which he published as a specimen. The Macarthurs, pipers to the Clan Macdonald of the Isles, noted their piobaireachds also, but with different vocables. Gesto had one very old-looking leaf of their noting, on which the vocables appeared very faint, but I did not look much at it.

In 1828 Gesto brought out a slim pamphlet entitled *Pibereach or pipe tunes, as taught verbally by the McCrimmen pipers in Skye to their apprentices.* It was the first publication in the medium of *canntaireachd*, and it contained 20 tunes, including the earliest published versions of 'The Lament for the Union', 'In Praise of Morag', and other famous pieces. Gesto's system lacked the precision of Campbell's Nether Lorn *canntaireachd.* It did not distinguish between certain intervals very clearly and it was riddled with typographical errors. In addition, he asked a steep price – a guinea – for it, which probably limited its distribution.

Here is Gesto's opening sequence for 'Donald Gruamach's March':

> I himbotrao hiodro, hodroradin hiodin,
> hindo botriea, hiedirieo, hadiriea hiodro,
> hobotrao hiodiriea, himborodin hiodin,

which would suggest something along the lines of:

Gesto also collected some of the stories attached to the tunes. They tended to be brief and bloody:

Donald Groumach. – Lament played in consequence of the death of Donald Groumach, who was shot, at the castle of Elandonan, in Kintail, about the ankle with a barbed arrow, and died from loss of blood before he was brought home to Sleat, in the Isle of Skye.

Lasson, alias the Flame of *Phadrig Chiegh*. Played by Patrick Maccrimmon at a time he, with his party, set fire to many houses in Kintail, in consequence of a quarrel between the Mackenzies and the Mackays of Lord Reay.

Even as Gesto wrote, however, staff-notation was becoming the dominant form and his collection – judging by its later scarceness – seems to have had limited contemporary impact. When the question of syllabically-notated scores arose again during the twentieth century, it was the system of Colin Mór Campbell of Nether Lorn that was accepted as the standard.

When the tack of Gesto expired in 1825, John MacLeod of MacLeod refused to renew it. Niel MacLeod had to quit the lands which his family had occupied for four hundred years and move to a rented house at Stein in Waternish which the Dunvegan MacLeods had previously sold to stem their mounting tide of debt. He died at Stein on 21 December 1836 and was interred in the old churchyard at Struan in Bracadale, looking towards Gesto across Loch Beag.

Niel MacLeod of Gesto is a very significant figure. The problems of bulk and cost to which *canntaireachd*-based notation systems were one solution was to remain in the forefront for many years, as we see in the work of C. S. Thomason below. Gesto's family was to be prominent in Scottish musical life for several generations. His grandson, Keith Norman MacDonald (1834–1913), edited *The Gesto Collection of Highland Music* (1895) and *Puirt-a-Beul* (1901), while his great-grandson, the painter Somerled MacDonald (1868–1948), was a founder member of the Piobaireachd Society. During the 1930s, Somerled, one of the leading amateur pipers of his generation, mounted a passionate defence of the traditional styles against the Society scores which he regarded as inaccurate and musically incompetent. When it became known that he was preparing a book on the old interpretations, however, he found himself ejected from the judging panel at the Northern Meeting and subject to a covert campaign of detraction and innuendo. Despairing of gaining a fair hearing, he abandoned the project. Judging by the high quality of his letters to the *Oban Times*, this represented a considerable loss to the subject.

Donald MacDonald (c.1767–1840)

Donald MacDonald was a pipe-maker, champion player and pioneering editor of *pìobaireachd* and light music for the Highland pipe. He is thought to have been born in Glenhinnisdal in Skye about the year 1767. His father, John MacDonald, was a noted tradition-bearer and, as a servant of Flora MacDonald, had been involved in the escape of Prince Charles Edward Stuart in the summer of 1746. He had later caught fish for Dr. Samuel Johnson's breakfast during the latter's Highland tour with biographer James Boswell. Both MacDonalds eventually moved to Edinburgh, with Donald working as a teacher and pipe-maker at a number of addresses in the city. He also served as piper to the 2nd Battalion Rothesay and Caithness Fencibles, raised by Sir John Sinclair in 1795, one of numerous home-service volunteer formations recruited during the Napoleonic wars. It was later renamed The Caithness Highlanders and after six years' service in Ireland was disbanded at Glasgow in 1802. Donald was still listed as its piper when he finished third in the Highland Society of London's annual competition held at Edinburgh in 1801. He was eventually placed first in 1817 and had to withdraw from further competition in accordance with the rules. Donald is thought to have been taught by the famous MacArthur dynasty and to represent their subtle and richly decorated style.

Donald MacDonald was also eminent as a pipe-maker. His instruments with their characteristic drum-shaped bells and wide bore were famous for their robust tone. Bagpipe making was not – in those days at least – the kind of trade in which fortunes could be made, even if, as in Donald's case, he spread his risk and 'carried on the business of Pipe-making in all its branches', manufacturing and offering instruction in the Lowland, Northumberland, Union and Highland pipes. Donald's sons, John, Donald jr., and James all predeceased him, and his widowed daughters and four grandchildren were left in poverty when he died.

One of the reasons for this was the financial reverses he had suffered as a publisher of pipe music. He had been working on the problems of recording pipe music in staff notation since the early years of the nineteenth century and the conventions he developed, namely setting melody notes with their stems down and ornamental figures in reduced type with their stems up regardless of their position on the stave, transformed the appearance and accessibility of the music. Donald thus established the basic way of writing bagpipe music accepted by all later editors. He published two bagpipe tutors (1808 and 1817), and in 1818/19 issued his *Collection of the Ancient Martial Music of Caledonia called Piobaireachd*. This contained 23 *pìobaireachd* arranged with left-hand accompaniments so they could also be played on keyboard instruments and some two dozen pieces of light music. He also compiled one of the most important early manuscript collections. It is dated 1826 and has 50 tunes with an accompanying section of tales and legends. Although the scores were later incorporated in C. S. Thomason's *Ceol Mor* (see below), it has not yet been published in its own right.

In the two generations following 1745 there was an explosion of creativity in Scottish music and song. The achievements of the brilliant galaxy of songwriters and fiddle composers who flourished at this time are well known, but pipers also made a distinctive contribution. Donald MacDonald was a contemporary of

Robert Burns and Carolina Oliphant (Lady Nairne), of Niel Gow and William Marshall. But pipers had to cope with the vagaries of self-appointed regulatory bodies like the aristocratic Highland Societies of London and Scotland which sought to promote the instrument and its music within a narrowly military context. The Societies were keen to get the music written in staff notation in order to speed up learning, and make judging at competitions easier. MacDonald evidently went ahead with *Ancient Martial Music* believing he had the Highland Societies' backing; but the Highland Society of Scotland subscribed for a mere five copies. Assuming a print run of about a hundred copies, and production costs of about £100, then at its selling price of one guinea MacDonald's pioneering venture was unlikely to do more than clear its costs, at best. In the event he seems to have suffered financially, so much so that his projected second volume remained unpublished. To make matters worse, his book had foisted upon it (presumably in an attempt to sustain the Societies' patronage) a high-flown antiquarian preface which has been the source of much subsequent misunderstanding. The preface to his book was obviously not written by MacDonald since it very much reflects the stereotypical views of the Anglo-Scottish establishment and contains statements he must have known were untrue. Yet it was from this, anonymous, source that the mistaken but much-repeated idea sprang that the pipes had been proscribed after the Rising of 1745 and that *pìobaireachd* was dying as a result.

After he had parted with his interest in it, Donald MacDonald's *Ancient Martial Music* enjoyed a modest success, being reprinted a further three times during the nineteenth century. In 1828 he brought out *A Collection of Quicksteps, Strathspeys, Reels, & Jigs. Arranged for the Highland Bagpipe* containing more than a hundred tunes. This went to at least three impressions during his lifetime and three subsequent ones after the plates were acquired by the Glen family, so that it remained in print for most of the nineteenth century.

Donald MacDonald and his father were regularly visited by the writer Alex MacGregor who left a vivid account of them:

> I remember calling on worthy John one evening . . . when we had a long discussion about pipe-music. John remarked that 'The gathering of the Clans', was a splendid piobaireachd, which was composed at the battle of Inverlochy. He repeated it in the syllabic manner [i.e. in *canntaireachd*] . . . When he had finished it he said, 'Let us go down stairs to hear the same fine piobaireachd from Donald on his large bagpipe'. We did so, and worthy Donald, who was a short, thick-set, very stout man, who weighed about twenty stones, did all justice to the piece of music in question. The aged father, however, who had listened very attentively, addressed his son, and said, 'Donald, my boy . . . you played such a part of the Crànnludh by far too slow, for it ought to be-

Hiodratatiti, hiodratutiti, hiodratititi, hiodratatiti'.

'Ah! very good, father', said Donald, 'very good, it is easy for these volatile, quivering lips of yours to articulate these notes rapidly, but not at all so easy for my stiff fingers, to extract them from this black, hard, hole-bored stick of mine!' (meaning his chanter).

MacDonald's *pìobaireachd* settings are rich and subtle and show a characteristic beautiful symmetry of development. For all his financial ups and downs, his championship of staff notation carried all before it, and although *canntaireachd* notation continued to attract interest, his work effectively displaced it as the main method of recording the music of the pipes.

Angus MacKay (1813–1859)

Angus MacKay is a towering figure in piping history. He committed more *pìobaireachd* to paper than almost anybody else, compiled one of the biggest early light music manuscripts, containing more than 500 tunes, and was one of the pioneers of the 'competition' march. MacKay's career shows some of the consequences for piping following the opening-up of the Highlands as an aristocratic playground. A lot of estates were coming on the market and being snapped up by southern money for sporting purposes as it became clear that this was more profitable than the large-scale sheep farming which had launched the main phase of the Highland Clearances. There was a role for piping under the new dispensation, but it tended to be part-time and largely decorative – summed up by the description of Sir Walter Scott's piper, John Bruce, as 'a good looking man [who] can make a noise'. The status of pipers fell correspondingly and most leading players migrated to the towns and cities where opportunities were better. Working in the landed sector during the nineteenth century involved a steady casualisation of the art as the piper was increasingly expected to undertake a range of additional non-professional duties such as fisherman, chauffeur, or gamekeeper. Angus Cameron, who won the Edinburgh medal in 1794, commented on the situation in the early 1840s where *arriviste* estate-owners with no personal knowledge of, or interest in, piping, could employ players in this incidental fashion. He said that there was no longer a single man in Appin 'who made the pipe his business' and dismissed the current crop of lairds in categorical terms: 'Ou, they're a' deed! an' they're a' puir! an' they're a' English!'

MacKay's appointment as first piper to Queen Victoria in 1843 established the instrument and its music in its modern position within the British establishment. His career also marks a further stage in the involvement of semi-official bodies like the Highland Societies of London and Scotland in standardising the music. This reflected the increasing prominence of competition and the need to present judges of high social standing but little musical experience with a manageable task.

Angus MacKay was born on 10th September 1813, probably in the Isle of Raasay where his father, John MacKay (1767–1848), worked as a piper. John MacKay was the leading composer and teacher of his generation. In 1823 he left Raasay to become piper to an English lord with a Welsh title, Peter Burrell, Lord Gwydir, later Lord Willoughby of Eresby, at Drummond Castle in Strathearn. The family trekked across the west Highlands with their belongings stowed in creels on a couple of Highland ponies. Gwydir occupied his position by virtue of his wife, the Right Honourable Sara Clementina Drummond, heiress of the Jacobite Duke of Perth and head of the Drummond name. He was an important figure in his own right, a key member of the royal household and an enthusiastic pioneer of the movement to 'Celticise' Scotland. He had led a party of Strathearn tenants, decked out in 'traditional' Highland style, during the famous visit of King George IV to Edinburgh in 1822. There were similar demonstrations when Queen Victoria toured the southern Highlands in 1842 and visited Drummond Castle: 'Lord Willoughby had about one hundred of his Gaelic-speaking tenantry drilled and dressed in the Drummond tartan, and armed with battle-axes, swords, and targets . . . as a guard of honour'. It is clear from similar scenes at Taymouth Castle, where John Bàn MacKenzie (1796–1864) was first piper, that the pipes had a prominent role in such entertainments.

Angus MacKay's first job was as boy piper to Lady Gwydir. He won a prize from the Highland Societies for setting pipe tunes in staff notation when barely twelve years old. In 1826 he won fourth prize at the Edinburgh competition and in 1835 the prize pipe itself. As a professional piper he followed 'new money'. He worked for the Campbells of Shawfield and Islay, who were ploughing Glasgow merchant fortunes into ancestral Hebridean acres, and the Wards of Birmingham (later Earls of Dudley) who acquired the bankrupt estates of the MacDonells of Glengarry. Queen Victoria had been much impressed by the Breadalbanes' show at Taymouth and wanted a piper of her own. On their recommendation, she selected Angus MacKay and he took up his new appointment on 25 July 1843.

MacKay went on to become one of the most influential collectors and editors of pipe music in nineteenth-century Scotland. His *Collection of Ancient Piobaireachd or Highland Pipe Music* (1838), dedicated to the Highland Society of London, contained 61 tunes written in staff notation. The music text was accompanied by extensive introductory material on the leading piping dynasties, giving the history of the Highland Societies' competitions from 1781 to 1838, and notes, topographical and antiquarian, on the tunes. The book appeared under Angus MacKay's name and the style of the music scores is very much his; but he seems to have had limited control of what went into the finished text. The selection of tunes included mediocre pieces associated with important aristocratic houses and major clans at the expense of great tunes like 'The Lament for the Children' and 'Scarce of Fishing', which seems to indicate the influence of the Highland Society. Meantime the Society's under-secretary, Aberdonian journalist/antiquary, James Logan (author of *The Scottish Gael*, 1831), wrote the various essays and notes which were to have such an important effect on the interpretation of this music in the wider world during the nineteenth and early twentieth centuries.

The collection had three aims: (i) to stabilise the repertoire for the purposes of competition and instruction; (ii) to replace the rich diversity of oral versions with a standard fixed score; and (iii) to substitute for the traditional varied palette of ornament a uniform simplified style. Behind this lay a desire to assert the institutionally sponsored score as the ultimate source of 'authority' in piping by systematically undermining the creative autonomy of the master players. This was very much the programme of the Highland Society of London; how much it reflected MacKay's personal intention remains an open question. Three editions of *Ancient Piobaireachd* appeared during the nineteenth century (1838, 1839, 1899) and it rapidly became the standard published source. Its scarcity and expense (a guinea and a half when new, later commanding substantial sums in the second-hand market) forced players to resort to written transcripts, and it may be doubted whether it ever became 'the pipers' bible', as was later claimed. But it certainly became 'the judges bible' as benches came to depend upon it as a source of instant expertise.

Ancient Piobaireachd represented merely part, perhaps a quarter at most, of a much larger manuscript collection and in 1841 MacKay offered this to the Highland Society of Scotland. It contained 183 tunes in all, written out neatly and accurately, and covered virtually the whole known repertoire in *piobaireachd*. But the Highland Society suffered a typical attack of caution and referred the papers to Sir John Graham Dalyell. His opinion when it came was characteristically negative. Dalyell was a gentleman antiquary specialising in the natural sciences, an 'expert' who, despite having organised the Edinburgh competitions for upwards of twenty years, was deeply unsympathetic towards the pipe and its music, as is apparent from his book, *Musical Memoirs of Scotland* (1849). It is also clear from his report that he could not read pipe music and had little personal knowledge of the form. There were a lot of tunes here he did not know, he explained, and he would need to hear them played before he could assess them; but anyway the best ones were probably already in MacKay's published book, and so the Society should not acquire the papers. And thus an attempt to widen knowledge amongst the judging class – a vital step if piping were to flourish within the new regulatory structures – was coolly rebuffed. This is a recurring pattern. The Highland Societies preened themselves on being generous guardians and protectors of what they fancied was 'tradition', yet tended to react with baffled incomprehension when they encountered the real thing. John Campbell, son of Colin Mór of Nether Lorn, had arrived at the 1818 Edinburgh competition bearing with him one of the volumes of his father's *canntaireachd* collection. But the assembled gentlemen of the Highland Society found it 'utterly unintelligible' and refused an offer from a leading piper to translate it for them. Worse still, one of them bought the volume from John Campbell, probably as a curio, and then lost it. Angus MacKay held on to his manuscripts, and after his death they were looked after by pipers who knew their value. As a result, unlike many of the Highland Society of London's own papers, they survive to the present day.

Ancient Piobaireachd has become notorious for typographical error and, to be sure, about a third of the tunes had mistakes in them, ranging from missing or wrong grace-notes to serious structural dislocation. Little of this would have caused problems of interpretation to an experienced player, however. The main difficulty with MacKay's painstaking, pioneering, and invaluable record is not the dog's dinner made of it by Victorian engravers, but its systematic mis-representation a century later by Archibald Campbell of the Piobaireachd Society who passed off his own arrangements as the work of MacKay and other dead masters. This has led to competing pipers – up to the present day – being induced to play what they think is Angus MacKay when they are actually playing Archibald Campbell.

MacKay's royal appointment ended in 1854. He became violently insane and was confined initially in Bedlam and then in the Crichton Royal Hospital near Dumfries which was noted for its humane and pioneering therapeutic regime. The onset of his illness seems to have been sudden. There is no indication of mental disturbance in the substantial collections of manuscript scores he assembled during the 1830s and '40s, which are a model of clarity and order.

On 21st March 1859, Angus MacKay was drowned while attempting to ford the River Nith. His body was never recovered. Angus MacKay's importance in the culture of the Highland bagpipe is frequently invoked, but it is largely symbolic. At the time of writing his published works have been out of print for nearly a generation and his manuscripts remain unpublished.

THREE NINETEENTH-CENTURY FAMILIES

The concentration on the early piping dynasties has led to the supposition that when the MacCrimmons, MacArthurs and MacKays of Gairloch ceased their activities, the tradition 'ended' with them, creating a misleading impression of decline and fall. But continuity in families of leading players, teachers and composers by no means died out. Powerful new groups rose to prominence, although sometimes they, too, had been active in the art for centuries.

Among the many areas of Scotland rich in pipers, few are more so historically than the lower reaches of Strathconon. The river Conon rises in the far north-west and finds its way towards the Cromarty Firth through a landscape as varied and pleasing as any in Scotland. Here, once, were found in profusion the 'three things considerable' in the making of good pipers – time, access to high-quality instruction, and the prospect of decent employment thereafter. And here lived a trio of great players and teachers, Donald Mór MacLennan of Moy, who trained some of the best pipers in nineteenth-century Scotland; John Bàn MacKenzie of Achilty, who became first piper to the Marquess of Breadalbane at Taymouth Castle, enjoyed a huge reputation as a player and composer, and whose almost equally famous nephew Ronald carried the family style well into the twentieth century; and, eclipsing them all in fame, the legendary Donald Cameron.

Donald Cameron (*c.* 1810–1868) was a player and teacher of outstanding fame and prestige and the most successful competitive piper of his generation. He was a son of Colin Cameron (*c.* 1770–1862), a farmer, and his wife, Mary Cameron (*c.* 1777–1865), and in 1841 married Margaret Mackenzie (1818–1877) from Kilmorack near Beauly, after whom one of the finest piping strathspeys, 'Maggie Cameron', was named. Their three sons, Colin (1843–1916), Alexander (1848–1923), and Keith (1855–1899), were all famous as pipers, the first two also becoming eminent teachers. Donald's own tutors included Donald Mór MacLennan, John Bàn MacKenzie, and Kenneth MacRae. He was also a friend and pupil of Angus MacKay. After spells with various local lairds, Donald worked for Keith Stewart-MacKenzie of Seaforth at Brahan Castle from 1849 until his death. He taught several leading players such as J. F. Farquharson, Sandy MacLennan, Donald MacKay (Angus's nephew) and Sandy MacDonald (father of John MacDonald of Inverness).

Donald was born in the Strathpeffer area, one of a cluster of straths branching off from the valley of the Conon, linking Contin, on the confluence of the Blackwater and the Conon, with Dingwall to the east on the shores of the Cromarty Firth. It was a fertile, wooded district, dotted at frequent intervals with the comfortable houses of the gentry, Coul, Kinellan, Fairburn, Scatwell, Brahan. It was also rich in 'tradition'. From the top of the extraordinary almond-shaped mountain, Knock Farril, with its vitrified fort, the warrior giant Finn MacCoull, it was said, had hurled down standing stones into the valley below; not far off, a little man of superhuman strength in a red nightcap had emerged from the loch, so the story went, to help the MacKenzies defeat the MacDonalds at the battle of Park. Coinneach Odhar, the mysterious Brahan Seer, who foretold the doom of the Seaforths, was a native of the district. When Donald was a boy, there was widespread belief in the power of dreams and supernatural warnings, and in wraiths, and fairies who stole away children before they were christened. Around ancient mounds and tumuli it was said that unearthly music might be heard by night and unearthly lights beheld.

Yet the old order was changing. The crofts which had supported the local people were being thrown together by 'improving' landlords to create great farms; land was being drained and enclosed; 'model' villages like Maryburgh were being built to hold the population cleared from the land. The Gaelic language was beginning to fade under the impact of English schooling and modern communications. Piping, too, was beginning to enter its modern phase.

Donald Cameron was described as 'shrewd and clever, full of Highland lore and tradition', and it is said that he would not take pupils who could not speak Gaelic. But within two generations of his death the piping world would be dominated by Scots and English speakers living in towns and cities. Indeed the professional renown of his own family and their pupils was based on the recently developed Highland games circuit and the emergence of events which did not oblige former winners to retire from future competition. Donald's successes included the prize pipe at Inverness in 1843 and at Edinburgh in 1844, gold medals at Inverness in 1849, 1850, and 1859, and the new Champion of Champions contest at Inverness in 1867.

Donald Cameron was hailed as the leading exponent of 'the true MacCruimen style' in *pìobaireachd*, and also made a distinctive contribution to the light music competition repertoire with the first full version of the classic march nowadays known as 'Highland Wedding'. His own collection, started in 1853 and completed by his son Colin, contains some 80 *pìobaireachd* set in a beautifully musical and idiomatic style. It is one of the most important Victorian manuscripts and may have been intended for publication, perhaps being forestalled by *Ross's Collection* in 1869. Colin Cameron won the prize pipe at Inverness in 1861 and the gold medal in 1865 and was piper to the Duke of Fife at Mar Lodge, Braemar. A handsome, burly man, he had fingers so strong he could crush a pipe chanter and he made numerous important contributions to the publications of David Glen and C. S. Thomason. Contemporaries regarded him as the greatest living authority on *pìobaireachd*. He was widely connected in the traditional music world. The fiddle virtuoso Scott Skinner wrote to him with a copy of his new march 'The Lovat Scouts' with a view to its publication as a pipe tune, saying 'Dear Colin Cameron . . . pray learn this & put on the flutterin' blades as only pipers can. Yrs. always J. Scott Skinner' (Monikie, 15 May 1908). Colin's brother Sandy, who won the Inverness prize pipe in 1867, and gold medal in 1870, was for a time piper to the Marquis of Huntly at Aboyne and had distinguished pupils.

Donald Cameron died at his home, Seaforth Cottage, in Maryburgh, on 7th January 1868, and was buried in his parents' grave at the High Church of Inverness. His line of teaching came down to the twentieth century through his own pupils, those of his brother Sandy, and, in the next generation, his sons

Colin and Sandy. Sandy the younger's leading pupil, John MacDougall Gillies, in turn taught numerous gifted players, including Willie Gray and Robert Reid.

The belief that there was a distinctive 'Cameron school', including Donald, his brother Sandy (1821–1871; prize pipe, Inverness, 1846; gold medal, Inverness, 1862), and their various sons and pupils is met with quite commonly; but there does not seem to have been a Cameron 'house-style' as such. Glen's and Thomason's collections which contain many settings supplied by members of the family and the Cameron manuscript itself suggest that each had his own individual approach.

In May 1949 Colin's son (also Colin Cameron), prompted by John MacDonald of Inverness, wrote to the Piobaireachd Society's president Sheriff J. P. Grant about the preservation of the Cameron papers:

> . . . my wife says, and I daresay rightly, that after our decease the whole lot might conceivably be burnt as rubbish. . . . I cannot read a note of it (if it was in the Tonic Solfa notation that would be a different matter!) neither, so far as I am aware, can my brother or sister. . . . In a word, then, I bequeath the whole of the Pipe Music, which I handed to Pipe Major Macdonald, to the Piobaireachd Society.
>
> Of course, I use the word 'bequeath,' but if you would prefer that this matter be a strictly commercial affair, I, being a Scotchman, do not refuse to see it in that light. I leave it then to yourself as to what financial value should be placed on the Pipe Music.

Colin later acknowledged Grant's cheque for £5, adding 'I am obliged. I consider it quite adequate'. The Society deposited the manuscript in the National Library of Scotland, along with some of the family's fascinating collection of light music. At the end of the twentieth century it was unpublished and virtually unknown.

The MacPhersons

Malcolm MacPherson (1833–1898), known as 'Calum Pìobaire' – Malcolm the piper – was the chief representative of the MacPherson family who, along with the Camerons, McLennans, Bruces, MacKenzies and MacKays, were so important to the transmission of *piobaireachd* during the nineteenth century. Malcolm was an outstanding player, but it is as a teacher that he is chiefly famed, and through him we gain insight into some of the traditional methods of instruction. He was born on 5th December 1833 at Snizort in Skye, son of professional piper Angus MacPherson (born *c.* 1800) and his wife, Effy MacLeod of Uig. He married Ann McDiarmid from Kildalton, Islay, (died 3 October 1903). Three of their sons, John (1863–1933), Norman (1869–1947) and Angus (1877–1976), also became champion pipers.

Like many great masters, Malcolm MacPherson had several teachers, including his own father, Angus MacKay, Archibald Munro, and Sandy Cameron (the elder). It is thought that Malcolm's grandfather, Peter MacPherson, moved from Badenoch to Idrigill in Skye and married a sister of the Bruce pipers. Malcolm's father Angus is said to have been taught by Iain Dubh MacCrimmon, John MacKay of Raasay, and John and Peter Bruce. The family was a byword for excellence in piping, as appears from the following tale collected by an American scholar in Barra:

> I heard my father say that a neighbour of his father, that is of my grandfather, was married twice, and had three children from the first marriage, and when married for the second time, a son and daughter. His second wife did not seem to be kind enough to the children of the first wife, neglecting their food and clothing and keeping them constantly at hard work in the fields at herding.
>
> One morning when the man and his second wife were returning from mass they passed the pasture where their cows were grazing and heard the enjoyable *skirrels* of the bagpipes. The father said, 'What may this be?' and going off the road found the eldest son of the first wife playing the bagpipes to his heart's pleasure; and asked him earnestly, 'How did you come to play the bagpipes so suddenly, or where did you get this splendid [set] of pipes?' The boy replied, 'An old man came to me while I was in the action of roasting pots in a pit-fire and said, 'Your step-mother is bad to you and in ill-will towards you.' I told the man I was sensible that that was the case, and then he said to me, 'If I give you a trade will you be inclined to follow it?' I said yes, and the old man then continued, 'How would you like to be a piper by trade?' 'I would gladly become a piper,' says I, 'but what am I to do without the bagpipes and the tunes to play?' 'I'll supply the bagpipes,' he said, 'and as long as you have them you'll never want for the most delightful tunes.' The male descendants of the boy in question were all famous pipers thereafter, and the last of them was a piper to the late Cluny MacPherson of Cluny. (W. Y. Evans Wentz, *The Fairy-Faith in Celtic Countries*, Oxford, 1911, pp.103–4)

A similar tale records that the famous MacPherson heirloom, 'The Black Chanter of Clan Chattan', was given to one of Calum Pìobaire's predecessors by a fairy woman who loved him. This is a motif which is attached to other important piping families, most notably the MacCrimmons.

In his teens Calum went to work in Greenock as a labourer, ship's carpenter, and piper on the revenue cutter *Prince Albert*. Greenock was a boom town, the main port of Glasgow, and then at the height of its commercial power. When the American Civil War broke out, every seagoing steamer on the Clyde disappeared to run contraband through the Yankee blockade. It was a paradise for ship-builders and awash with quick money. Half the west Highlands lived in it. It was a raffish, riotous, notoriously drunken town. When Calum arrived he would have found nearly 200 public houses awaiting his custom and a chaotically vigorous street-life. At the Martinmas fair in 1862

> . . . lads and lassies made furious demonstrations of love and of animosity in sonorous Gaelic or sweet broad Scotch . . . The blind whistler . . . was in attendance . . . also a blind fiddler, who sung dissonant duets with a girl possessing a gruff contralto. Two tawny sharp skinned fellows in kilts, the one a bagpiper and the other a dancer, made their appearance, and a couple of short women in mutches stood opposite one another and sung a doleful ballad entitled 'The parting of Jessie M'Lachan with her Husband and Child' . . . (*Greenock Telegraph*, 'Feeing Market', 22/11/1862, p.4).

But Calum MacPherson was not the only major piper in town. Here, also, had come Donald Cameron's brother, Sandy, following a business career which had taken him first to Edinburgh and now to Greenock, where he ran the imposing Museum Hotel at 9 William Street, much frequented by pipers. MacPherson lived nearby at 15 Hamilton Street. Calum studied with Sandy Cameron and they played together in the 10th R.R.V., the local battalion of The Renfrewshire Rifle Volunteers, popularly known as 'The Greenock Highlanders', of which Sandy Cameron was honorary pipe-major. As we have seen, the Volunteer movement was everywhere in Victorian Scotland, with its fancy uniforms, and vigorous social life – bazaars, balls, soirées and dinners and much showy 'marching out'. It may have been in Greenock that the first modern pipe band was created, including pipers playing ensemble with their own dedicated corps of drums as a detached unit, and not as an offshoot of a military band. If so, then we see two players, generally regarded as masters of 'tradition', involved in the very latest development. But on this last point we have as yet no direct evidence.

Malcolm MacPherson went on to a glittering competitive career. He domi-nated the competition circuit for nearly a generation, winning prizes at the games at Birnam, Portree, Blair Atholl, Aberfeldy, Kingussie, Grantown and Dunkeld. He was awarded the prize pipe at the Northern Meeting in 1866, and gold medals at Inverness (1871) and Oban (1876), followed by the championship of the world for *pìobaireachd* at the Edinburgh Exhibition of 1886. A contemporary wrote: 'Malcolm MacPherson was a terror to pipers when he appeared on the games field . . . as a player of piobaireachd unsurpassed'. It was not just a question of tone and technique, it was his matchless musical artistry that gave him the edge. Pipe-Major Robert Meldrum (1851–1941), who had often heard him play, said: 'At piobaireachd playing Malcolm MacPherson was the father of us all; it may not be too much to say that for musical expression and taste he was the best ever heard by me; of course as regards fingering and production there may have been many just as good'.

Calum followed his father as piper to MacPherson of Cluny in about 1865, and at his home at Catlodge on Speyside, near Kingussie, gave instruction to pipers from all over Scotland. Some went on to become the leading players and teachers of their day, including John MacDonald of Inverness, Robert Meldrum, Angus MacRae and William MacLean of Kilcreggan. Calum's repertoire was enormous: it is said when asked in later life how many *pìobaireachd* he knew, he replied: 'Well, once I could play a terrible skelp of tunes, but I believe I could yet manage six twenties'.

People had been teaching and learning the pipes for centuries but little is known about the processes of instruction, and Calum MacPherson is the earliest master teacher whose methods have been recorded. Singing seems to have been central to his approach, both in repertoire-building and in the inculcation of interpretation and style. His most famous pupil, John MacDonald of Inverness, wrote:

Calum was easily the best player of piobaireachd I have ever known. He hardly ever played March, Strathspey and Reel; only piobaireachd and Jigs. Each morning, he used to play Jigs on the chanter while breakfast was being got ready – he would sit on a stool near the peat fire as he played. But his heart was in piobaireachd. He excelled in heavy low hand tunes. It was inspiring to hear him play 'My King has Landed in Moidart'; another grand tune of his was 'Cillechriosd'; I never heard anyone play 'Donald Dugald MacKay' in a way that appealed to me so much. Calum had very strong fingers, and I never once heard him missing Crunluath gracenotes. As I have said Calum played a few Jigs on the practice chanter before breakfast, I can see him now, with his old jacket and his leather sporran, sitting on a stool while the porridge was being brought to the boil. After breakfast he would take his barrow to the peat moss, cut a turf, and build up the fire with wet peat for the day. He would then sit down beside me, take away all books and pipe music, then sing in his own canntaireachd the ground and different variations of the particular piobaireachd he wished me to learn.

It was from these early associations of Malcolm MacPherson that I realised that piobaireachd must be transmitted by song from one piper to another in order to get the soul of it; the lights and shades. Most of the piobaireachd players of the present day rely on the score, but you cannot express in musical notation what you would like to. It is really impossible. (*Oban Times*, 4/04/1942, p.5)

The past may be closer than we think – the concept of instruction with on-site accommodation, adopted by the National Piping Centre a century later, is reproduced in miniature here, and perhaps on a larger scale by Sandy Cameron the elder, running what looks rather like an urban college of piping in Greenock in the 1860s.

Malcolm MacPherson fell into Loch Coultree on a fishing trip when trying to recover an oar. He was carried to a nearby cottage at Burnside and died the following evening, 9th July 1898. John MacDonald played 'The Lament for the Children' at the funeral at Laggan Bridge churchyard on 13th July. A memorial was dedicated at Catlodge in August 1960.

In the next generation, Calum's sons became leading figures in the piping world, especially John, known as 'Jockan' (1863–1933, gold medals at Oban, 1889, and Inverness, 1920), and Angus MacPherson (1877–1976, gold medal, Inverness, 1923). Angus became piper to the millionaire philanthropist Andrew Carnegie at Skibo Castle and in New York and became well known as a composer, judge and writer. His autobiography, *A Highlander Looks Back* (Oban, 1953, reprinted 1970), gives an interesting account of his life and times. Angus was for many years tenant of the Inveran Hotel on the river Shin, which was much favoured by anglers and pipers and was destroyed by fire on 19th June 1949. Angus's son, Malcolm Ross MacPherson (1906–1966), was also an outstanding performer (gold medal, Inverness, 1927; clasp, Inverness, 1930, 1937), and the main informant for Dr. Roderick Ross's *Binneas is Boreraig* (5 vols., Edinburgh, 1959–67), a radical new approach to *pìobaireachd* editing based on a three-line stave and aiming to reflect the stylings of a single master player. Two of Calum's sons, Norman and Malcolm, emigrated to North America where their descendants and pupils still play.

One often hears talk of a 'MacPherson school' of piping, and the history of *pìobaireachd* playing in the twentieth century is sometimes viewed in terms of its rivalry with the so-called 'Cameron' school. When this is explored, it usually turns out to involve little more than minutiae, the 'Cameron' style supposedly being more smooth and flowing, while the 'MacPherson' style was thought to be more abrupt and cut. John MacDonald of Inverness, who had studied with members of both families, stated that all the old master players had a broadly similar approach regardless of who had taught them, although the value placed upon thoughtful and sensitive interpretation led to a significant variety of personal styles.

The McLennans

The McLennans traced their descent back to the early sixteenth century and claimed to be coeval with the MacCrimmons. One of their leading representatives, Lt. John McLennan (1843–1923), wrote: 'Donald (ower) MacCremmen was tennant in Auchterneed, Strathpeffer in 1507. Next we find Iain (ower) MacCremmen, supposed to be son or nephew of Donald, piper and harper to Alasdair Crotach MacLeod of Dunvegan in 1533, being nine years after

Murdoch McLennan [1504–1574] was appointed Town Piper in Inverness' (*Oban Times*, 3/5/1919, p.3). One of the family, Murdo MacLennan, had played at Culloden; another, Duncan MacLennan of the Black Watch, had played at Waterloo. One of his five sons, G. S. McLennan's great-uncle Donald Mór MacLennan of Moy (born *c.* 1783), taught a whole generation of Victorian master players. Two of Donald of Moy's sons, Sandy (1811 – 1896, prize pipe, Inverness, 1857, gold medal, 1860) and John (1817–1906, prize pipe, Inverness, 1848, gold medal, 1854), were important players and teachers, Sandy being taught by Donald Cameron, and John by his father and John Bàn Mackenzie.

G. S.'s cousin, William MacLennan (1860–1892), was also a champion piper and dancer (Inverness prize pipe, 1878, gold medal, 1879) and a pioneer of the new, more technically elaborate style of play in competition light music. Following the death of his parents, he was brought up by G. S.'s father, Lt. John McLennan, whose pupil he became. He went on to work as a newspaper reporter before qualifying as an architect. His study of ballet in Paris and the sophisticated personal style of Highland dancing to which this led was widely influential. A theatrical impresario, he formed his own concert party, the Royal Edinburgh Concert Company, which included the fiddle virtuoso James Scott Skinner, and toured Canada. He died of meningitis in Montreal at a tragically early age. William taught his younger brother Donald G. MacLennan (1869–1965), who became the leading teacher of dance in Scotland and editor of *Highland and Traditional Scottish Dances* (Edinurgh, 1950). Their nephew, Capt. Hamish MacLennan (1899–1964), was the first manager of the Edinburgh International Festival. Meantime G. S.'s half-brother, Capt. Donald Ross ('D.R.') McLennan (1901–1984 gold medal, Inverness, 1956; gold medal, Oban, 1956) had gone on to become a distinguished pipe-major in the army, one of the earliest professional pipers to become a member of the Piobaireachd Society, and the most important reed-maker of his generation.

In piping, Lt. John McLennan (1843–1923) was the leading representative of the family during the later nineteenth and early twentieth centuries, a superintendent of police in Edinburgh, and a noted commentator on the art. He was, as one contemporary remarked, 'known by the sobriquet of "Big John" (not because of his personal bulk, but in honour of his well-deserved fame as an authority and proficient performer of piobaireachd)' (*Oban Times*, 8/12/1883, p.6). Although a gifted teacher (in William and G. S. McLennan, he produced the two outstanding technicians of their generation), it was as a writer and editor of pipe music that John McLennan made his greatest impact. In books like *The Piobaireachd as MacCrimmon played it* (1907) and *The Piobaireachd as performed in the Highlands for ages, till about the year 1808* (1924) he challenged all kinds of contemporary assumptions. His powerful, largely self-taught, mind combined a great deal of clear, logical and forcefully expressed thinking with a curious strain of the irrational. He believed, for example (although there was no written evidence to support this), that there had been a revolt of the master teachers following the '45, and that this led them to conceal the true metrical values of the music and teach their pupils 'wrong'. The nineteenth century written record produced by these pupils was therefore hopelessly corrupt. Many false beliefs had consequently arisen about *ceòl mór*, chief amongst which was that it possessed no regular pulse. McLennan's own published scores were designed to counteract this tendency. He adopted the minim rather than the crotchet as the basic unit of time in order to establish more precise rhythmical patterns and used this to work his way back to what he believed to be the true idiom. His scores were typeset following the conventions descending from MacDonald and MacKay, but he was able to get a whole tune on to a single folio page by means of a new and ingenious system. Each bar was numbered and the order of playing was specified in a numerical table so that whole parts could be fitted into a single line. McLennan believed that terms of art such as 'taorluath' and 'crunluath' were distortions of a once simple descriptive system derived from Gaelic cardinal and ordinal numbers to indicate which fingers were involved in execution. He suggested that these movements had been written inaccurately for almost a century, appearing with an extra, or 'redundant', low A which was not sounded in playing and that notational practice should be revised to reflect this. This latter suggestion was quickly adopted by other editors and arrangers, although it was later to trigger serious controversy.

McLennan published some twenty *piobaireachd* settings in all and, although his approach was highly didactic and theorised, he presented his scores merely as an aid to artistically sensitive performance, insisting that they were not intended to possess the prescriptive force claimed for those of the Piobaireachd Society. Along with his friends, Charles Bannatyne and David Glen, he mounted a sustained attack on the Society's authoritarian and musically insensitive approach, over a period of very nearly twenty years, writing that

> . . . when another man puts out a book which will be more simple, more concise, more intelligent, more musical, easier to learn and retain in the memory, I shall be the first to applaud him, and admit that I have been superseded . . . other writers as well as myself wrote as we thought proper, and forced no man to play our setting. The Society, on the other hand, put out their tunes as the ancient music of Scotland, and bind pipers with chains of gold to play them . . . The piper may have a far better setting of the tune, but he dare not play it, and his own natural abilities are curbed; he must simply play note for note what is put before him; he is simply a tracer or a copyist, and is not allowed to become an artiste (*Oban Times*, 14/05/1910, p. 3; 23/10/1920, p.3).

These criticisms were not received well, and there is consequently no reference to the McLennan family in the history of piping prefixed to Archibald Campbell's

Kilberry Book of Ceol Mor and only a handful of passing references in later studies such as Seumas MacNeill and Frank Richardson (*Piobaireachd and its Interpretation*, 1987), and Roderick Cannon (*The Highland Bagpipe and its Music*, 1988, 2002). When an unsold cache of John McLennan's books was discovered in 1988, they were advertised in the *Piping Times* with a notice warning potential purchasers that 'the ideas put forward are not authentic' (Vol.41, no.1., Oct., 1988, p.5). Until Angus Fairrie's overview in *The Northern Meeting, 1788–1988* (1988), and Bridget Mackenzie's many details in *Piping Traditions of the North of Scotland* (1998), it was by no means easy to form an idea of the achievement of this remarkable family, despite the outstanding personal fame of George Stewart McLennan (see below). In terms of direct and traceable influence, the McLennans were at least as important as the MacPhersons or the Camerons, yet they have been largely excluded from the picture for much of the twentieth century.

EDITORS

Many people have edited bagpipe music, some master pipers, some not. Famous players like Willie Ross (1878–1966) have also won fame as editors of pipe music, but the three chosen, William Ross (1823–1891), C. S. Thomason (1833–1911), and David Glen (1853–1916), are seminal figures in their own right and together indicate something of the range of people involved.

William Ross

William Ross – usually known by the Gaelic form of his name *'Uilleam'* (pron: *Oo*yum) by pipers, to distinguish him from the later Willie Ross, was a grand-nephew of John Bàn MacKenzie. An imposing-looking man, he was born in Knockbain by the Beauly Firth and served as pipe-major of the Black Watch, winning the prize pipe at Inverness in 1853. From 1854 to 1891 he was first piper to the Queen.

Pipe-Major Robert Meldrum, who knew him well and was intended by Ross to be his successor, describes his career:

> When he had got settled down in Buckingham Palace, he asked the Queen to make him an allowance for living outside the palace. This was granted, and he immediately began to make pipe reeds and bags, and engaged a turner and began to make pipes. He supplied the five kilted regiments that were in existence at that time, and made a big business.
>
> As Pipe-Major of the 93rd . . . I sometimes handed him sums of £20. The full ivory mounted pipes won by me at the Northern Meeting were made by Ross . . . he often said he was to recommend me for his post on his retirement. But he died suddenly in 1891 . . . It is told that Lord

Rollo, getting into conversation . . . at a dinner of the Highland Society of London, asked him what the amount of his income was. Ross replied that he had 10d a day Army pension, £200 a year and all found with the Queen, £30 from the Highland Society, £20 from the Gaelic Society, besides his profits on the sale of pipes and pipe equipment. Lord Rollo at once exclaimed 'You d – – fellow! You are better off than I am.' (*Oban Times*, 6/07/1940, p.5)

Ross's Collection was published in 1869, with a second extended edition in 1875/6, and by the time of the third edition in 1885, it had expanded to 40 *pìobaireachd* (from 20 in 1869) and more than 400 pieces of light music (from just over 200 in 1869). His work alone is a rich contradiction of the twentieth-century dogma, much repeated, that all later piobaireachd was a copy of Angus MacKay. The price, remaining at 30/- throughout, indicates the dramatic fall in the cost of printing and publishing this material, enabling Ross to offer twice the content in 1885 that he could in 1869. The purchaser got a lot for his money – a large and choice collection of tunes, attractively arranged in the very latest style. Each *pìobaireachd* was published in staff notation for the first time and included some of the greatest tunes in the tradition: 'The Lament for the Children', 'Scarce of Fishing', 'The Lament for Donald Bàn MacCrimmon', 'In Praise of Morag', 'MacCrimmon's Sweetheart', 'The Lament for Mary MacLeod', 'The Battle of the Pass of Crieff', 'The Lament for the Only Son', 'The Old Woman's Lullaby', and 'The Blue Ribbon'. Though publishing by subscription, Ross exercised an editorial freedom denied to Angus MacKay.

Above all, the volume contained input from a key group of Victorian players, including Sandy MacDonald (father of John of Inverness), Colin Cameron and Duncan Campbell of Foss. Sandy worked for the Earl of Fife at Mar Lodge, a short distance from Balmoral, and the development of Deeside as an aristocratic playground meant that during the summer months the strath was full of leading players. The numerous pipers on upper Deeside, including Sandy's brother William MacDonald, a noted composer who was piper to the Prince of Wales at Abergeldie, used to meet at Peter Coutts's home at Tullochmacarrick in Glengairn. Coutts had been a piper to the Queen at Balmoral and later to Farquharson of Invercauld. Bob Nicol said that sometimes he would hear John MacDonald play something really nice and on enquiring would be told 'Oh, that's my father's setting; you'll get it in Ross's book'.

The light music of the pipes had been a typically eclectic blend of song airs and borrowed fiddle tunes; but from the middle years of the nineteenth century the pipe began to develop a specialised light-music repertoire of its own. This was marked by the appearance of specialist publications like Donald MacDonald's *Collection of Quicksteps, Strathspeys, Reels, & Jigs. Arranged for the Highland Bagpipe* (1828 and later editions), the first collection specifically devoted to the light music. This was followed by Angus MacKay's *The Piper's Assistant* (1843 and later editions) and a number of publications by the Glen family of Edinburgh. These were unpretentious little oblong-shaped volumes typically containing a hundred or so tunes and selling at about 6/-. They contained a companionable mixture of Highland and Lowland airs, little two-parted affairs very lightly graced, and with titles like 'Woo'd and married and a'', 'There cam' a young man to my daddie's door', 'O'er the Muir amang the Heather' and 'The Rock and the Wee Pickle Tow'. They presented a fairly low level of technical demand. Indeed the lightness of ornament is sometimes really quite striking to a modern eye, slurs and cuttings being used sparingly, sometimes only when absolutely necessary to separate two notes at the same pitch.

Ross's Collection had a major influence on the repertoire. It contained versions of many of the new-style competition tunes, including the marches 'The Marchioness of Tullibardine', 'The Edinburgh Volunteers', 'The Balmoral Highlanders', 'Abercairney Highlanders', 'The Glengarry Gathering', 'The Stirlingshire Militia', 'Highland Wedding', and 'Leaving Glenurquhart'; strathspeys like 'Tullochgorm' and 'The Cameronian Rant'; and reels like 'The Rejected Suitor', 'Over the Isles to America' and 'The Smith of Chillichassie'.

The material was more technically formidable, and much closer to the distinctive pipe idiom than anything that had gone before. It is clear that Ross's influence upon the present is much greater than has been supposed. Turning from MacDonald and the early Glens to *Uilleam* Ross is like experiencing a sudden vision of the future. Ross and his circle should receive acknowledgement for what increasingly appears a major achievement as the founders of the modern light music tradition.

C. S. Thomason

Charles Simeon Thomason was born in India, at Azamgarh in the North-West Provinces on 25th May 1833, the son of James Thomason lieutenant-governor and his wife Maynard Grant. His mother's family were the Grants of Elchies on Speyside, and it was mainly here that he was brought up following her death in 1839. In a rich musical environment he learned Gaelic and studied the flute and the pipes. His grandfather, J. W. Grant, had studied as a gentleman amateur with Donald MacDonald, and it was to him that MacDonald sent the manuscript of his proposed second volume when it became clear that his financial difficulties would prevent its publication. Thomason noted:

When MacDonald's first volume was published Mr. Grant was in India. The second volume alluded to so freely in the first as about to contain historical notes pertaining to both volumes was eagerly looked forward to & formed the subject of many a letter from Mr. Grant when postal communication was the sport of long sea voyages in sailing ships via the Cape. I have heard my grandfather relate how, after many fruitless attempts to extract a reply, at last, to his great surprise, a letter was received by him from MacDonald together with his second vol. in manuscript. This vol. though containing historical notes on many of the piobaireachdan in it, unfortunately contained no such notes pertaining to those in the first vol. as promised. MacDonald wrote that he had been almost ruined by the publication of the 1st vol., & not being in a position to undertake that of the 2nd. begged to present to my grandfather its MS original, in the hopes that he, who of all his patrons had evinced the greatest interest in his work, would some day find himself in a position to perpetuate it (C. S. Thomason, 'Ceol Mor Legends', National Library of Scotland MS 3749, ff.83–4).

A copy of the manuscript was presented to Thomason along with his grandfather's pipes when he was commissioned in the Bengal Engineers in 1852. An enthusiastic amateur player, Thomason had studied with Sandy MacLennan (Donald of Moy's son), and Sandy Cameron (the elder). He wrote:

I was fortunate enough to come to terms with Donald's brother, Sandy, who then had a small place in the High Street, where all pipers of note were accustomed to congregate when in Edinburgh. A full size and a half size stand of pipes lay always at hand on the table for the use of all comers; music was always kept well agoing. I must there have heard the best pipers in Scotland, though they were unknown to me even by name. I was too much a tyro to form any opinion as to the merits of the performers, but I used to listen greedily to their conversation regarding the capabilities of the several pipers of the day . . . (*Oban Times*, 02/01/1904, p.3).

Copies of Angus MacKay's book had become so scarce that Thomason had to borrow one and transcribe it, which first turned his inventive mind towards the possibilities of an abbreviated system of notation. As it transpired, he lost the lot in the fall of Delhi during the Indian Mutiny in the summer of 1857, although he managed to escape and took part in the later siege of the city, being one of the sappers who blew in the Kashmir Gate at the height of the British assault. So, he had to start all over again; but he was no longer focused on the problems of merely personal learning.

The Victorian period was the first great age of mass communication, the powerful urge to include *everybody* within the orbit of the print media. Thomason was convinced that the whole of the *piobaireachd* repertoire must be made available in print to pipers at a price they could afford, and he saw clearly that traditional methods could not achieve this. To reproduce the whole repertoire in the style of MacDonald and MacKay would not only be prohibitively bulky but also punitively expensive. It was useless looking to existing institutions like the Highland Societies of London or Scotland who had already done all they seemed ever likely to in this field; so Thomason concluded that he must do it himself. As a first step, then, something had to be done about the notation.

Assisted by a leading contemporary player, Donald MacKay (Angus MacKay's nephew, and pupil of Donald Cameron), Thomason began to develop a system of musical shorthand. This used a range of signs adapted from standard musical notation and also a series of special new symbols which enabled conventional *pìobaireachd* movements containing many notes to be represented by a single token. Various kinds of brackets were used to indicate repeated sections and first and second endings; each division of the tune was numbered and a system of abbreviations adopted ('L' for Leumluath, 'T' for Taorluath and so on) to indicate the type of variations to be played. It took Thomason more than 20 years to perfect the system, but eventually he was able to represent any piece of *ceòl mór* in a precise but highly compressed manner, like this:

When tunes were arranged in this way, the structural links between the parts became more obvious than with the older notation. Thomason's conclusions about this, embodied in the extensive introductory sections to *Ceol Mor* and in numerous letters to the *Oban Times*, represented the first serious work on *pìobaireachd* structure for more than a century. Thomason established the structural principles underlying 'Primary Piobaireachd', the form assumed by at least half the repertoire, and his work on piping ornament was unsurpassed in its range and particularity. Armed with such insights, he was able to emend a number of important tunes which had not been transmitted accurately, including 'I got a Kiss of the King's Hand' which had appeared in Angus MacKay in a mutilated form and had been played in this fashion, warts and all.

Thomason's approach to the problem of cost was typically bold and effective: he engraved the music plates himself. The day after he retired in 1888, he set about the gigantic task at 'East Laggan', the home he had designed for himself by the lake at Naini Tal in the foothills of the Himalayas in northern Uttar Pradesh. By this stage he had risen to considerable eminence, ending his career as Secretary for Public Works for Central India, and he could make the imperial service in British India do things that ordinary mortals could not. As a result the completed plates were reproduced by the military surveying service, using the latest methods in photo-zincography, and published by Thomason himself at below cost in order to place the classical music of the pipe 'within the reach of poor pipers'.

The results, when bound, contained virtually the whole tradition within a plump volume that could be carried within a capacious Victorian sporran. Returning to Scotland and his other home, 'Laggan House' near his grandfather's place on Speyside, he distributed copies of Ceol Mor among the senior players, inviting comment and support. The object was a new, more accurate, and above all collectively sanctioned edition of the work. Although the system *looked* complicated, such was the conventional nature of the music that it could quickly be learned. Some of the master players, including John MacDonald and his pupils, received it enthusiastically; but others rejected it out of hand. On minds that were not closed, Ceol Mor had a powerful effect, leading directly to the formation of the Piobaireachd Society and an invitation to Thomason to become its president. For the first of the Society's competitions held at Oban on 13th September 1904 copies of the set tunes, taken from Ceol Mor, were distributed free to intending competitors. When it was boycotted by a few leading players, this enabled a faction within the Society hostile to the new system to depose Thomason. Most of the founding members thereupon resigned.

His enemies attempted to blacken his reputation by suggesting that his motives were pecuniary and that he had joined the Society simply to promote sales. To a scrupulously honest man like the General (who had envisaged no personal gain whatever from the project) such insinuations were deeply wounding. Indeed the brutality with which he was treated may seem surprising until we recollect that Thomason was not quite regarded by the Scottish establishment as 'one of us'. For one thing he was an 'Indian' officer and there was distinctly greater cachet attached to appointments on the 'Home' establishment. Then, too, he was an engineer, a useful enough calling but hardly what a well-connected and wealthy young man would aspire to. Many contemporaries would have thought there was something suspect about a gentleman who had so close an affinity with 'trade' that he could – as Thomason could – design a harbour or irrigation system or make a set of pipes with his own hands (and play them). The flash end of the British Army was occupied by the likes of the Marquis of Tullibardine who served in the Household Cavalry (Blues and Royals). Tullibardine was a member of the Piobaireachd Society and actively involved in the anti-Thomason campaign.

So the General went away and thought for a while, and then decided it was no good setting about things in a top-down fashion, as the Piobaireachd Society was doing – steps to ensure the future prosperity of piping had to involve the active participation and support of the players, and there were a number of questions which urgently required to be addressed. He had been anxious for some time about developments in the pipe scale and the widely varying characteristics of contemporary chanters, and with Colin Cameron he had been testing samples from various periods. It looked as if the pitch had gradually been rising, that modern manufacturers were moving progressively away from a timbre suitable for playing *ceòl mór*. Then there was the wide variety of fingerings used to sound the various notes, which was causing confusion in competition as people could be penalised for favouring one method of execution rather than another. So Thomason called a meeting in Edinburgh in the spring of 1907 attended by all the leading players at which these problems were discussed and a committee was set up to explore the matter further. Thomason was also one of the first to attempt to assemble the verbal lore of the pipe, and he compiled a substantial collection of such material, from a variety of written, printed and oral sources, to which he gave the title 'Ceol Mor Legends'. It remains unpublished.

In 1909 a public dinner was organised in his honour, at which he was presented with an illuminated scroll; his health was pledged with Highland Honours while the pipes played 'Stand Fast Craigellachie'. But Thomason presented both a puzzle and a challenge to the contemporary power élite. He stood outside the structure and would not let himself be manipulated either by the old guard, or by the dissident Campbells and their supporters when they later regained control of the Society. Although from a landed background, he represented a different strand of society from the general run of self-appointed cultural guardians in nineteenth-century Scotland. He had not attended one of the great English public schools, he refused to mount the bench and sit in judgement on players better than himself, and he mixed frequently and on an easy footing with pipers.

Thomason is yet another reminder that the wellbeing of the music of the pipes was in the hands not of institutions, or organisations, or clubs, or societies, but of gifted individuals like himself, often with little encouragement or support. He was Donald MacDonald's heir, summing up all that had come before, and pointing the way (although it was never properly followed up) to the future. His book, *Ceol Mor*, was the greatest single contribution ever made to the editing of *pìobaireachd*. However, just like all the other musically accurate sources, it fell victim to the Piobaireachd Society monopoly. It was allowed to go out of print and stay there. After about 1920 it was impossible to get a copy for love or money until the English publishers EP brought it briefly back into print during the 1970s.

Thomason's quiet persistence in the face of every obstacle, his great knowledge, his considerable musical talent which made him a notable composer as well as an editor and theorist, his selfless desire to further the art, his uncompromising honesty, his openness and affability as a human being which made him welcome alike to high and low, mark him as one of the most interesting and impressive people who has ever had to do with the music of the pipe.

General C. S. Thomason died at his home at 103 Warwick Road, Kensington on 12th July 1911, and is buried in Inverallan Churchyard, Grantown-on-Spey.

David Glen

Thomason's work is one of the twin summits of the golden age of *pìobaireachd* editing which fell during the second half of the nineteenth century. The other was the creation of a very different man from a very different background – David Glen, pipe-maker and music publisher of Edinburgh. Although they took strikingly different approaches, each offered distinctive solutions to the problems of scale and expense which had dogged the publication of bagpipe music from the beginning. Thomason went for miniaturisation; Glen used another of the great Victorian devices – namely serialisation – which parcelled a big and expensive product into affordable units, in effect permitting purchase by instalments. The technique also enabled operations to proceed on a larger scale than was possible in a single-volume collection. Glen's *Ancient Piobaireachd* (1880–1907) eventually ran to 100 tunes, more than twice as many as *Uilleam* Ross. At the same time, he was able to substitute for the rather home-made appearance of Thomason's self-engraved plates a high-quality typographically attractive product which was a joy to look at and possess.

David Glen was born in Edinburgh on 3rd April 1853 at 30 St Andrew Square, home of his father Alexander Glen (1801–1873), bagpipe maker, and his second wife, Ann Marshall (born *c.* 1816). The extended Glen family was a prominent one in the musical life of nineteenth and twentieth-century Edinburgh. David's cousins John (1833–1904) and Robert (1835–1911), of the firm J. & R. Glen, were also important instrument makers and key figures in the early-music movement. David's own firm, David Glen & Sons, were leading pipe-makers and pre-eminent as publishers of pipe music during the later nineteenth and early twentieth centuries.

Glen was taught by Gilbert Gordon, piper to Lord Panmure, and was said to be a fine player. His work marks the highest development of the staff notation conventions of Donald MacDonald and Angus MacKay, and was an important – perhaps the decisive – influence in the long transition of pipe music from an oral to a predominantly literate form. There had long been complaints from reformers about the oral/aural context in which pipers taught and learned. It was claimed that 'learning off the fingers' of another player was primitive, and led to multiple versions of any given tune, restricting the possibilities for ensemble play. Glen's pleasing settings from their sheer omnipresence – there can have been few pipe cases in Scotland which did not contain at least one of his volumes – must have been an important means of drawing ever larger numbers of the performer community within the circle of musical literacy during the later nineteenth and early twentieth centuries.

Glen published several collections, any one of which would entitle him to an important place in the history of the pipe. The sheer scale of his activities is striking when compared with the earlier tradition: for example, his light music edition, *David Glen's Collection of Highland Bagpipe Music* (1876 – 1900), ran to seventeen parts in all and eventually contained more than one thousand tunes. Attractively arranged and containing an appealing mixture of new and older pieces, it was a convincing demonstration of the huge creative effort of the generation following Angus MacKay and the, by now, impressive range of the light music of the pipe. Its influence was great: it sold about eighty thousand copies and remained in print for nearly a century. In Glen's fascinating pages one could watch the tradition negotiate with itself and all kinds of things in process of transformation into something better. They form a source of unparalleled richness for studying the development of light music idiom during the second half of the 19th century.

Glen's *Collection of Ancient Piobaireachd or Highland Bagpipe Music* (1880–1907) appeared in seven parts containing one hundred tunes, covering the core of the competition repertoire. It could be bought as single tunes, or in separate parts, or altogether as a bound volume with historical notes by Henry Whyte, 'Fionn', providing entry at different levels, each at an appropriate price. *Music of the Clan MacLean* appeared in 1900. This contained a number of hitherto unpublished and little-known *pìobaireachds* supplied by John Johnston of Coll, whose style perhaps reflected that of the Rankins of Mull. Glen's last big enterprise was *The Edinburgh Collection of Highland Bagpipe Music: Pibrochs, Marches, Quicksteps, Strathspeys, Reels & Jigs* (1903–1908), issued in eleven parts and containing more than five hundred tunes. There were numerous con-temporary compositions and the collection was marked throughout with a powerful sense of a vigorously creative and ongoing tradition. Indeed Glen was innovative in nearly everything he did: Fionn's notes to the big *pìobaireachd* collection went at least some way towards achieving Thomason's goal of assembling the verbal lore of the pipe; the MacLean book focused on a neglected aspect of the tradition and was based on the repertoire of a single player. It was fifty years before this was done again by Dr. Roderick Ross in *Binneas is Boreraig.*

Glen was an indefatigable collector, and his manuscript *pìobaireachd* collection containing some 190 tunes (National Library of Scotland, MS. 22120) is amongst the largest ever compiled. Yet he was merely one of a close-knit group of editors and players active in the field. These included Charles Bannatyne (1867–1924), John McLennan and C. S. Thomason, who between them owned most of the historically important unpublished collections. Meanwhile players like Colin Cameron and John MacDougall Gillies (1855–1925) also supplied him with rare material. Between them they published the entire *pìobaireachd* repertoire, carefully edited to reflect traditional idiom and stylistic variety. But the formation of the Piobaireachd Society in 1903 changed this situation dramatically for the whole of the following century. When the Society began to publish set tunes for competition in controversial versions edited by its own members, Glen offered to supply the scores at a reduced price in a musically reliable form. But the Society insisted on its own settings, taking out a series of advertisements in the *Oban Times* stating, 'To Pipers. Caution . . . This is the only Edition authorised . . . and from which the competitors will be judged' (*Oban Times* 01/04/1905). Its control of the competition circuit enabled it to establish a monopoly position and end the publication of *pìobaireachd* on the open market. And so the dynamic movement by people who were first and foremost players to make the repertoire freely available in print which began with Donald MacDonald and reached its apogee in the work of Thomason and Glen was brought to an abrupt halt.

Glen's *pìobaireachd* scores retained their prestige among leading performers, John MacDonald of Inverness describing them in 1940 as 'the most reliable we have today'; but they became increasingly scarce. By the end of the twentieth century few pipers had access to a copy, even in the greatest libraries. David Glen died in Edinburgh of a stroke on 25th June 1916.

PLAYERS AND COMPOSERS

The great succession of master players is one of the most prominent features of the pipe, and a subject of absorbing interest to players and *aficionados* alike. Yet they were seldom performers merely: all the great players taught, most of them composed, and a good many of them were also editors of bagpipe music. The present small selection drawn from the last century-and-a-half could be greatly extended but those appearing here are chosen because their careers are representative and reflect some of the larger movements within piping at the time.

[114]

John MacDougall Gillies

John MacDougall Gillies's family came from Glendaruel, in the heart of the beautiful province of Cowal. It is a fertile shallow glen, with the eighteenth-century Kirk of Kilmodan standing at its centre, and the graves of numerous Gillies's in its churchyard. It used to be the destination of the summer mystery tours by horse charabanc for trippers from Dunoon, stopping at the tea pavilion at the Glendaruel Hotel, a classic piece of Victoriana now, alas, no more. Looking up the glen on a lovely summer afternoon, it does not seem at all the kind of place one would willingly leave for the grimy backstreets of Aberdeen. But employment, opportunity, the sheer excitement and bustle of city life drew many from the land, including the parents of Jack MacDougall Gillies, who is widely acknowledged as one of the greatest teachers of the twentieth century.

John MacDougall Gillies was born on 20th May 1855 at 126 Gallowgate, Aberdeen, the first of two piping sons of John MacDougall Gillies, marble polisher (born c.1826) from Glendaruel, and his wife, Isabella Smith from Glasgow (born c. 1826). He became a master house painter to trade, and began his playing career with the Aberdeen Volunteers under Pipe-Major Alex Fettes, who composed the classic 6/8 march, 'The Glendaruel Highlanders', in the family's honour. Robert Meldrum knew him in his early days, recollecting: 'We were about the same age. I was getting taught at the barracks by Willie Murray, PM of the Depot, and I used to pass on my knowledge to John. He had a brother, Alec, who was a better player'. But John MacDougall Gillies had a real affinity with *piobaireachd* and made great strides under Sandy Cameron the younger when the latter was piper to the Marquis of Huntly at Aboyne Castle, Deeside. Gillies went on to win all the top awards in *piobaireachd* playing, including the Braemar gold medal (1875), the Inverness prize pipe (1882), the Oban gold medal (1884) and the gold medal for previous winners at Inverness in 1885. He was the first-ever winner of the clasp for former gold medallists at Inverness in 1896.

In 1886 Gillies became first piper to the Marquis of Breadalbane at Taymouth Castle in Perthshire. It was a high-profile appointment in what was probably the biggest private piping establishment in Scotland. Some of the largest estates relied on local players but the Breadalbanes always went for top-flight professionals. Gillies's famous predecessors, John Bàn MacKenzie (1796–1864) and Duncan MacDougall of Aberfeldy (c. 1837–1898), had been able to turn out around two dozen pipers for lavish 'Highland' entertainments where guests included numerous crowned and titled parties including Queen Victoria and Prince Albert. In Duncan MacDougall's day, the Duke of Cambridge had complimented him on turning out the finest pipe band he had ever heard, which was no doubt gratifying, but when the captains and the kings departed, the real piping resumed. One contemporary recollected of Gillies that he and . . . Sandy Cameron used to adjourn to the Tower and there play to their hearts' content. Mr. Gillies used to say he never heard anything finer than Sandy's playing of 'The Ribean Gorm' on a fine summer evening with a gentle breeze carrying it far up the glen. Variation after variation of this most symmetrical and beautiful tune, rolled around singlings, doublings, and treblings, embedding the urlar in the crunluath-a-mach as even as a wheel on a mill-lade . . . ('The Late Mr J. MacDougall Gillies', *Oban Times*, 26/12/1925, p.3).

But employment in such settings was losing its attraction for pipers as they were increasingly expected to carry out a range of menial duties in addition to their musical role. A defining moment came when Lady Breadalbane arrived at Taymouth from her Park Lane residence in 1888:

Her Ladyship, not in the best of moods, had heavy gambling losses . . . On her last night in London she had lost £72,000 on the turn of a card.
　　She sent for the factor and ordered all those pipers doing nothing but playing pipes to sweep the drive. MacDougall Gillies . . . fetched his pipes and belongings and left . . . (quoted in Donaldson, *Highland Pipe*, p.194).

By Lady Breadalbane's standards this was a fairly minor reverse. She was the first person in history to lose a million pounds in a night at the tables in Monte Carlo. Gillies returned to Aberdeen, but did not remain there long. Trade in the city was depressed, and when in January 1890 his wife Margaret Low died, he moved to Glasgow, lodging in the Cowcaddens with his old teacher Sandy Cameron, who was at that time piper to the Lord Provost. Gillies worked at his trade for a while and from about 1903 until a week before his death was manager of Peter Henderson's the pipe-makers. In Glasgow he developed into an outstanding teacher, and many brilliant young players studied with him including William Gray, George Yardley, and Robert Reid – who was widely regarded as his successor. Reid always said that *pìobaireachd* had been brought to its highest artistic development by Gillies and Cameron in the city of Glasgow during the closing years of the nineteenth century.

City life also offered the chance to become involved with pipe bands, and Gillies was one of the earliest players of the foremost rank to work in a competitive setting. He served from 1891 as honorary Pipe-Major of the 1st (later 5th) Volunteer Battalion H.L.I., pioneering competitive ensemble play and winning the first Cowal open pipe band championship in 1906, with a further four wins up to 1912. He was also pipe-major of the Glasgow Highland Club and president of the Scottish Pipers' Association, formed in 1920.

Gillies was at the centre of an extensive network of knowledge and enquiry about piping. Robert Meldrum recollected gaining access to an old roll of tunes which had once been in the possession of John Bàn MacKenzie at Taymouth Castle. This contained the scores of two hitherto unpublished pieces, namely 'The Lament for Captain MacDougall' and 'I am proud to play a pipe'. Meldrum immediately transcribed them and sent copies to Gillies. The tunes were later published in the collections of Thomason and Glen.

In the summer of 1890, the historian Henry Whyte ('Fionn') published in the *Oban Times* a set of traditional words for 'MacFarlane's Gathering', and appealed for further information:

> *Thogail nam bò,*
> *Thogail nam bò,*
> *Thogail nam bò thèid sinn;* (repeat)
> *Thogail nam bò,*
> *Ri uisge 's ri ceò,*
> *Ri monadh Ghlinn-crò thèid sinn.* [etc]

(The general import is of sallying forth, whatever the hazard, to lift the cattle. The MacFarlanes were famous cattle-raiders – so much so that in the south-west Highlands the moon was commonly known as 'MacFarlane's Lantern'). 'Fionn' was anxious to trace the pipe tune which related to these words, which he could find in none of the published collections. There was no response to his enquiries in the *Oban Times*, but such appeals often led to private correspondence, and in due course Gillies recovered the tune, since published as 'The MacFarlane's Gathering' and now one of the best-loved pieces in the tradition. He collected it in 1894 from a man called John Leitch from Glendaruel, then living in Dumbarton (apparently through the agency of the town's Provost MacFarlane), and took it down from Leitch's playing on the fiddle. The setting published in Thomason's *Ceol Mor* a few years later was thus presumably Gillies's transliteration back into pipe idiom of a tune which had started off there originally but had since migrated into the repertoire of another instrument. Gillies's setting as published by Thomason is a subtler affair than the version ascribed to him in the Piobaireachd Society's *Collection* which is the one that modern pipers play.

Gillies was employed as a professional adviser and instructor to the Piobaireachd Society from its earliest years, and its first series of competition scores (1905–12) were mainly published by his firm. Several early twentieth-century master players had links with the Society in this way, including John MacDonald, Gavin MacDougall, Sandy Cameron (the younger), John MacColl and Willie Ross. The Society tended to do business behind a protective screen of professional pipers whose advice it sought (but seldom followed). Mounting dissatisfaction with this led to the formation in November 1910 of the Scottish Pipers' and Dancers' Union, with Gillies on the committee. The aim was to regain control of the way the music was played and escape from the unrelenting diet of competition by organising lectures and recitals. The First World War brought this initiative to an end, however, and these problems were unresolved at the end of the twentieth century.

The Society's main editor, Archibald Campbell (1877–1963), demonstrates the characteristic gentleman/piper relationship. He had lessons from Gillies and later, after Gillies's death, frequently invoked his name to justify his (Campbell's) personal settings of tunes in the Society's published *Collection*, although these differed considerably from the elegant stylings in Gillies's manuscript book. Campbell took Gillies's papers after he died. It is not known what the original extent of these may have been, or what proportion eventually found its way back into the public domain. Gillies was a skilled and energetic committer of *ceòl mór* to the written page and his settings are amongst the best in the tradition from a musical point of view. His main manuscript, begun in 1879 and now in the library of the University of Glasgow (MS Gen. 1457), records more than 70 of the great tunes in a very pleasing and subtle style, but it remains unpublished and little known at the end of the twentieth century.

Gillies was said to be an exacting teacher with pupils whom he thought worth the trouble. The folklore says that he kept Robert Reid on one tune – 'Too Long in this Condition' – for a whole year, although his approach seems to have varied. One pupil, a gentleman amateur who later went on to become a senior judge, recalled being taught almost wholly by singing: Gillies would come into the teaching room and lay his practice chanter on the table. At the end of the lesson, he would pick it up and leave, having played not a note on it in the meantime.

John MacDougall Gillies died at his home at 409 Great Western Road, Glasgow, on 17th December 1925.

John MacColl

John MacColl (1860–1943) was one of the leading figures on the Highland games circuit during the second half of the nineteenth century. In him we see the principle of competition introduced by the Highland Societies almost a century before carried to its highest point by someone with a sufficiently all-round gift to exploit the system to the full. The scale of the late-Victorian Highland Games movement meant that as a piper, dancer and athlete MacColl could make a comfortable living at it. Had this been all, he would appear as a minor statistic, at best, in the copious annals of competitive piping. But MacColl was gifted: there was hardly anything he did not do outstandingly well. As a composer, especially of competition marches, he is one of the best the tradition ever produced, and his beautifully melodic and inventive tunes remain classics to this day.

John MacColl was born at Kentallen in Duror, Argyllshire, on 6th January 1860, youngest of the four sons of piper and fiddler Dugald MacColl, the tailor of Kentallen, and his wife, Elizabeth McInnes. Pipers seem to flourish in beautiful places, and there are few more appealing in the whole of the central Highlands, with the hills of Appin behind and a dramatic prospect to the west across Loch Linnhe to Ardgour and Sunart. It is classic Stevenson country. Just a mile or two up the road, in the woods of Lettermore, Colin Campbell of Glenure, 'The Red Fox', was shot by (maybe) Alan Breac Stewart whose foster-father, James of the Glen, was sentenced to be hanged for the deed at Ballachulish by a court at Inverary packed with Campbells.

John MacColl got his early teaching from his father and later from the pipe-maker and music publisher Donald MacPhee (1841–1880), whom he had first heard playing at Bonawe Highland Games in 1877. He went to work at Bonawe Quarry to save up to study with him in Glasgow. After MacPhee's death in December 1880, MacColl continued his lessons with Pipe-Major Ronald MacKenzie (died March 1911, a Skyeman, ex-pipe-major, Black Watch; prize pipe, Inverness, 1873 and gold medal, 1875 – not to be confused with the other Ronald MacKenzie, 1842–1916, pipe-major of the 78th and nephew of John Bàn) with whom he worked as a piper for Neil M. MacDonald, grandson of Niel MacLeod of Gesto, at Dunach a little south of Oban. 'Johnny' MacColl was early identified as an outstanding prospect, 'an *educated* player . . . sweet and powerful in expression', and he went on to a hugely successful competitive career, winning all the major awards (gold medal at the Argyllshire Gathering, 1881; silver cup for previous winners, 1883; prize pipe at Inverness the same year; special centenary gold medal, Inverness, 1888; and the clasp in 1900; plus first prize, Paris Exhibition, 1902). Like a number of contemporaries, he was in the Volunteers, serving as pipe-major of the 3rd Battalion, Black Watch, and then with the Scottish Horse. He also trained pipers in the Volunteers during the winter months and acted as an instructor for the Piobaireachd Society.

Improving income, leisure and transport links during MacColl's youth and early manhood created the modern mass entertainment industry, bringing the music hall, the seaside holiday, and, in Scotland, the Highland games circuit into vigorous existence. This had a considerable impact on opportunity for top pipers who could make significant sums going the rounds of Dunoon, Braemar, Oban and Inverness, and a host of smaller events. It provided an escape route from 'service' in landed families, and independent spirits like MacColl and his friend William McLennan, who moved into showbiz as a travelling impresario, were quick to seize it. He was a talented athlete and dancer as well as a piper. His son described him

> finishing a dance, throwing off his kilt (having running shorts underneath), competing in the hundred yards race and then putting his kilt and things on ready for the next dance . . . He was away from home practically all summer travelling round the Games . . . he could earn £40 in an afternoon from piping, dancing and athletics (quoted in Donaldson, p.201).

This implied an income considerably in excess of the lower professions. Indeed MacColl could earn more in a summer month than his distinguished contemporary, schoolmaster and folk-song collector Gavin Greig (1856–1914), could earn in a year – rather ironical in view of the fact that if MacColl ever did the round of the smaller North-East games, he would probably have encountered Greig (something of a piping *aficionado*) on the judges' bench. But there was more involved than money and the status that flowed from it. It meant that top pipers could once again afford leisure; MacColl was a skilful yachtsman and golfer (playing off a 2 handicap), a shinty internationalist, a fiddle player and a Gaelic singer.

MacColl's *piobaireachd* playing was sometimes criticised for lacking expression, but John MacDonald of Inverness described his interpretation of 'I got a Kiss of the King's Hand' at Birnam one year as 'one of the most harmonious performances I have listened to'. On the other hand, by general consent he was the best march player of his generation, one contemporary adding: 'His dapper figure marching round the platform was a delight to see'.

John MacColl, along with William Laurie (*c.* 1881–1916) and G.S. McLennan, was one of the brilliant trio of light-music composers of the early twentieth century who set the standard by which everything that happened afterwards was judged. His original *piobaireachd* compositions include 'Donald MacPhee's Lament' and 'N. M. MacDonald's Lament', but he was best known for his characteristically beautiful marches, including 'John MacFadyen of Melfort', 'Arthur Bignold of Lochrosque', 'Jeannie Carruthers', and 'Mrs John MacColl', which set new standards in technical demand and brilliantly exploited the expressive possibilities of the form.

MacColl became manager of the pipe-makers R. G. Lawrie of Glasgow in 1908, and retired about 1936. He died on 8th June 1943, at his home 34 Claddens Quadrant, Glasgow. 'The Lament for the Children' was played at his funeral by John MacDonald of the Glasgow Police.

John MacDonald of Inverness

John MacDonald was born on 26th July 1865 in Glentruim, near Kingussie, eldest son of Alexander MacDonald (*c.* 1835–1883) and his wife Jane Lamont. He was one of a brilliant family of MacDonald pipers from Speyside, which included his uncles William (piper to the Prince of Wales and composer of 'Leaving Glenurquhart') and Duncan (who wrote 'The Braes of Castle Grant'), and of course his father, Sandy MacDonald, piper to the laird of Glentruim, and later to the Earl of Fife, a pupil of Donald Cameron and an important master in his own right, from whom John got his early instruction in piping. John MacDonald studied in addition with several master teachers, including Sandy and Colin Cameron and George and Angus MacDonald of Morar. However, his most important teacher was Malcolm MacPherson, 'Calum Pìobaire'. The folklore has several stories about this famous encounter, such as Calum remarking to his son Jockan who had been giving John some lessons, 'you have made him good; now I will make him great'.

In his 'Piping Reminiscences' (*Oban Times* 4/4/1942) MacDonald gave a detailed account of his training by Calum Pìobaire, stressing its strongly oral character, and the huge size of the repertoire imparted. His training in *pìobaireachd* was derived, therefore, from most of the major nineteenth-century teachers. He was linked, through the MacPhersons and Camerons, with the MacKays of Raasay, the Bruces of Skye and Glenelg and the later MacCrimmons – an outstanding pedigree which he referred to in his characteristically self-effacing way as 'the Apostolic Succession'. John MacDonald first competed at Inverness in 1889, and came third in the *pìobaireachd*, observing: 'the judge on that occasion informed me that I would have been placed higher up in the prize-list if I had marched off on the left foot instead of on the right'. He won the Inverness gold medal in 1890, followed by the clasp in 1903, and went on to dominate competitive *pìobaireachd* playing, eventually amassing eight clasps, a record which was to stand for many years. For the generation which came to maturity during the first half of the twentieth century, 'John MacDonald' and '*pìobaireachd* playing' were synonymous terms. He was also an outstanding light-music player and in high demand as a teacher. He had been an instructor and adviser to the Piobaireachd Society from its foundation in 1903 and, like everybody else in this position, faced a number of dilemmas. Regarding the art as an end in itself, he found himself frequently dealing with powerful people to whom the pipes were merely a means to promote military efficiency. He was eventually to counsel against wasting time and money on what he described as '*purely military* piping'.

MacDonald, like many contemporary pipers, served in the Volunteers and from 1890 was pipe-major of the 4th (VB) Cameron Highlanders. This meant direct contact with leading members of the Piobaireachd Society including Lord Dunmore, its President, who was C.O. of the 4th Camerons, and Simon 14th Lord Lovat (1871–1933), who was one of its senior officers. Lovat was a remarkable character, an important Highland landowner, ex-Household Cavalry (1st Lifeguards), who had raised a battalion of Highland sharpshooters called the Lovat Scouts for service during the Boer War and went on to command the Highland Mounted Brigade at Gallipoli. He followed Dunmore as President of the Piobaireachd Society upon the latter's death in 1907, and did much to foster its already strong connections with the British Army. Like others before him concerned with the morale of Highland formations, Lovat saw a pressing need to do something about the generally deplorable state of playing in the regular army. Unlike his predecessors, however, Lovat had the persistence and the contacts to get something actually done about it. In 1909 he obtained the agreement of the

War Office that candidates for appointment as pipe-major in the regular army should first undergo training by the Piobaireachd Society's chief instructor, John MacDonald. The idea was that with their technique and knowledge of *piobaireachd* strengthened and renewed, piping N.C.O.s would return to their units and train their junior colleagues in turn, thus leading to a general improvement in standards. Lovat got the War Office to agree that military pipers could reach the rank of pipe-major only with a certificate from the Piobaireachd Society, which thus gained a very considerable power. There were difficulties, of course: the Army objected to John MacDonald as instructor because he was a civilian, as indeed he was. The ethos of the Volunteer movement was utterly unlike that of the regular army, as we have seen. Nevertheless the Army Class duly came into being, although it meant an ostensibly civilian body – the Piobaireachd Society – paying the instructor. The first course was held at Inverness in October 1910 and John MacDonald's teaching won golden opinions. Between 1909 and 1914 he also ran classes in the Uists for six weeks every summer under the auspices of the South Uist Piobaireachd Society. Only the outbreak of war prevented his moving to Edinburgh to establish what eventually became the Army School of Bagpipe Music. The war seriously disrupted civilian piping and created major problems for professional teachers whose income depended on a steady flow of pupils. So MacDonald took a full-time job as a commercial traveller for the drinks firm Youngers in the North and West Highlands, turning down the position as instructor to the Army Class when it was revived in 1919.

John MacDonald's expressive gift and marvellous execution kept him at the top for fifty years. He won eight clasps, five of them after the age of sixty. In 1927 he made the first commercial recordings of *piobaireachd* with Columbia, playing the grounds and opening variations of 'Lament for the Children', 'MacCrimmon's Sweetheart', 'The Little Spree' and 'Lament for Patrick Og'. J. P. Grant of Rothiemurchus and General Frank Richardson (two of his leading amateur pupils) sought funding for further recordings in the 1930s but without success.

R. U. Brown and R. B. Nicol had many stories about him. They heard him for the first time at a recital and they thought 'that man surely canna be a good player, he's far too fat'. But a perfect pipe struck up and the Bobs were dazzled. They said it was just as good as you could possibly imagine. At first they went up to Inverness for lessons separately, but later they arranged to go together so that they could effectively double the benefits of their period of instruction. Nicol would get one set of tunes and Brown another and then they would swap them. John MacDonald was very self-contained – he did not make contact in human terms very easily, but he liked the Bobs and they spent long hours by his fireside while he smoked his pipe and told them stories. He frequently played for them on the pipes and they often remarked that 'he played best in his carpet slippers'. MacDonald was a very dry blower and Bob Nicol a very wet one (the latter would sigh, 'It's always been my problem; I could get a set of pipes wringing wet in half an hour'). At the games when they were all competing, if it was hot, dry weather Johnny would get Bob Nicol to blow in the pipe for him about twenty minutes before he was due on the boards. He would appear, listen for a second and say, 'I think that will do, Nicol'. If it was wet he got Bob Brown to do it. MacDonald was also an accomplished fiddle player – indeed his sister Helen declared that the 'real' piper in the family was brother Andrew.

John MacDonald could be horribly crushing and abrupt while teaching. Bob Brown used to say, 'He was the kindest man imaginable – until you opened the pipe box. Then, oh boy . . . he could make you feel so low, that you could have gone out under the door wearing a tile hat'. The Bobs were sitting outside his room one day waiting for their lesson, and Johnny was labouring inside over a fumbling pupil (who turned out to be Seton Gordon – 'oh it was terrible', said Bob Brown, 'him with his amateur's fingers') – and bellowing 'No, no, no!' They felt like picking up the pipes and quietly leaving.

MacDonald had a slight stroke in 1935 and stopped playing on medical advice, although he remained active as a teacher. Yet as the Piobaireachd Society's texts accumulated, his position became increasingly awkward. There was growing alarm inside the Society during the 1930s about what was being done in its name, and MacDonald was in contact with two members of the Music Committee, Somerled MacDonald and Seton Gordon, who were trying to get the current series of publications edited by Archibald Campbell scrapped. They wanted John MacDonald to be made a member of the Society (as a professional player he was technically barred), and to become editor of its publications. But MacDonald, already 73 years old, had had enough. He wrote to Seton Gordon:

> I don't see why the P.S. Music Committee do so much altering of the tunes they publish . . . I am not too happy, and in my opinion they dont add to the beauty of the melodies, and unfortunately these go down to posterity as the correct settings . . . I would not like you to bring up a motion that I should be consulted in the settings of the tunes or anything in connection with their publications. . . . To me, it seems quite evident, from results of the last 15 years [i.e. since the start of the Society's second series edited by Archibald Campbell] that the preservation of our ancient and traditional music, with all its beautiful and melodious airs, and sentiment, has passed into the wrong hands, and it will take a long time, if ever, before it can be restored to its original standard . . .

It may be that he had had his advice ignored too often and, having been unable to prevent the current situation developing, felt he was unlikely to be able to retrieve it. More to the point perhaps, he had been obliged to teach Archibald Campbell's settings. He wrote in 1949 to Seton Gordon that he was no longer going to do this, declaring: 'I am not continuing teaching the tunes for this year's competitions as written by the P.S. I am too old now to adopt the modern ideas of Piob. – and am quite happy to keep what I got from the old Pipers'.

John MacDonald was awarded the M.B.E. for services to piping in 1935, and was made honorary piper to King George V. He died at his home, 3 Perceval Road, Inverness, on 6th June 1953, and was buried on 8 June at Cluny Hill Cemetery, Forres, in the grave of Helen Gibb, his second wife. Neither honour is mentioned on his tombstone.

Willie Ross

William Collie Ross was born on 14th June 1878 at Camsorie, Glen Strathfarrar, near Beauly in Inverness-shire. His father was Alexander Ross (1854–?), head forester of Struy on the Lovat estate, and his mother, Mary Collie (1854–1944), came from Monar at the head of Glen Strathfarrar. Alexander Ross was a piper and fiddler and all his children could play, but Willie and his brother Alec (who also made his mark as a piper and composer) were the main musical representatives of the family in their generation. Most of Willie's piping tuition came from his mother although he had lessons, too, from his father and his mother's uncle, Aeneas Rose (1832–1905), piper to the Duke of Atholl. Some thought that Willie was inclined to inflate his piping pedigree. Bob Nicol – who was his rival in competition latterly – used to joke that nobody knew who his teachers were: 'He gie'd oot that it wis the Camerons, but he was never near them . . . the auld chancer'. Willie Ross joined the Scots Guards in 1896, saw active service in the Boer War and became pipe-major of the 2nd battalion in 1905. He also served throughout the Great War until invalided home in June 1918. He was based for many years in the capital, and he spoke of long sessions on *piobaireachd* with the younger Sandy Cameron in the Tower of London.

Willie married Edith McGregor (?–1942), a housemaid, and they had a son, William, who died, aged about seven, and a daughter Cecily, who was musically gifted. Edith McGregor was a beauty and Ross himself a tall and strikingly handsome man. They used to turn heads in the Strand as they walked out, she dressed in the highest fashion and he resplendent in the full No.1's of a pipe-major in the Scots Guards.

Willie Ross was the most successful all-round competitor of his generation. His awards in *piobaireachd* included the gold medals at Inverness in 1904 and Oban in 1907, followed by eight clasps at the Northern Meeting. In the light music he won eleven former winners' march, strathspey and reel events at Oban and Inverness. He was one of the Piobaireachd Society's teachers and was appointed instructor of the Army Class at Edinburgh Castle in 1919. This happened in circumstances of some confusion. In the spring of 1919, John Grant, a minor civil servant and teacher of boys, found himself appointed as instructor of the Army Class. He was by no means the premier player and teacher in the country, and during the first (and only) course he ran, all the students wrote to their commanding officers asking to be returned to their units (one of the few respectable forms of mutiny in the British Army). The Piobaireachd Society quickly dispensed with Grant's services, but they could not get the person they wanted, their chief instructor John MacDonald of Inverness. The problem was that the Army Class was part-time, and only paid a salary for six months of the year; the rest had to be made up from other sources, private instruction and so on. John MacDonald was unwilling to give up a secure, full-time and well-paid job with the drinks firm Youngers in order to do this. And so Willie Ross was parachuted in, being one of the few contemporary master players, thanks to his army pension, who could afford to consider the post. His income was supplemented by peripatetic teaching throughout the Highlands and Islands in the summer months and his appointment as pipe-major of the Lovat Scouts (for all practical purposes the Piobaireachd Society's private regiment, raised by its President, Lord Lovat, and commanded by his successor, Col. J. P. Grant of Rothiemurchus). Willie Ross turned the Army Class into a position of immense influence. He refused a commission, and went on to preside over the piping world from his eyrie in Edinburgh Castle for the next forty years. He did not know when he took on the job that his employers meant to replace him with John MacDonald as soon as they could raise a full-time salary.

The courses for aspiring pipe-majors ran for six months each winter. As many candidates had been orally taught, they were expected to learn to read and write music in staff notation, master the basics of musical theory and widen their knowledge of *piobaireachd*. About 90 people went through the School in this phase of its existence. When the Second World War began, the Piobaireachd Society placed Willie Ross at the disposal of the War Office and the only higher-education centre for piping in Scotland was transformed overnight into a crammer. Willie's one-month crash courses in elementary regimental piping were intended to help staunch the haemorrhage of players, 'wastage' being estimated at 80% per year. By the end of the war Willie Ross had taught more than 700 students in this new scheme. In 1945 he was awarded the M.B.E. for his services. It is doubtful whether any of the wartime pupils went on to major careers in piping, but through them Willie Ross influenced the whole of Scotland's popular instrumental tradition: after it was all over, they went back to their fiddles and accordions with repertoires stuffed full of pipe tunes.

There are many stories of Willie at the Castle and the atmosphere of 'despotism tempered by epigrams' that characterised his régime. He could be very exacting. It is said that he insisted that music copying be done with parade-ground accuracy, everything ruled off to the millimetre and aligned *just so*; if it wasn't, the offending page would be unceremoniously ripped from the student's work book and the task begun all over again. Yet the atmosphere could be very relaxed and companionable: round a fire kept well going with a pot of seasoning bubbling on it, the students would sit with their teacher while he enthralled them with stories. Willie could not bear failing people and found all sorts of inventive excuses for returning them to their units without this stigma; likewise, he could not always conceal his disappointment when the examining board (dominated by Piobaireachd Society personnel) failed his candidates. At the end of the 1952–3 course, J. P. Grant wrote: 'The Board went off without any "incidents" and passed 2 & "ploughed" 3 candidates. I think we were generous. Ross, I regret to say again behaved abominably on being told the result . . . I wish he would resign, in everyone's interest; but there appears to be no sign of it & clearly we can't sack him after all these years of good service'.

Willie Ross was the most prolific teacher of his generation, many of whose pupils, including Donald MacLeod, John MacLellan (his eventual successor at the Army School) and John D. Burgess, went on to achieve fame in their own right. His amateur pupils included Archibald Campbell, Kilberry (who described himself as 'an intensive pupil of his'), and Edward, Prince of Wales, later Edward VIII.

Even so, Willie Ross's position was, if anything, even more difficult than John MacDonald's. As the employee of the Piobaireachd Society he was obliged to teach Archibald Campbell's scores, and, like MacDonald, he spent a good deal of his time preparing pupils for success on the competition circuit where the senior benches were occupied by the likes of J. P. Grant and Archibald Campbell who expected their scores to be played. Willie's mother is reported to have once stormed in while a pupil was playing, and shouted 'Rubbish. Do you tell me my son is teaching you that rubbish?' Willie explained to the pupil: 'My mother is quite right. But . . . if you want to get prizes that's the way you must play . . .'

There was a further irony in the situation, in that Ross was himself an outstandingly able music editor. In the arena of light music, where there was no attempt at cultural control, he showed his true stature. Indeed the ineptitude of Campbell's scores is in stark contrast with the masterly style of Willie Ross. The five volumes of *Pipe Major W. Ross's Collection of Highland Bagpipe Music* (1923–1950), containing some 240 tunes, became the definitive source for the modern competition repertoire in the light music and remained in print throughout the twentieth century. There must be few pipers who do not have at least one of Willie Ross's books. Several of his own classic compositions are included, like 'Leaving Port Askaig', 'Center's Bonnet', and 'Brigadier General Ronald Cheape of Tiroran'. His settings did much to promote the modern, more heavily ornamented style in march playing, which had been gathering momentum since the days of William MacLennan and John MacColl, and of which Ross himself was a leading exponent.

Gramophone recordings and radio broadcasts gave Willie Ross an enormous audience and he enjoyed a reputation as 'The King of the Castle' and 'The

World's Pipe-Major'. Following one Empire broadcast, letters of congratulation came from as far afield as South America, the West Indies, South-East Asia and southern Africa from where an enthusiast wrote, 'I had an urgent message from a friend to come to his house as Pipe-Major Ross was to give a piping recital that evening. The road to his house is appalling; but I would have tackled the Pentland Skerries rather than miss Pipe-Major Ross. The reception was perfect; the tone and harmony of the pipes were magnificent and his fingering was faultless'. Since the B.B.C. studios gave pipers no time to settle the instrument, Willie always had another player stand behind him to give the drones a touch as they began to drift, so the pipes sounded in perfect tune.

After the War, the six-month pipe-majors' courses resumed at the Castle and Willie Ross sailed on into a robust and seemingly indestructible old age. But behind the façade, there were serious problems. For one thing he was now nearly 70 years old. The Army refused to take responsibility for the post, and moves within the Piobaireachd Society to replace him were steadily opposed by Archibald Campbell, who thought that none of the younger generation of master players, including R. U. Brown, R. B. Nicol and Donald MacLeod, was up to the job. These difficulties were compounded by the fact that the Society could afford to pay Willie's salary, or provide him with a pension, but not both: if he retired, they could not replace him with another teacher. This impasse dragged on for nearly ten years, until eventually Willie was taken seriously ill and had to undergo a series of abdominal operations which stopped him playing. Willie wrote: 'I am not now able to blow even a chanter so will miss that very much'.

Willie Ross died in the Earl Haig Home in Edinburgh on 23rd March, 1966, and was buried beside his wife in Morningside Cemetery. Except for his tombstone, at the time of writing neglected and vandalised, there is no proper memorial to him in Edinburgh, or in Scotland.

G. S. McLennan

Many people who know little otherwise about the pipe and its music have heard of G. S. McLennan, probably the single most famous piper since the eighteenth century, whose compositional skills and dazzling technique have set the standard of excellence in the three generations since his death. Less well known is the fact that he came from a widely extended and richly gifted family which had made an important contribution to the music of the pipe for several centuries.

George Stewart McLennan was born on 9th February, 1883, in Edinburgh, a son of John McLennan, and his first wife Elizabeth Stewart who died in 1889. 'G. S.' (as he is always known by pipers) was first taught by his father at the age of four and then by his uncle, Pipe-Major John Stewart. He had lessons in Highland dancing from his cousin, William MacLennan. He was a child prodigy and played before Queen Victoria by royal command at the age of ten; she called him 'this marvellous boy'.

He was determined to become a sailor but, anxious to prevent this loss to piping, his father enlisted him as a boy piper in the 1st Gordons in October 1899. He became pipe-major in 1905. McLennan saw service in Ireland and at various garrison towns in England, spending most of the Great War at the Gordons' depot at Aberdeen until early in 1918 when he joined the first battalion in France as a Lewis gunner. He won all the major awards, including the Argyllshire and Inverness gold medals in 1904 and 1905 and the clasp in 1909, 1920 and 1921. As a *piobaireachd* player he was strongly influenced by his father's view that playing had become too slow and unrhythmical. He took his tunes at a brisk tempo, therefore, and would march in time to them round the boards, which provoked a good deal of controversy. He followed his father, likewise, in placing great value on the musical independence of the player. He refused to teach the Piobaireachd Society's prescribed scores in the manner set by the Society, although he was almost alone amongst the master pipers of the day to take such a stand. As a result they would not employ him as an instructor. He was the last major player to reach the rank of pipe-major in the British Army before the Piobaireachd Society was given control of appointment procedures in 1910 and was the last important solo player to have a piping career which did not depend on their sanction.

G. S. McLennan was noted for his melodious pipe (a lovely silver-and-ivory mounted set of Henderson's) and brilliant technique. His tone was robust; yet leading Aberdonian player, George Cruickshank. reported that he found the pipes delightfully free and responsive when G. S., in a characteristically generous gesture, lent them to him at a competition. McLennan's skill as a reedmaker would certainly have had some bearing on this. His hands were so strong that spectators could distinctly hear the fall of his fingers on the chanter as he marched round the boards. In the light music he was a leading pioneer of the faster and more heavily decorated style which developed during the later nineteenth and early twentieth centuries. It appears that McLennan did not play in the 'round' style, which some have inferred from the strings of even quavers and semi-quavers in his published books, but 'pointed' his marches, strathspeys and reels in the normal fashion.

G. S. McLennan was the outstanding composer of light music in the first half of the twentieth century. His tunes were published in a number of sources, two of them appearing during his lifetime. These are the appendix of his father's book, *The Piobaireachd as Performed in the Highlands for Ages, till about the Year 1808* (1924); and G. S.'s own collection, *Highland Bagpipe Music*, published in Aberdeen in 1929. His untimely death prevented the appearance of the second volume of his collection which was to be entitled 'Tunes from a Silent Chanter'. This material was eventually published in *The Gordon Highlanders Pipe Music*

Collection (1983–5). McLennan's light-music settings differed interestingly from those of his lifelong friend and colleague, Willie Ross. In Ross's case, everything was dotted and cut to within an inch of its life and the preferred rhythmical pattern was made very explicit. G. S., although his settings were in every way as developed and technically demanding, left much more room for performer choice.

McLennan's style as a composer was highly distinctive, and he contributed a number of classic tunes to the repertoire, including 'Pipe Major John Stewart', 'Mrs. MacPherson of Inveran', 'The Jig of Slurs' and 'The Little Cascade'. 'The Little Cascade' in particular was to achieve very much a cult status. G. S. McLennan was pre-eminent amongst the multi-talented group of late nineteenth and early twentieth-century composers who established the light music of the pipe at a new level of musical sophistication and technical demand. Yet he did not neglect *ceòl mór* and his compositions in this genre showed a similar level of originality and musicality to that displayed in his light music.

When he retired from the army in 1921, McLennan settled in Aberdeen as a bagpipe maker with premises at 2 Bath Street, and his home at 48b Powis Place became a centre for music-making in the city. He numbered the great fiddle player and composer James Scott Skinner amongst his friends and also the prominent lawyer and piping judge, Alfred E. Milne, to whom he dedicated an attractive competition march. But G. S.'s lungs had been damaged on active service and his health was affected thereafter. He died just before midnight on 31st May 1929. Alfie Milne lived out of the city in the village of Blackburn and would have no truck with telephones, and it was long remembered by Aberdonian pipers that the Highland dancer Mary Aitken ran ten miles through the night to bring him the news of G. S.'s death.

G. S. McLennan never made recordings, and he did not broadcast. He lived in an age before television and media hype. Yet he achieved a level of fame and public regard that would make a modern champion piper gasp. At the funeral on 4th June, the Gordons pulled out all the stops. In a coffin mounted on a gun-carriage and preceded by forty pipers, the body of G. S. McLennan was born through the city of Aberdeen. The crowds brought the traffic to a halt. He was buried in the McLennan family's plot at Echobank (later Newington) Cemetery in Edinburgh. At the time of writing the grave is neglected and overgrown.

Donald MacLeod

The only rival to G. S. McLennan's fame as a composer during the twentieth century was Donald MacLeod, who was taught both by Willie Ross and John MacDonald. Donald MacLeod was born at 5 Newton Street, Stornoway, on the Isle of Lewis, on 14th August 1916. His parents were Donald MacLeod and his wife Donaldina MacDonald. He began learning the pipes – just like McLennan –

at the age of four with his father who was Pipe-Major of the Lewis Pipe Band, going on to more advanced study with Willie Ross and John MacDonald of Inverness. He recollected that their styles were very different. Willie rewarded excellence with squares of chocolate; but MacLeod came home from his first lesson with John MacDonald in tears, declaring that he would never go back, although he did – eventually for more than twenty-five years.

Donald MacLeod became a piper in the 2nd Battalion Seaforth Highlanders in 1937. When World War II broke out, he went with his battalion and the rest of the 51st Highland Division to France and was captured at St Valéry in May 1940. He made a daring escape, and eventually found his way back to Scotland. When talking about the episode later, he would dismiss it with a typically self-effacing reference to his slight stature, saying, 'Ach, the Germans threw the tiddlers back'. He became Pipe-Major of the 7th Seaforth, returning to France with them and eventually piping them across the Rhine in the spring of 1945. John MacDonald watched anxiously for his safety during the war years, writing, '*McLeod of the Seaforths* . . . in my opinion is likely to be one of the best Piob. players. He has got a natural aptitude and has got a mind of his own to stick to what he gets instead of copying anyone he may hear play . . .' Donald MacLeod went on to become a major champion. He won the gold medals at Inverness in 1947 and Oban in 1954, and eight clasps at the Northern Meeting between 1948 and 1964. He was also an outstanding light-music player, winning eight silver stars, the premier award for march, strathspey and reel playing, between 1952 and 1959. Yet it was not all plain sailing. Donald recollected how, when he won the Inverness medal, he hurried round to John MacDonald's house and proudly played his tune, 'Glengarry's March': 'There was a deathly hush when I finished . . . "MacLeod", he said, "Did they give you the medal for that?"'

Although he was acknowledged to be the best player and teacher in the army, Donald MacLeod was not appointed as Willie Ross's successor when the military finally assumed responsibility for providing the instructor at the Army School of Piping. At the time, he was teaching junior pipers at the Bridge of Don barracks in Aberdeen, and he stepped into the breach when Willie was unable to complete the 1958/9 pipe-majors' course. The senior class was transferred to Aberdeen the following year and MacLeod taught it with great success. He retired from the army in 1962, and became a partner in the Glasgow bagpipe-making firm of Grainger and Campbell. He toured and taught in America, Canada, Sweden, South Africa, Rhodesia, New Zealand and Australia. A gifted and positive teacher, he quickly recognised the potential of recorded lessons and his teaching tapes, which show a style similar to that of fellow-MacDonald pupils R. U. Brown and R. B. Nicol, were very influential. MacLeod gave frequent recitals on radio, including a series on 'Piobaireachd for the Beginner'. In 1978 he was awarded the M.B.E. for services to piping.

These achievements alone would have given Donald MacLeod an honoured place in the annals of piping, but his outstanding contribution was as a composer and arranger. He began to compose at the age of twelve and eventually published six classic volumes of light music, *Pipe Major Donald MacLeod's Collection of Music for the Highland Bagpipe* (Glasgow, from 1954 onwards) and one of original *pìobaireachd*: *Donald MacLeod's Collection of Piobaireachd Book 1* (Glasgow, n.d.), containing some twenty pieces composed by himself. A number of projects were left uncompleted at his death including an intended publication to be entitled '1001 tunes', and much additional material. Had Donald MacLeod been merely prolific, there might be little more to say, but his work was of consistently high quality, and his critical standards were exacting. A colleague reported that one would quite often hear Donald at work on some interesting-sounding phrase or part, only to find it in the waste-paper basket the following morning. He was an admirer not only of the great piping composers, but also drew widely upon the traditional fiddle, accordion and song repertoires. He was much taken with the west-coast style of accordionist Bobby MacLeod whom he commemorated in the classic 6/8 march, 'MacLeod of Mull'. Donald made a distinguished contribution to all the genres, but his jigs were particularly fine and tunes like 'Glasgow Police Pipers', 'The Seagull', 'Donald MacLennan's Tuning Phrase' and 'The Hammer on the Anvil' are to be heard wherever pipers assemble. Some thought his *pìobaireachd* compositions rather slight, describing them as 'slow airs with variations', but since their regular airing at the Donald MacLeod Memorial Competition, an invitational event established in his honour in 1994 by the Lewis and Harris Piping Society, where Donald MacLeod compositions have to be played, it may be that some will join the select group of modern tunes to establish themselves in the standard repertoire.

Donald MacLeod died in Glasgow, on 29th June 1982. His teaching tapes are currently being re-issued on digitally remastered CDs by Lismor Recordings under the series title *The Classic Collection of Piobaireachd Tutorials by Pipe Major Donald MacLeod M.B.E.*

THE BOBS OF BALMORAL

Born and brought up within a few miles of each other on Deeside, and working as gamekeepers on the royal estate at Balmoral, R. U. Brown and R. B. Nicol were close friends and colleagues, and the leading pupils of John MacDonald during the middle years of the twentieth century. They became the most influential players and teachers of the period, attracting two generations of master class pupils to their various homes on Deeside, thus continuing the piping pre-eminence the Strath had enjoyed in the days of Sandy MacDonald and *Uilleam* Ross. The famous pair were also the first major players to be born after the Piobaireachd Society was founded and to come to maturity in an ethos dominated by its activities.

Superficially, at least, their characters could hardly have been more different. Bob Brown was a man of dazzling charm. None of the photographs gives the slightest sense of his immense presence. He was usually to be found in comfortable tweed plus-fours, but the writer encountered him at Balmoral one Sunday shortly after church – where he was an elder – wearing a well-cut dark lounge suit. It absolutely transformed him. If somebody had said this was the ambassador of a major power, you would have believed it at once. He was a master of language as well as music, like his sister Bessie Brown, who was extraordinarily like him, even to the set of her hands on the chanter. Witty and sardonic, they could terrorise the life out of you if they liked; and they sometimes did like. It is something of an art-form in Aberdeenshire. Bessie once reported how Bob Brown and Bob Nicol had rescued their colleague Jimmy MacGregor from an altercation in a beer tent at the games. 'Aye, min, ye can jist see him,' she cried, bristling with comic bellicosity, '*Tiger Brown*.' Once when Bob had been down in London competing successfully for the Blue Banner, he got off the train at Ballater and met an acquaintance who asked, 'My, Bob, did you get anything in London?' The reply was characteristic: 'Ach, I won a bit clootie' ('clootie' = small cloth or rag).

At the same time the Browns had a warmth that was utterly unforgettable. The world and time shrank to things of little consequence in the magical atmosphere they carried about with them. The writer vividly remembers sitting in Bessie's cottage in the wood above Banchory on a summer afternoon in the '70s, the golden green light, the creak of her antique wooden-framed wheel-chair (she had polio as a child), and her work-table full of richly-coloured fishing flies (which was her living), and the person herself, apple-cheeked, bright-eyed, razor-sharp, and dangerous (if you were a piper): she was a penetrating critic and had notebook upon notebook full of who had played what, where, and how, going back for years and years. Altogether, the Browns were the most extraordinarily vital people with enough personality between them to equip half-a-dozen normal human beings. Meeting them was like being struck by lightning.

Bob Nicol was utterly different: grave and reserved in public, watchful, a little stiff, perhaps, with strangers. His features were slightly asymmetrical as a result of a shooting accident in which he had lost an eye, and perhaps it was this which gave his expression when at rest a slightly frozen, reconstructed look. One had the feeling that Bob Brown trusted the world; but Nicol didn't. And Brown, although he had a deep affection and admiration for him, constantly pulled his leg: 'Aye,' he would say in later years as his colleague grew increasingly stout, 'he was a fine figure of a man, Bob Nicol. What a chest he had; but it slipped'. Yet Nicol had great natural dignity and conveyed a sense of inner power every bit as formidable as Bob Brown's.

In recent years the Bobs have been increasingly presented as key figures in the 'authentic' oral transmission of *pìobaireachd* during the twentieth century, but the real situation may be a good deal more complex.

Robert Urquhart Brown

Bob Brown was born on 1st May 1906 at Blackhall on the south bank of the River Dee about two miles west of Banchory where his father, Frank Brown, was head keeper. After completing his education at Banchory Academy, he joined his father as an assistant keeper at Blackhall, working next on the neighbouring Park estate and then, finally, on the royal estate at Balmoral, living for much of his time there at the lodge of Garbhalltshiel. Nearly all of his family played the pipes and Bob began his formal instruction at the age of 11. Like many master players, he studied with a number of teachers and, although the fame of most of his earlier instructors has not endured, they were people of calibre and represented an interesting combination of influences. His first teacher was William Fraser, a pupil of G. S. McLennan; next he went to Jonathan W. Ewen, piper to the Marquis of Huntly at Aboyne (gold medal, Inverness, 1885), a pupil of Sandy Cameron; then he studied with Peter Ewen (or Ewing) of Aberdeen, a pupil of John or Alec MacDougall Gillies; chief amongst his early teachers was G. S. Allan (gold medal, Inverness, 1906), pipe-major of the Royal Scots and one of the best competitive players of his generation. The most important by far of all Bob Brown's teachers, however, was John MacDonald of Inverness, with whom he studied from 1927 until the latter's death in 1953. Brown went on to become one of the two or three leading *pìobaireachd* players and teachers of his generation.

He used to urge a thorough course of instruction on the practice chanter and the pipes until complete technical mastery was attained (apparently he was eighteen months on the practice chanter before he was allowed to progress to his first tune); when this stage was reached, he advised leaving the practice chanter alone (he claimed never to have touched his, except for teaching purposes, in the thirty years since he had met John MacDonald) and then to concentrate the whole attention on playing sweetly and idiomatically on the pipes. He saw this latter as the main failure of the coming generation of players: they had good instruments and accurate technique but they tended to play in a very mechanical and wooden way, as if the music were a mere set of exercises.

Bob Brown went on to a successful competition career, winning the gold medals at Inverness in 1928 and Oban in 1931, the clasp in 1947 and again in 1951, and the Gillies Cup in London on numerous occasions. He saw war service as pipe-major of the 5/7th and latterly 1st Gordons, and frequently travelled to give recitals, record, and teach in North America, South Africa, Australia and New Zealand. He enjoyed immense authority abroad: indeed an R. U. Brown Piobaireachd Society of South Australia was founded in his honour. He and Nicol were also pioneers of tape-recording as an aid to instruction and the transmission of the tradition. This happened in the early 1950s as a result of a group inside the Piobaireachd Society including J. P. Grant and R. L. Lorimer, a publisher who had links with the School of Scottish Studies. They were troubled that the opportunity to record John MacDonald had been squandered and were anxious to use the new technology to make a permanent record of MacDonald's pupils. On a bitterly cold winter night in 1953 in an unheated house in Braemar which Lorimer had borrowed from the Invercauld estate, and after an exhausting day down on the Esk culling deer, the Bobs made a series of formal recordings, later issued commercially by the School of Scottish Studies (*Scottish Tradition Cassette Series* nos. 2–3, Tangent Records Ltd., TGMMC 502–3). They were unhappy about the quality of these and wanted to re-record them, but the opportunity never arose. Lorimer also left them a large reel-to-reel tape recorder and instructed them in its use so that the Society could have self-recorded examples of their playing whenever it chose. It is not clear whether such recordings were ever actually made, but Bob Brown certainly used the machine to make an extensive series of teaching tapes for the pupils of Dr. Kenneth MacKay in Laggan, and these were widely copied on and distributed throughout the piping world. They form part of the current commercial CD series of digitally re-mastered lessons by Brown and Nicol, distributed under the title *Masters of Piobaireachd* by Greentrax Recordings.

When cheap cassette recorders became available in the 1960s, many pupils taped their lessons with the Bobs, and routinely copied them on to other people – with their instructors' blessing: they were very enthusiastic about the potential of the new medium. There must be a huge amount of such material in existence. The writer's own collection contains about 140 *piobaireachd*, 99 taught to him directly by Bob Nicol, the remainder coming through various intermediaries from R. U. Brown and others. The tape revolution enormously extended Brown's range as a teacher; indeed he was probably the first master teacher of *ceòl mór* to reach a truly global audience. He went on to make a number of commercial recordings in America and New Zealand, issued as LP's entitled *The Cairn on the Hill* and *The Pipes of Balmoral*, both released around 1972.

After John MacDonald's death, Bob Brown became a Piobaireachd Society instructor and ran classes for them in Aberdeen from 1953 to 1963. He succeeded MacDonald as the person the Society tended to consult in cases of doubt or difficulty. For example, when Sheriff J. P. Grant was trying to publish the 'Nether Lorne Canntaireachd' in its entirety in 1957, it was to Bob Brown he turned when Robin Lorimer and Francis Collinson of the School of Scottish Studies proved to have insufficient knowledge to assist him. Brown, on the other hand, responded with great enthusiasm, and set himself to master the system during the quiet winter months. Eventually the project fell through when the owners of the manuscript raised difficulties and the Royal Celtic Society, which was sponsoring the venture, withdrew. Brown and Grant became quite close at this time, and he was presented with some of the Sheriff's piping books after the latter's death in 1963. Unlike Bob

Nicol, Bob Brown considered Grant a real authority; Nicol retorted, 'Weel, he *hid* tae say that, the Sheriff gie'd him the medal'.

In 1958 when Willie Ross fell ill and gave up the Castle, Bob Brown was widely canvassed as his successor, a proposal which met with an enthusiastic response from the military, but this did not go ahead. In 1968 he was awarded the M.B.E.

Bob Brown was a marvellous all-round piper and he was very adept technically. Once, regarding a pupil's poorly maintained drone reeds, he cried, 'Good lord, look at that. That bridle's just falling off. There's hemp and rosin over there, away and re-tie it'. And when the student flushed and said, 'Well, um . . .', Bob swept a glance of humorous horror round the room, where several other students in a like condition were strenuously avoiding eye-contact. 'Call yourselves pipers,' he exclaimed, 'and ye canna tie a bridle! Look, you do it like this . . .' And there was a blur and there was a bridle, beautifully tied. Then he picked up another reed and there was another blur and another bridle just like the last one. And then he slowed it down and showed the various steps until we could all manage it in the approved manner. As a result of which the writer can do bridles; even if he cannot manage the blur. Bob did dramatic things with chanter reeds too. Students were poor, and reeds were dear, and maybe they were not just so adept as they would be later on, so when they were adjusting chanter reeds, they did it like mice nibbling at the last of the cheese, a little file here, a little scrape there. Not Bob. On one occasion he flagged a pupil down: 'That reed's off', he said, 'and it's making you work too hard. Give it here'. He surveyed it briefly, and with a sudden bold gesture, carved a great slice off it. I remember it yet, flying through the air. You could have heard the intake of student breath in Banchory. 'Ah well,' he smiled, 'kill or cure.' He had an intriguing mannerism which a number of his students followed: he had a rubber sealing ring from an old-fashioned beer bottle stopper round the bass drone tuning pin, at the point where the pipes were just coming in and ready to give a stable performance. Normally this section of the drone is behind the piper's left ear and he cannot easily see it; so that when Bob felt the resistance of the ring he knew he was ready to go.

Bob Brown was a lovely light-music player but *pìobaireachd* was his main interest. His repertoire seemed bottomless and he was an exciting and much-sought-after teacher. He taught mainly by singing, and his pleasing and expressive baritone voice is preserved on thousands of miles of tape in the hands of pupils and the pupils of pupils all over the world. His energy and generosity are well summed up by a story from the Breton piper, Jackez Pincet, who stayed with him for a couple of weeks for lessons in the later '60s. He would be awakened at the crack by Bob with a beaming smile and a big cup of tea and the words 'Come on, MacCrimmon, time for work'.

Bob Brown was not active as a composer, but he did compile the later variations for the *pìobaireachd* 'John MacDonald's Prelude' to make it into a complete tune.

He was taken ill during an Australian tour in 1972 and died, just after his return home, on 24th April 1972. He is buried at Crathie.

Robert Bell Nicol

Bob Nicol was born on 26th December 1905 at West Lodge, Durris, Kincardineshire, son of David Nicol, a salmon-fisher from Banchory and his wife, Mary McDonald. On leaving Banchory Academy, he worked as stalker, fisherman and piper, first on the Cowdray estate near Aberdeen and, from 1924 onwards, on the royal estate at Balmoral. Taught by local players as a boy, he went on to master-class instruction from John MacDonald of Inverness, beginning in 1926 until MacDonald's death in 1953, going up for instruction for several weeks annually during the '20s and '30s. Nicol went on to win most of the top piping awards, including the relatively rare feat of winning both the gold medals at Oban and Inverness in a single year, 1930. He won the clasp in 1932 and the Bratach Gorm in 1939. From 1942 to 1945 Nicol saw active service as pipe-major, 2nd battalion Gordon Highlanders. He was also a fine reedmaker, and often spoke about this. He said it had taken him a long time to develop his own chanter reed. It was not a matter just of having good cane and your tools sharp, you had to be in the mood. You could address yourself to the job till you were blue in the face, but if they were not coming you might as well give over. Sometimes they just flowed out of him. You could renovate reeds, too, he said. Once he had taken Bob Brown's chanter reed, undone the whipping, removed the blades, cleaned them with methylated spirits, boiled the staple which brought it up again like new, opened it out slightly again at the top, re-whipped the blades, bringing them very slightly further down the staple than they had been – effectively shortening them, 'And Brown took the clasp with it the following day'.

Bob Nicol recollected the first time he had ever played at the Northern Meeting as a boy of sixteen. His tune was 'The Battle of the North Inch of Perth', and when he came out of the hall, he was standing with an older man, no relation, when an old fellow with a white beard came up and said 'I liked your tune', and assuming Bob's companion to be his father, added, 'He's going to be some player that laddie of yours'. The speaker was the legendary Sandy Cameron.

Nicol's musical background drew both on the North-East and on his family's West Highland connections. His mother was a Gaelic speaker and he set a number of her songs for the pipes. He recalled his grandmother's stories of the Clearances in Moidart, how they were reduced to living under tarpaulins on the shore, eating mussels and limpets boiled in a pot, saying: 'It never struck me until I was a grown up man that it was true; it had actually happened to us; I thought that they were just fairy stories from long ago'. Speaking of *pìobaireachd*, he would say, 'There's a great sorrow in that tune; oh aye, there's a great rage and indignation too, but at the bottom of it there's this desperate sorrow. I think it was the poverty – it must have been – the terrible grinding poverty – that gave such sadness to their music'.

Bob was unmarried and lived for a good many years at the bothy of Invergelder, coming home at the weekend to his mother's house, Kincluny Cottage, near the Park bridge on the River Dee. Later he lived with his sister Jean at Mill of Cosh further up the river, and latterly at 3 Blacksmith's Cottages, Birkhall, a couple of miles west of Ballater on the south Deeside Road. The Bobs worked in one of the most famously lovely Highland straths but were still quite close to major centres of population and consequently had many pupils. Indeed a number of able student pipers elected to study at the University of Aberdeen because of their fame as teachers. Although his student group eventually became world-wide, Bob Nicol refused to charge for instruction, saying, 'Na, it cam' for nothing, it will go for nothing'.

Nicol's teaching method was predominantly oral, with singing and talk making up the bulk of the lesson. He has been described after his death as never using the book, but this would apply mainly to favourites like 'The Glen is Mine' or 'Black Donald's March' and the tunes set for competition in any particular year. Outside this range he frequently consulted the Piobaireachd Society scores, in cases of doubt, supported by a number of the older collections, such as MacPhee and Glen. His personal copy of Thomason's *Ceol Mor*, full of his own pencil annotations, had been stolen from the pipers' room at Balmoral Castle and he was much grieved by its loss. He would begin by discussing the tune to be studied in general terms, sometimes directing that note values in the scores be amended, or cadence movements added or removed; then he would sing the tune, pausing from time to time to expound various points of interpretation. It is rather rare for master instrumentalists to have pleasing singing voices, and Nicol's intonation would best be described, perhaps, as a thoughtful croak. Indeed he would sometimes shake his head self-deprecatingly and say, 'I'm nae Caruso ye ken', yet he was extraordinarily effective in conveying tempo and rhythm and idiomatic nuance. He would then illustrate finger-technique on his practice chanter. This latter was quite a sight: he turned an alarming magenta colour when he played, and he shut his good eye, fixing the pupil with the blazing, sightless glass eye he had acquired following his shooting accident. If the pupil was at the stage of playing the tune on the pipes, Nicol would conduct him with precise and shapely gestures, his hand raised a little from the arm of his chair, as Sandy Cameron and John MacDonald did.

As the use of cassette recorders spread, Bob Nicol enthusiastically collaborated with his students in taping lessons. Believing that it was an excellent extension of the teacher's method, he deplored that the technology had not been available a generation before. At the same time, he was keenly aware of the danger that fixed audio texts would simply replace fixed printed ones, and urged his pupils to do their best by study, reflection and educated listening to cultivate an individual style. He always said that taped lessons were not to be treated as a source of instant expertise, just a useful additional aid to understanding and expression. Yet within a couple of decades of his death, as perhaps he may have feared, his recordings were being issued in commercial form (*Masters of Piobaireachd*, Greentrax) as providing direct and uncomplicated access to 'tradition'.

It was interesting to watch Nicol recording: he always controlled the microphone and would switch it off when he felt the siren call of scandalous piping folklore (which was fairly often). At the beginning of a tune he would raise his hand in a characteristic gesture, and say: 'This is the way that ever I had it from Old John', and it was plain that he was following scrupulously what he had himself been taught. On the rare occasions when a pupil asked for a tune he had not got from MacDonald, he would say, 'Well, I did not get this from John, but I've given the tune some study, and this' – with a characteristically self-deprecatory shrug – 'is the way *I* would play it'.

Nicol frequently stressed the strength and flexibility of the oral method as a teaching medium (of which he regarded recording as a simple extension), and is on record as declaring, 'The book, the book, the bloody book; I can't be doing with it at all'. But this was a comment specifically directed against the publications of the Piobaireachd Society: he described Archibald Campbell as 'no musician', and would not have the *Kilberry Book of Ceol Mor* in the house. Yet Nicol was by no means opposed to written or printed scores as such. When the enterprising Yorkshire firm EP Publishing began to issue reprints of the classic old *piobaireachd* collections in the early 1970s, the writer contacted them to enquire if they had plans for further titles. Since the new plate-glass British universities were being built, and there was a significant demand for standard works from libraries trying to build research collections from scratch, and since, perhaps more significantly still, the new technology meant that EP did not have to sell very many copies to at least cover their costs, they responded positively, and asked what they might consider next. So the writer consulted Bob Nicol, who unhesitatingly recommended the remaining volumes in the series (*Ross's Collection*, and *The Bagpipe Works of Donald MacPhee*), stating concisely what their significance was and why they should be reprinted. After a little additional gathering of information, the recommendation would go to EP and about six months later the new volume would duly appear with an introduction by Seumas MacNeill. An invaluable resource was created, and it was most unfortunate that within a very few years EP were taken over by another company before reaching Glen's *Collection of Ancient Piobaireachd*, which was the next on the list. The new owners allowed the series to drop, and it is now virtually unobtainable.

In the days of Bob Nicol, print and the power that flowed from it, for good or ill, could not be ignored. Like his teacher, John MacDonald, he had to work in a situation where, if you wanted to 'succeed' as a player, you could not depart too dramatically from the Piobaireachd Society scores which dominated competitive *ceol mor* playing in Scotland throughout the twentieth century. Like MacDonald, he condemned these as coarse and unmusical, declaring: 'The timing of the tunes has been altered, they drew lines, and so many notes have to go in there, and so many in here . . . something's drifted'. But he and Bob Brown had been sent to John MacDonald at the behest of the Society. This involved a long and awkward journey to Inverness, and we may recollect that there was a master player within an easy day's travel in the city of Aberdeen to whom they were pointedly not sent, namely G. S. McLennan. From 1953 to 1958 Nicol was the Society's instructor in the Uists. Brown was in close contact with J. P. Grant and Archibald Campbell during the 1950s and seems frequently to have consulted the latter about permissible interpretations of the set tunes from year to year. He was on the Society's judges' list and therefore presumably also a member. Following Brown's death, Nicol himself was recruited by the Society. He reported going down to a meeting and seemed little impressed. He saw Archibald Kenneth as the leading figure, but the rest were 'jist doctors and lawyers. They're "enthusiasts", that's aboot a' ye can say for them; eence ye've said that, ye've jist aboot exhausted the subject'. Kenneth, in turn, found him a difficult colleague, writing, 'Nicol is the most pleasant of men. But as a judge he has the defect that he won't give an opinion backed by reasons . . . this does nothing to simplify reaching a decision. He will neither put up a reasoned case for his favoured candidates; nor will he reason against mine – he didn't even say he disliked their performances, but I was left to infer it from his studied refusal to comment on any such, and his reiterated support for the ones that took his fancy. I think it is the old story – too much politeness and the fact that we know each other so well . . .' Interestingly, it does not seem to have struck the gentleman amateur why the professional piper was unwilling to enter into discussion with him. We see here again the dilemma of master players involved with musically limited people of superior social standing: did you try to increase their knowledge only to find yourself hopelessly implicated, as John MacDonald did, when a week or so later they set up as 'experts'; or, like Bob Nicol, did you refuse to enter dialogue at all, because there was so little common ground between the gentlemen who fancied they knew so much, and the great pipers who knew so much more than was dreamed of in the gentlemen's philosophy?

Nicol was a complex man, who mistrusted his temperament, his susceptibility to what he called 'rushes of blood', and when he fell ill in later life and stopped playing the pipes for a number of years, he was disturbed that the music itself might have left him. Yet he was an electrifyingly good player, particularly of the light music, which he played very fast and light with superb 'lift' and attack. It must have been about 1972 that the writer heard him give a thrilling display in his house at Birkhall. Bob was preparing for his last attempt at the Bratach Gorm and his pipes were singing. Classic competition marches, strathspeys and reels poured from his chanter in dazzling profusion; it was so utterly unlike the pedestrian, over-cautious modern approach, that it left his little student audience

– few of whom had actually heard him play the pipes – quivering with surprise and delight. He played the tunes in groups of six: the competition marches 'MacLean of Pennycross', 'Abercairney Highlanders', 'The Braes of Castle Grant', 'The Stirlingshire Militia', 'John MacDonald of Glencoe', and 'Millbank Cottage'; followed by strathspeys and reels: 'Delvinside', and 'Lochiel's away to France'; 'Tullochgorm' and 'Iain son of Hector's Big Reel'; 'MacBeth's Strathspey' and 'Pretty Marion'; 'Arniston Castle' and 'Charlie's Welcome'; 'The Shepherd's Crook' and 'The Flagon'; 'Blair Drummond' and 'Cabarfeidh' with seemingly inexhaustible grace and style and idiomatic resourcefulness. The marches proceeded with beautiful fluency and the 'light lilt' which he always said should characterise this form. In the strathspeys and reels, the tempi were those of the dance, for all that these were 'heavy' competition pieces. It was noticeable, too, that the ornamentation wasn't 'shown' as if it were a separate department of the tune, but incorporated sweetly into the melodic flow and executed with lightning speed and accuracy. Finishing, Nicol permitted himself a chuckle. 'Aye,' he said, 'I was fair travellin'.'

The summer of 1972 had seen Bob Nicol teaching in Brittany, under the auspices of the Ministère de la Jeunesse et des Sports. It was the first time a Scottish piper had taught *pìobaireachd* in Brittany. Bob held classes in Rennes and Saint-Nazaire, and there was talk of his becoming official instructor to a new Breton school of *pìobaireachd*. He broadcast on French radio (ORTF), gave newspaper interviews, and created a considerable stir. The students were impressed by his light music, but even more by 'his fantastic knowledge of *pìobaireachd*'.

Bob Nicol also took an active part in the community of Ballater, and was much esteemed. He regularly played (great as he was) for the children dancing on the green, and cherished the fine belt with the Clanranald arms worked upon the buckle (for his mother's side of the family) presented to him in recognition of his services. In the same spirit he taught many local children from beginner level upwards. In the 1970s he reported interestingly on how difficult a task this was becoming. In the old days, an inbuilt knowledge of the idiom of the light music – coarse or subtle – could be taken for granted, even in beginners; but, thanks to television and radio and recorded commercial music, this had gone, he thought, and idiom had to be formally taught, just as in *pìobaireachd*. He was keenly conscious of how challenging a task this was.

Bob Nicol died at his home at Birkhall on 4th April 1978, and was buried at Kirkton of Durris on 8th April 1978. The funeral was impressive, attended by hundreds of pipers from all over the country, and with two clergymen officiating: his own, Catholic, priest, and the Presbyterian minister of the parish. The priest was long-haired, given to leather jackets and motor cycles; the minister grave and grey-haired, black-gowned, with starched Geneva bands. The priest spoke of the wonderful mysteries of God, of musical gifts inscrutably given, and as inscrutably taken away; the minister about how *useful* and *respectable* a man Mr. Nicol had been. There are many Scotlands, and two rather contrasting ones were visible that day. The 23rd Psalm was given out, to the tune of 'Crimond', and the great company of pipers took it up. Any expectation of the usual meagre congregational singing was instantly blown away: it was shattering, overwhelming in expressive power and feeling. Not only can pipers – usually – sing, but their colleague had been much loved: they meant every note of it.

And so the age of the Bobs passed. They were commanding figures in their generation, and, of course, the folklore made free with them. One contemporary recollected: 'I mind the first time I met Bob Nicol. In a foxhole. Just before the 51st Highland Division crossed the Rhine. I never knew how Bob Nicol managed to get into the army. He must have pulled strings. He only had one eye. I went thirty years to Bob Nicol; learned all he knew; had him through all the stuff I wanted'. The speaker went on, as others have done, to criticise Bob Brown, saying that Nicol was the real master, and that Brown used to come secretly to Nicol's every week for instruction, and went on to claim that Bob Brown's phrasing was too jerky and cut, as Nicol's also was sometimes. The account continued how they were faulted for this by Calum Pìobaire's grandson, Malcolm R. MacPherson, at a gathering of pipers one night at Mill of Cosh. 'There was this great enormous stone pig of whisky and we played the night away till the dawn came up. My God we were fu'. Bob Nicol's glass eye was whurlin' roond.'

Being a piper during the past two or three centuries has involved a wide range of activities and many different kinds of social opportunity. The top people during the eighteenth century, such as the MacCrimmons and MacKays of Gairloch, occupied the decent middle rungs of society. But during the nineteenth and early twentieth centuries, when institutional efforts were at their height to 'rescue' and 'preserve' the music of the pipe, the players experienced a steady decline in status. They went from being people who *had* servants, to people who *were* servants. Their personal fame and reputation might be great, but their worldly circumstances were often rather modest. The second half of the twentieth century saw this situation change again. Pipers have always been able people, good at all kinds of things as well as piping: in the old days, they often administered the estates on which they worked; and so as affordable higher education became widely available in post-war Britain, they availed themselves of it in numbers. As a result, the top players today – although they are exactly the same kind of people they always have been – tend to be lawyers and doctors and business executives rather than gamekeepers, valets, or fishermen. They are linked down the centuries by the opportunity to pursue this richest and most fascinating of arts.

TUNES

'Black Donald's March'

The following example shows how the various elements which go to make up a *pìobaireachd* are combined. Before starting, however, we need to remind ourselves about the conventions of written bagpipe music. Melody notes are written with their stems pointing down, regardless of position on the stave, while ornamental figures are set in reduced type with their stems pointing upwards. This can be a little ambiguous in contexts where it may not be absolutely clear what is a melody note and what is an ornament, but the system on the whole is elegant, and makes for easy sight-reading with a little practice.

The tune nowadays known as 'Black Donald's March' is preserved in a number of manuscript and published sources, the earliest complete score appearing in Donald MacDonald's book, *A Collection of the Ancient Martial Music of Caledonia, called Piobaireachd,* published in Edinburgh in 1818/19. MacDonald set the Ground, or *ùrlar,* like this:

An inherent ambiguity in MacDonald's system means that some of the small notes have no time value, but some of them do, as a result of which the melody would probably have been timed like this:

MacDonald follows this with a thumb variation:

This would have been timed somewhat thus:

The framing of variations at this time lay within the artistic discretion of the performer, and MacDonald could have elected (a) not to have a thumb variation at all, or (b), to develop it at considerably greater length as was done by one the foremost players of the following generation, Angus MacKay (National Library of Scotland, MS 3753, i, 192–194), thus:

Both MacDonald and MacKay proceed to a leumluath variation here, Mac-Donald's version going like this:

This would be timed something like:

At this point, MacDonald repeats the Ground (MacKay does not), then proceeds to a Taorluath variation:

This would be timed roughly thus:

Following the Taorluath, the Ground is re-stated by both MacDonald and MacKay, and each goes on to a Crunluath variation, in MacDonald's case as follows:

The timing would be roughly thus:

The tone row which supports the whole structure

is progressively revealed, at the same time being decorated with increasingly elaborate ornament. This is a fundamental procedure found throughout *piobaireachd*.

Probably the easiest way to think about the phrase pattern of 'Black Donald's March' is of a single short figure: 'a' repeatedly asserted, and alternating with other set figures to produce an antiphonal 'call-and-response' sequence. This is both very economical, and produces an insistent, highly charged effect. Here is the Ground in outline showing this pattern:

Readers who want to learn more about this should consult the writer's e-series on the 'Set Tunes' for 2001–4 in *Piper & Drummer Online* which contains examples and background information with musical extracts from numerous rare early printed and manuscript sources. This can be accessed at *www.piperanddrummer.com* and then clicking on the 'Archive' section on the home page.

'The Breadalbane Fencibles' Quickstep'

(Angus MacKay's MS, National Library of Scotland, MS 3755, f.27).

'Lord Breadalbane's March'

Noted by C[olin]. Cam[eron]. composed by D[onald]. Cam[eron]. B.[rahan] Castle 1856', ('Music of Colin Cameron 19th–20th Century, assembled by A. G. Kenneth', National Library of Scotland, Acc.9103/21)

'Seaforth Highlanders Quickstep'

Composed by John Bàn MacKenzie, 1821

The tune is recorded in 'Five quarto volumes of *pìobaireachd* of Pipe-Majors Ronald and Alexander MacKenzie and Charles Scott', National Library of Scotland, MS 22126 (63–75).

'John MacFadyen of Melfort'

This is reproduced from what appears to be the earliest published version, David Glen's *Edinburgh Collection of Highland Bagpipe Music*, vol. 10, 1906, p.11.

G. S. McLennan, 'Piobaireachd'

From Alfred E. Milne's MS, Aberdeen University Library, MS 2904, ff.306–7. (The manuscript does not include a *crunluath* doubling although presumably one is intended; space was left for this but it was not written in.)

Ground

1st Var.

Taorluath

Doubling of Taorluath

Crunluath

John MacDonald, 'Prelude'

R. B. Nicol, Gaelic air from his mother's singing

(The above is from Nicol's own sung version; ornamentation is by the writer.)

REFERENCES

Short references appear within the text; the remainder are given below. Unless otherwise indicated, all manuscript material is held by the National Library of Scotland. Further information on most of the topics discussed here will be found in my book *The Highland Pipe and Scottish Society*, Tuckwell Press, East Linton, 2000.

Percy Scholes quote (p. 9), *Oxford Companion to Music*, 10th edn., 1970, p.67.

G. S. McLennan story (p. 9), John McLennan, The *Piobaireachd as MacCrimmon Played it*, Edinr., 1907, p.1.

Sandy Cameron story (p. 15); for a slightly different version see Christine Knox Chambers, 'Non-Lexical Vocables in Scottish Traditional Music', Ph.D. Dissertation, Edinr., 1980, pp.50, 311.

Willie Ross story (p. 21), Bob Nicol in conversation with the writer, Ballater, 10th June 1975.

Andrew MacDonald and the judges (p. 21), Seton Gordon Papers, Acc.5640/2 (1), Archibald Campbell to Seton Gordon, 26/09/1929.

Amateurs judging with professionals (p. 22), see Piobaireachd Society Papers, Acc.9103/10, 26/07/1953.

Willie Ross story (pp. 22–4), narrated by Hector Ross, 'Pipeline', Radio Scotland, 22/11/1998, first broadcast 1967.

'Lament for the Children' story, (p. 30), Donald MacDonald Manuscript, MS 1680, f.8.

James Hogg story (p. 32), see Douglas S. Mack, ed., *James Hogg Selected Poems*, Oxford 1970, p.141.

'Lord Lennox's March' (p. 38), from 'A Collection of National Music for the Great Highland Bagpipe . . . compiled by Robert Millar and others for John C. Cameron, bagpipe maker, Dundee, 1838', McLennan Papers, Acc.11516/2.

William Laurie story, (p. 42), see G. I. Malcolm of Poltalloch, *Argyllshire Highlanders 1860–1960* (Glasgow: Halberd Press, n.d.)., p. 143

John MacDonald on the *Kilberry Book* (p. 58), letter from MacDonald to Seton Gordon, in Seton Gordon Papers, Acc.5640/2 (1), 28/01/1949.

Archibald Kenneth's tunes (p. 59), see *The Seumas MacNeill Collection of Bagpipe Music*, Glasgow, 1960, p.27.

Archibald Kenneth on revising the *Piobaireachd Society Collection* (2nd series), (p. 59), see 'Re-publishing of Piobaireachd?', *Piping Times*, vol 24. no.10, July 1972, pp.8–11.

Archibald Campbell on Piobaireachd Society publishing monopoly (p. 59), Piobaireachd Society Papers, Acc. 9103/11, 05/01/1956.

The ex-President of the Piobaireachd Society on the credibility of the current system (p. 61), see David Murray, 'My Month', *Piping Times*, vol.52, no.11, August 2000, p.27.

On Ceol Sean see 'Early collections available on CD-Rom', *Piping Today*, no. 11, 2004, pp. 12–13.

Elizabeth MacCrimmon story (p. 66), see John Johnston of Coll in 'Dr. K. N. MacDonald and Bagpipe playing', *Oban Times*, 12/09/1896, p.3.

Donald MacPhedran story (p. 66) is given by 'Cean-na-Drochaid' (J. Mac-Pherson) in 'MacPhedran's Pipe Tunes', *Oban Times*, 08/09/1906, p.3.

Nell Ackroyd story (p. 67), see *International Piper*, vol.2, no.8, 1979, p.11.

Gaelic terms of art (p. 74); for the latest thinking here, see Colm Ó Baoill, 'Moving in Gaelic Musical Circles', *Scottish Gaelic Studies*, vol.19, 1999, pp.172–194.

Alexander Campbell story (pp. 86–7), see 'Slight Sketch of a Journey made through parts of the Highlands & Hebrides in Autumn 1815', Edinburgh University Library, La 111: 577, ff.47–50.

Alexander MacGregor on Gesto's manuscripts (pp. 87–8), see 'Canntaireachd, or Articulate Music', *Celtic Magazine*, vol.5, 1880, pp.483–4.

Iain Dubh MacCrimmon's stories about the tunes (p. 89), see 'Remarks by Captain MacLeod as far as he has been informed by the late John Mac-Crimmon, Piper, Dunvegan, Isle of Skye', *Celtic Magazine*, vol.8, 1883, pp.434–5.

John and Donald MacDonald story (pp. 91–2), see Alex. MacGregor, 'John MacDonald-an Adherent of Prince Charles', *Celtic Magazine*, vol.3, 1878, pp.462–6.

Angus Cameron story (p. 92), see Henry Cockburn, *Circuit Journeys*, Edinr., 1888, pp.107–8.

Scott Skinner quote (p. 97), Piobaireachd Society Papers, Acc. 9103/21, 'Music of Colin Cameron 19th–20th century, assembled by A. G. Kenneth'.

Colin Cameron's manuscripts (p. 98), Piobaireachd Society Papers, Acc. 9103/9, 'Correspondence, 1929–1950', 11/05/1949.

Robert Meldrum on the pre-eminence of Calum Pìobaire (pp. 100–101), see 'Pipe-Major Meldrum on Champions Past and Present', *Oban Times*, 13/07/1940, p.3.

Robert Meldrum on the Gillies brothers (p. 115), see 'Pipe-Major Meldrum on Champions Past and Present', *Oban Times*, 20/07/1940, p.5.

MacFarlane's Gathering story (p. 117), see 'Celtic Scraps', *Oban Times*, 07/06/1890, p.3.

John MacColl's promise as a player (p. 119), see 'Bagpipe Competition' by J. C., *Oban Times*, 01/12/1883, p.6.

John MacColl playing the 'King's Hand' (p. 120), see 'The Piping Reminiscences of John MacDonald M.B.E. Honorary Piper to His Majesty The King', *Oban Times*, 04/04/1942, p.5.

John MacDonald on corruptions in the Piobaireachd Society scores (p. 123), see Seton Gordon Papers, Acc.5640/2 (1), 11/09/1938, 13/01/1939, 30/03/1939, 08/09/1940, and 02/07/1941.

John MacDonald refusing to go on teaching the Piobaireachd Society scores (p. 124), see Seton Gordon Papers, Acc.5640/2 (1), 28/01/1949.

Willie Ross objecting to Piobaireachd Society failing his candidates (p. 126), Piobaireachd Society Papers, Acc.9103/10, 14/04/1953.

Willie Ross's mother criticising his style (p. 126), see I. MacKay, 'James Matheson, Lairg', in *Piping Times*, vol.42, no.10, July 1990, p.21.

Willie Ross's broadcasts (p. 127), see 'Piping to the Empire. John MacDonald M.B.E. and William Ross', *Oban Times*, 15/12/1934, p.5.

Willie Ross on his illness (p. 127), see Piobaireachd Society Papers, Acc. 9103/12, 05/06/1958.

John MacDonald praising Donald MacLeod (p. 130), see Seton Gordon Papers, Acc.5640/2 (1), 18/07/1940.

John MacDonald criticising Donald MacLeod (p. 130), see 'Some Memories of John MacDonald' by Pipe Major Donald MacLeod, *Piping Times*, vol.14, no.6, March 1962, pp.6–7.

Bob Nicol criticising Archibald Campbell and condemning the influence of 'the book' (p. 138–9), see School of Scottish Studies Archive, Edinburgh University, SA 1972/246 and 1977/164.

Archibald Kenneth on Bob Nicol as a judge (p. 139), see Piobaireachd Society Papers, Acc.9103/7, 17/05/1971.

Bob Nicol teaching in France, (p. 140) see P. Mollard, 'Robert B. Nicol in Brittany', *Piping Times*, vol.25, no.1, October 1972, pp.29–30.

Bob Nicol and the whisky pig story (p. 141), Bert Barron in conversation with the writer, St. Andrews, 1990.

ACKNOWLEDGEMENTS

Particular thanks are due to Neal Murray of Aberdeen for original photographs and for reproduction from newspaper sources, and to the owners and staff of the *Oban Times* for access to master copies. Grateful acknowledgement is also due to the following for assistance with illustrations as numbered: Falkirk and District Council, 7; Scottish National Portrait Gallery, 9, 11; the Royal Caledonian Club of London, 10; Mrs Lesley Ross Alexander, 27; Dr. William Wotherspoon, 30; the *Piping Times*, 33, 34.

I am indebted to the staff of the Mitchell Library (Glasgow), the Wighton Collection in Dundee City Library, the University Libraries of Aberdeen, Edinburgh and Glasgow, the National Library of Scotland and the British Library Newspaper Library at Colindale. Invaluable assistance has been provided by the Carnegie Trust for the Universities of Scotland with access to libraries and with copying of manuscript collections for this book as well as my earlier study, *The Highland Pipe and Scottish Society* and with the 'Set Tunes' *pìobaireachd* series 2001-4 in *Piper & Drummer Online* at *www.piperanddrummer.com* The Open University's Flexible Fund also gave assistance towards travel and accommodation costs.

This book draws on my own experience of Scottish instrumental music and song which owes much to the knowledge and kindness of many people living and dead, too many, indeed, to be named here, but I would like particularly to record my thanks to Bob Brown, Margaret Buchan, Ian Duncan, Peter Forbes, Bill Fraser, Mary Jane Gatt, Donald Grant, Andy Hunter, Donald MacPherson, Bob Nicol, Edward Ross, Jean Ross, Mary Bell Strachan, Jack Taylor and Bill Wotherspoon.

INDEX

(musical quotations appear in **bold** type)